SENTENCE SKILLS
A Workbook for Writers

SENTENCE SKILLS
A Workbook for Writers

John Langan
Atlantic Community College

McGraw-Hill Book Company

New York St. Louis San Francisco Auckland Bogotá Düsseldorf
Johannesburg London Madrid Mexico Montreal New Delhi Panama
Paris São Paulo Singapore Sydney Tokyo Toronto

Library of Congress Cataloging in Publication Data

Langan, John, date
    Sentence skills.

    Includes index.
    1. English language—Rhetoric.   2.   English
language—Grammar—1950—   I.   Title.
PE1408.L3183   808'.042   78-26361
ISBN 0-07-036255-6

SENTENCE SKILLS: A Workbook for Writers

1234567890   DODO   7832109

This book was set in Times Roman by Monotype Composition Company, Inc.
The editors were William A. Talkington and Susan Gamer;
the designer was Merrill Haber;
the production supervisor was Dominick Petrellese.
R. R. Donnelley & Sons Company was printer and binder.

Cover: Painting by James Nelson, 1976.

ACKNOWLEDGMENTS

Selection c on page 219, selection a on page 223, and selection a on page
226: Rita K. Baltus, adapted from *Personal Psychology for Life and Work*.
Copyright © 1976 by McGraw-Hill, Inc.

Selection a on page 219: Al Brooks, adapted from *Car Crime Prevention*.
Copyright © 1978 by Shell Oil Company.

Selection a on page 221 and selection a on page 230: Paul R. Ehrlich,
Richard W. Holm, and Irene Brown, adapted from *Biology and Society*.
Copyright © 1976 by McGraw-Hill, Inc.

Selection b on page 230: Joseph A. Kriz and Curtis J. Duggan, adapted from
Your Dynamic World of Business. Copyright © 1976 by McGraw-Hill, Inc.

Contents

Preface

This book has two main concerns. First, it will help you master the basic writing skills you need to be successful in your schoolwork or career. Second, and just as important, the book will show you how to transfer these basic skills to realistic writing situations. All too often, people can demonstrate such skills in isolated practice activities, but they cannot apply the same skills in their own writing. This book will make you a skillful editor and proofreader—a person able to recognize and correct errors in writing.

Part 1 presents all the basic skills needed for writing clear, error-free sentences. Each skill is self-contained so that you can turn directly to the areas that give you trouble. Explanations are brief and clear, and formal terminology is kept to a minimum. Typically, the main features of a skill are presented on the first page of a section; secondary points appear later. Numerous and varied activities are provided so that you can practice skills enough to make them habits. To help you transfer basic skills to your own writing, you are asked not just to supply correct answers but to write sentences applying the skill in question. An answer key starting on page 188 allows you to check your answers to the practice exercises in Part 1. To encourage you to use the answer key as a learning tool only, answers are *not* given to the review tests at the end of each skill section.

While Part 1 gives you practice on skills within individual sentences, Part 2 gives you practice on many of the same skills within full compositions. You are asked to rewrite a series of compositions, correcting in each of them a number of mistakes involving a single sentence skill. The rewriting activities serve as a middle ground between isolated sentence work and your own compositions. In short, the activities increase your chances of transferring the sentence skills to your everyday writing. Part 2 also helps you to develop the habit of careful proofreading. A progress chart on page 232 will help you track your performance as you move through the sequence of steps in Part 2.

The mastery and editing tests in Part 3 reinforce the basic writing skills in the first part of the book. The mastery tests may be used as homework assignments, supplementary activities, in-class quizzes at the end of a section, or review tests at any point during the semester. (Such review helps ensure that skills covered at earlier points in the semester will not be forgotten.) The editing tests offer practice in a variety of sentence skills and further work in proofreading. A progress chart on page 281 makes it easy for you to score your answers to the tests in Part 3.

The first three parts of the book help you to write clear sentences; Part 4 shows you how to write varied and interesting sentences. Through work in sentence combining, you will develop a sense of the many different options open to you when expressing a given idea. You will learn to compose sentences that impart variety and ease to your writing style.

Part 5 provides a number of writing assignments so that you can apply the basic writing skills you have learned. The surest way to achieve a transfer of such skills is to apply them in actual writing situations. A progress chart on page 336 encourages you to rewrite assignments as often as necessary to achieve error-free compositions.

While the five parts of the book have been described in sequence, the format is extremely flexible. For example, practice in a given skill in Part 2 can be followed by a guided composition activity in Part 2 or a mastery or editing test in Part 3. Sections of Parts 4 and 5 may be covered at any point during the semester. Or, you and your instructor may choose to do extensive work at one time in a single part of the book.

Sentence Skills, in sum, will help you learn, practice, and apply the basic writing skills you need to communicate clearly and effectively. You know that competent writing is important—not just in your English classes but in your other courses, in everyday life, and in your career. What remains is your personal determination to do the work needed to become an independent writer. If you decide—and only you can decide—that you want to learn to write effectively, this book will help you reach that goal.

Acknowledgments

Reviewers who have contributed to this book through their helpful comments include Marian C. Bashinski, Florida State University; Elaine Newman, Queens College; Eric Hoem, Mount Hood Community College; Anna Y. Bradley, C. S. Mott Community College; and Cecilia Macheski, LaGuardia Community College. I am grateful also for the assistance of Ruth K. Crozier. And I owe special thanks to my wife, Judith Nadell, whose own work in the teaching of writing has helped shape sections of this book, and whose extraordinary editing gifts have made *Sentence Skills* a stronger text than I could have managed by myself.

John Langan

PART 1
Sentence
Skills

INTRODUCTION

Part 1 explains the basic skills needed for you to write clear, error-free sentences. While the skills are presented within four traditional categories (grammar, mechanics, punctuation, and word use), each section is self-contained so that you can go directly to the skills you need to work on. Note, however, that you may find it helpful to cover "Subjects and Verbs" before turning to other skills. Typically the main features of a skill are presented on the first pages of a section; secondary points are developed later. Numerous activities are provided so that you can practice skills enough to make them habits. The activities are varied, and range from underlining correct answers to writing complete sentences involving the skill in question. One or more review tests at the end of each section offer additional practice opportunities.

Use the answer key that begins on page 188 after you finish each practice activity. You want to learn right away if you have understood and applied correctly the skill in question. Talk to your instructor about any answers that do not seem clear. Answers are *not* given for the review tests at the end of each section or for the mastery tests in Part 3. These tests will evaluate your final mastery of the skills.

Subjects and Verbs

The basic building blocks of English sentences are subjects and verbs. Understanding them is an important first step toward mastering a number of sentence skills.

Every sentence has a subject and a verb. Who or what the sentence speaks about is called the <u>subject</u>; what the sentence says about the subject is called the <u>verb</u>.

People <u>gossip</u>.
The <u>truck</u> <u>stalled</u>.
<u>He</u> <u>waved</u> at me.
That <u>woman</u> <u>is</u> a millionaire.

A SIMPLE WAY TO FIND A SUBJECT

To find a subject, ask *who* or *what* the sentence is about. As shown below, your answer is the subject.

Who is the first sentence about? <u>People</u>
What is the second sentence about? The <u>truck</u>
Who is the third sentence about? <u>He</u>
Who is the fourth sentence about? That <u>woman</u>

A SIMPLE WAY TO FIND A VERB

To find a verb, ask what the sentence *says about* the subject. As shown below, your answer is the verb.

What does the first sentence *say about* people? They <u>gossip</u>.
What does the second sentence *say about* the truck? It <u>stalled</u>.
What does the third sentence *say about* him? He <u>waved</u>.
What does the fourth sentence *say about* that woman? She <u>is</u> (a millionaire).

A second way to find the verb is to put *I*, *you*, *he*, *she*, *it*, or *they* in front of the word you think is a verb. If the result makes sense, you have a verb. For example, you could put *they* in front of *gossip* in the first sentence above, with the result, *they gossip*, making sense. Therefore you know that *gossip* is a verb. You could use the same test with the other three verbs as well.

PRACTICE 1   Adding Subjects

In the following sentences, the verbs are underlined twice. The subjects (the *who* or *what* words) have been omitted. Fill in your own subjects to make the sentences complete.

1. The _____ shouted.

2. _____ gave me a stereo receiver as a birthday present.

3. The _____ slipped out of my hand and fell into a puddle.

4. Using matches, _____ lit up the gas stove.

5. The _____ must be emptied.

6. The _____ is turned on too loud.

7. The elderly _____ rested on the park bench with his eyes closed.

8. While _____ painted the living room, _____ was downstairs paneling the basement.

9. _____ were so high in the store that _____ refused to buy anything.

10. The _____ pushed the old lady and grabbed her purse, but _____ surprised him with a karate chop.

PRACTICE 2   Finding Subjects

Underline the subjects in the following sentences. Verbs have already been underlined twice. Remember that you find a subject by asking *who* or *what* the sentence is about.

1. Most students <u>took</u> one hour to finish the essay exam.
2. My socks <u>wore</u> thin after only three months.
3. Melanie <u>has driven</u> her car across the country on three separate occasions.
4. The windstorm <u>blew</u> over the storage shed in the backyard.
5. The video game <u>was played</u> by the entire family.
6. Pretzels and chips <u>are</u> his favorite evening snack.
7. The window fan <u>made</u> a clanking sound and <u>kept</u> them awake at night.
8. The wind <u>blew</u> our storm door off its hinges.
9. The children <u>stared</u> in wide-eyed wonderment at the Thanksgiving Day floats.
10. The shrubs <u>are growing</u> too close to the side of the house.

PRACTICE 3 Adding Verbs

In the following sentences, the subjects are underlined. The verbs have been omitted. Fill in your own verbs to make the sentences complete.

1. <u>I</u> _____ an entire pizza by myself.
2. <u>Barracuda</u> _____ in that lake.
3. <u>Clyde</u> _____ down to the playground with his son.
4. <u>Sally</u> _____ the biology test.
5. The television <u>movie</u> _____ suddenly.
6. The <u>dancer</u> _____, badly twisting her ankle.
7. <u>Brian and Sue</u> _____ the fence in one weekend.
8. <u>I</u> _____ three books for that course.
9. The <u>man</u> suddenly _____ to the ground, as if a bullet _____ him.
10. The <u>sky</u> quickly _____ overcast, so <u>we</u> _____ indoors.

PRACTICE 4   Finding Verbs

Draw a double line under the verbs in the following sentences. Subjects have already been underlined. Remember that you find a verb by asking what the sentence *says about* the subject.

1. <u>Barbara</u> believes in extrasensory perception.
2. <u>Most</u> of my friends like my new hairstyle.
3. The <u>drawer</u> of the bureau sticks on rainy days.
4. The <u>sun</u> reflecting off the lake blinded my eyes.
5. Her part-time <u>job</u> limits her study time.
6. The <u>game</u> was called because of darkness.
7. The <u>picture</u> fell suddenly to the floor.
8. The checkout <u>lines</u> at the supermarket moved very slowly.
9. An old <u>newspaper</u> tumbled down the dirty street.
10. <u>He</u> starts every morning with a series of yoga exercises.

PRACTICE 5   Finding Subjects and Verbs

In each of the following sentences, draw one line under the subject and two lines under the verb.

Ask *who* or *what* the sentence is about to find the subject. Then ask what the sentence *says about* the subject to find the verb.

1. Carol works for a candlestick maker.
2. My Timex watch never loses time.
3. His car broke down on the freeway.
4. Cotton shirts feel softer than polyester ones.
5. The fog rolled into the cemetery.
6. Sparrows live in the eaves of my porch.
7. My car needed a tune-up for weeks.
8. A green bottle fly stung her on the ankle.
9. Russ expected a better grade on the paper.
10. I ran ten miles in my first week of jogging.

MORE ABOUT SUBJECTS AND VERBS

Distinguishing Subjects from Prepositional Phrases

The subject of a sentence never appears within a prepositional phrase.   A *prepositional phrase* is simply a group of words that begin with a preposition. Following is a list of common prepositions:

about	before	by	in	on	through
above	behind	during	inside	onto	to
across	below	except	into	out	toward
among	beneath	for	of	over	under
around	beside	from	off	past	with
at	between				

Cross out prepositional phrases when looking for the subject of a sentence.

~~Under my pillow~~ I found a quarter left ~~by the Tooth Fairy.~~
One ~~of the yellow lights at the school crossing~~ began flashing.
The funny pages ~~of the newspaper~~ disappeared.
~~In spite of my efforts,~~ Bob dropped out ~~of school.~~
~~During a rainstorm,~~ I sat ~~in my car~~ reading magazines.

PRACTICE

Cross out prepositional phrases.   Then draw a single line under subjects and a double line under verbs.

1. The attractive woman over there in the corner is my former wife.
2. The dishes in the sink must be washed before tomorrow.
3. Both of my house keys are missing.
4. The hamburger on sale at 89¢ a pound looks several days old.
5. In the middle of the movie, the screen suddenly went blank.
6. The water stain on her suede shoes disappeared with brushing.
7. The last rays of the sun faded into darkness.
8. During the baseball game, my twin brother ate five hot dogs.
9. Without the help of a calculator, I could not balance my checkbook.
10. Over the river and through the woods to Grandmother's house we will go.

Verbs of More Than One Word

Many verbs consist of more than one word.   Here, for example, are some of the many forms of the verb *talk*:

talk	were talking	will be talking
talks	have talked	must talk
does talk	has talked	would talk
is talking	had talked	can talk
are talking	had been talking	should have talked
talked	should talk	could be talking

Following are sentences that contain verbs of more than one word:

Diane <u>is</u> not <u>working</u> overtime this week.
Another book <u>has been written</u> about the Kennedy family.
We <u>should have stopped</u> for gas at the last station.
The game <u>has</u> just <u>been cancelled</u>.

Note: Words like *not, just, never, only,* and *always* are not part of the verb although they may appear within the verb.

PRACTICE

Draw a single line under subjects and a double line under verbs. Be sure to include all parts of the verb.

1. He has been sleeping all day.
2. The wood foundations of the shed have been attacked by termites.
3. Sally should have gone Christmas shopping earlier.
4. The teacher had not warned us about the quiz.
5. Carol and Arnie have both received raises in their salaries.
6. You should not pet that temperamental hamster.
7. I have not washed my car for several months.
8. He could make a living with his wood carvings.
9. The bus must have been delayed in Atlanta.
10. They have just been married by a justice of the peace.

Compound Subjects and Verbs

A sentence may have more than one verb:

My heart <u>skipped</u> and <u>pounded</u>.
Frank <u>drove</u> home from work, <u>showered</u>, and then <u>walked</u> over to Julie's house.

A sentence may have more than one subject:

<u>Psychology</u> and <u>history</u> are my favorite subjects.
The <u>radio</u> and the <u>tape player</u> were stolen from Clyde's car.

A sentence may have several subjects and several verbs:

<u>Dave</u> and <u>I</u> <u>prepared</u> the report together and <u>presented</u> it to the class.
<u>Judy</u>, <u>Carol</u>, and <u>Will</u> <u>met</u> for lunch together and then <u>went</u> to a movie.

PRACTICE

Draw a single line under subjects and a double line under verbs. Be sure to mark off *all* the subjects and verbs.

1. The mother and daughter wore identical outfits.
2. Many people laughed and cried during the movie.
3. Tuna and dolphins were trapped in the fisherman's net.
4. The hospital will serve you only decaffeinated coffee with your meals.
5. The first hundred people at the theater will be admitted at half price and be given a mystery gift.
6. My sister and I often play games like Monopoly and chess.
7. John and Marilyn looked back in disbelief at the flashing lights of the police car behind them.
8. I sprayed the trees with insecticide and spread weed killer on the backyard lawn.
9. During the baseball season the Dodgers, Reds, and Giants all occupied first place for several weeks.
10. One student sat quietly and never volunteered answers to the teacher's questions.

REVIEW TEST 1

Draw one line under the subjects and two lines under the verbs. Cross out prepositional phrases where needed to help find subjects. Underline all the parts of a verb. And remember that you may find more than one subject and verb in a sentence.

1. I did not hear about the cancellation of the class.
2. James should have gotten an estimate from the plumber.
3. The family played badminton and volleyball at the picnic.
4. A solution to the problem popped suddenly into my head.
5. The game has been postponed because of bad weather.
6. I have not been eating in the cafeteria this semester.
7. Ruth will be studying all night for the test.
8. I may hitchhike to the Mardi Gras this year.
9. She does not drive her car at night.
10. Every other night, garbage trucks rumble down my street on their way to the town dump.

REVIEW TEST 2

Follow the directions given for Review Test 1.

1. The doctor spoke gently to the tearstained little boy with the broken finger.
2. During a lecture in his Economics 101 class, David fell asleep.
3. Diesel trucks with heavy exhaust fumes should be banned from the road.
4. One of the new dental assistants in the clinic is my cousin.
5. With their fingers, the children drew pictures on the steamed window.
6. Three buildings down the street from my house have been demolished.
7. Rats, squirrels, and bats took over the attic of the abandoned house.
8. Jack and Bob will anchor the long-distance team in the track meet.
9. Reluctantly, I crawled out of bed and stumbled to the bathroom.
10. Tiddledywinks, pick-up-sticks, and hearts were our favorite games as children.

Sentence Fragments

Every sentence must have a subject and a verb and must express a complete thought. A word group that lacks a subject or a verb and that does not express a complete thought is a *fragment*. Following are the most common type of fragments that people write:

- Dependent-word fragments
- *-ing* and *to* fragments
- Added-detail fragments
- Missing-subject fragments

Once you understand the specific kind or kinds of fragments that you may write, you should be able to eliminate them from your writing. The following pages explain all four fragment types.

DEPENDENT-WORD FRAGMENTS

Some word groups that begin with a dependent word are fragments. Here is a list of common dependent words:

after	unless	even (even though, even if)
since	before	when (whenever)
because	if	who (whoever)
while	as (as if)	which (whichever)
although, though	so that	where (wherever)
until	that	

Whenever you start a sentence with one of these words, you must be careful that a fragment does not result. The word group beginning with the dependent word *After* in the selection below is a fragment.

> After I arrived in Chicago by bus. I checked into a room. Then I went to a diner to get something to eat.

A *dependent statement*—one starting with a dependent word like *After*—cannot stand alone. It depends on another statement to complete the thought. "After I arrived in Chicago by bus" is a dependent statement. It leaves us hanging. We expect in the same sentence to find out *what happened after* the writer arrived in

Chicago. When a writer does not follow through and complete a thought, a fragment results. To correct the fragment, simply follow through and complete the thought:

> After I arrived in Chicago by bus, I checked into a room.

Remember, then, that *dependent statements by themselves are fragments.* They must be attached to a statement that makes sense standing alone. Here are two other selections with dependent-word fragments:

> Brian sat nervously in the dental clinic. While waiting to have his wisdom tooth pulled.
>
> My daughter likes to make paper boats. Which she floats in the tub during her nightly bath.

"While waiting to have his wisdom tooth pulled" is a fragment; it does not make sense standing by itself. We want to know in the same statement *what Brian did* while waiting to have his tooth pulled. The writer must complete the thought. Likewise, "Which she floats in the tub during her nightly bath" is not in itself a complete thought. We want to know in the same statement what *which* refers to.

How to Correct a Dependent-Word Fragment

In most cases you can correct a dependent-word fragment by attaching it to the sentence that comes before or the sentence that comes after it:

> After I arrived in Chicago by bus, I checked into a room.
> (The fragment has been attached to the sentence that comes after it.)
>
> Brian sat nervously in the dental clinic while waiting to have his wisdom tooth pulled.
> (The fragment has been attached to the sentence that comes before it.)
>
> My daughter likes to make paper boats which she floats in the tub during her nightly bath.
> (The fragment has been attached to the sentence that comes before it.)

Another way of correcting a dependent-word fragment is simply to eliminate the dependent word:

> I arrived in Chicago by bus and found a place to stay.
> He waited to have his wisdom tooth pulled.
> She floats them in the tub during her nightly bath.

Do not use this second method of correction too frequently, however, for it may cut down on interest and variety in your writing style.

Notes:

1 Use a comma if a dependent-word group comes at the *beginning* of a sentence (see also page 133):

After I arrived in Chicago by bus, I checked into a room.

However, do not generally use a comma if the dependent-word group comes at the *end* of a sentence:

Brian sat nervously in the dental clinic while waiting to have his wisdom tooth pulled.

2 Sometimes the dependent words *who, that, which,* or *where* appear not at the very start but *near* the start of a word group. A fragment often results:

I spent the evening visiting Hilda Cooper. A friend who was in the hospital. I was frightened by her loss of weight.

"A friend who was in the hospital" is not in itself a complete thought. We want to know in the same statement *what about* the friend who was in the hospital. The fragment can be corrected by attaching it to the sentence that comes before it:

I spent the evening visiting Hilda Cooper, a friend who was in the hospital.

PRACTICE 1

Turn each of the dependent-word groups into a sentence by adding a complete thought.   Put a comma after the dependent word group if a dependent word starts the sentence.

Examples After I got out of high school

After I got out of high school, I spent a year traveling.

The man who came to dinner

The man who came to dinner stayed for the night.

1. While shopping at the market yesterday

    _____

2. Because the car would not start

    _____

3. When I finished eating breakfast

    _____

4. Since I was tired

    _____

5. The party that I went to

    _____

PRACTICE 2

Underline the dependent-word fragment(s) in each selection. Then rewrite the selections, correcting the fragments by attaching them to the sentence that comes before or the sentence that comes after—whichever sounds more natural. Put a comma after the dependent-word group if it starts the sentence.

1. After I slid my aching bones into the hot water of the tub. I realized that there was no soap. I didn't want to get out again.

    _____

    _____

    _____

2. The peas and carrots had a flat taste. Since they had come from a can. I forced myself to eat them.

    _____

    _____

3. Because he had eaten and drunk too much. He had to leave the party early. His stomach was like a volcano. That was ready to erupt.

    _____

    _____

    _____

4. I used to believe that you had to wait exactly an hour after eating. Until you could go in swimming. If you tried to sneak in after only fifty-six minutes. Your stomach would know and you would drown immediately.

    _____

    _____

    _____

    _____

5. Today Pam got a call from James Wood. A boy that she had dated in high school. She agreed to have lunch with him. Although she had no intention of breaking off with her present boyfriend.

    _____

    _____

    _____

    _____

-ING AND *TO* FRAGMENTS

When an *-ing* word appears at or near the start of a word group, a fragment may result. Such fragments often lack a subject and part of the verb. Underline the word groups in the selections below that contain *-ing* words. Each is a fragment.

1   I spent almost two hours on the phone yesterday. Trying to find a garage to repair my car. Eventually I had to have it towed to a garage in another town.

2   She was at first very happy with the blue sports car she bought for only $500. Not realizing until a week later that the car averaged 7 miles a gallon of gas.

3   He looked forward to the study period at school. It being the only time he could sit unbothered and dream about his future. He imagined himself as a lawyer with lots of money and good women to spend it on.

People sometimes write *-ing* fragments because they think the subject in one sentence will work for the next word group as well. Thus, in the first selection, they think the subject *I* in the opening sentence will also serve as the subject for "Trying to find a garage to repair my car." But the subject must actually be *in* the sentence.

How to Correct -*ing* Fragments

1 Attach the fragment to the sentence that comes before or the sentence that comes after it, whichever makes sense. Selection 1 could read: "I spent two hours on the phone yesterday, trying to find a garage to repair my car."

2 Add a subject and change the *-ing* verb part to the correct form of the verb. Selection 2 could read: "She realized only a week later that the car averaged 7 miles a gallon of gas."

3 Change *being* to the correct form of the verb *be* (*am, are, is, was, were*). Selection 3 could read: "It was the only time he could sit unbothered and dream about his future."

How to Correct *to* Fragments

When *to* appears at or near the start of a word group, a fragment sometimes results:

I plan on working overtime. To get this job finished. Otherwise, my boss may get angry at me.

The second word group is a fragment and can be corrected by adding it to the preceding sentence:

I plan on working overtime to get this job finished.

PRACTICE 1

Underline the *-ing* fragment in each of the selections that follow. Then make it a sentence by rewriting it, using the method described in parentheses.

Example   A thunderstorm was brewing. A sudden breeze shot through the windows. Driving the stuffiness out of the room.

(Add the fragment to the preceding sentence.)

A sudden breeze shot through the windows, driving the stuffiness out of the room.

1. He works ten hours a day. Then going to class for 2½ hours. It is no wonder he writes sentence fragments.

(Correct the fragment by adding the subject *he* and changing *going* to the proper form of the verb, *goes*.)

_____

_____

2. After the alarm rang, he lay in bed ten minutes longer.   Wishing that he had $100,000.   With money he would not have to leave his beloved bed, except when he wanted to.

   (Add the fragment to the preceding sentence.)

   _____

   _____

3. Charlotte loved the movie *Gone with the Wind,* but Clyde hated it. His chief objection being that it lasted four hours.

   (Correct the fragment by changing *being* to the proper form of the verb, *was*.)

   _____

   _____

PRACTICE 2

Underline the *-ing* or *to* fragment(s) in each selection. Then rewrite each selection, correcting the fragments by using one of the three methods of correction described on page 16.

1. I could not find a space until I drove to the last parking lot. As a result, being late for class.

   _____

   _____

2. Martha Grencher is pleased with the carpet of Astro-Turf in her kitchen. Claiming that crumbs settle in the grass so she never sees them.

   _____

   _____

3. Looking down at the grass, which had suddenly begun to seem very squishy. I realized I had hiked into a marsh of some kind.

   _____

   _____

4. Some students show through body language that they don't want to get involved in a class. Hiding in the back or in a corner. But by sitting where you can have eye contact with teachers. You can make a favorable impression on them.

_____

_____

_____

_____

5. At the age of ten I had to recite a poem in church. I was afraid of the adults in the audience. Knowing they would pity me if I forgot my lines. I was also worried that the kids would giggle at me. To make me laugh if possible.

_____

_____

_____

_____

_____

ADDED-DETAIL FRAGMENTS

Added-detail fragments lack a subject and a verb. They often begin with one of the following words:

for example   also   except   such as   including   especially

See if you can locate and underline the one added-detail fragment in each of the selections that follow:

1 Clyde read in a consumer magazine that the ingredients in many cold medicines do not help a cold. Except for the aspirin in them. He could buy aspirin by itself at a much lower price.

2 The class often starts late. For example, yesterday at quarter after nine instead of at nine sharp.

3 He failed a number of courses before he earned his degree. Among them, English I, Economics, and General Biology.

People often write added-detail fragments for much the same reason they write *-ing* fragments. They think the subject and verb in one sentence will serve for the next word group as well. But the subject and verb must be in *each* word group.

How to Correct Added-Detail Fragments

1 Attach the fragment to the complete thought that precedes it. Selection 1 could read: "Clyde read in a consumer magazine that the ingredients in many cold medicines do not help a cold, except for the aspirin in them."

2 Add a subject and a verb to the fragment to make it a complete sentence. Selection 2 could read: "The class often starts late. For example, yesterday it began at quarter after nine instead of at nine sharp."

3 Change words as necessary to make the fragment part of the preceding sentence. Selection 3 could read: "Among the courses he failed before he earned his degree were English I, Economics, and General Biology."

PRACTICE **1**

Underline the fragment in each of the selections below. Then make it a sentence by rewriting it, using the method described in parentheses.

Example   I am always short of pocket money. <u>Especially for everyday items like magazines and sodas.</u>

(Add the fragment to the preceding sentence.)

<u>*I am always short of pocket money, especially for everyday items like magazines and sodas.*</u>

1. Bill is very accident-prone. For example, managing to cut his hand while crumbling a bar of shredded wheat.

   (Correct the fragment by adding the subject *he* and changing *managing* to the proper form of the verb, *managed*.)

   _____

   _____

2. The first load of wash should be white things. Such as bed sheets, pillowcases, towels, handkerchiefs, and underwear.

   (Add the fragment to the preceding sentence.)

   _____

   _____

3. I am the only woman I know who plays all kinds of card games for money. For example, poker, blackjack, and pinochle.

   (Correct the fragment by adding the subject and verb *I play.*)

   _____

   _____

   _____

   _____

PRACTICE 2

Underline the added-detail fragment in each selection. Then rewrite that part of the selection needed to correct the fragment. Use one of the three methods of correction described on page 19.

1. I could feel his anger building. Like a land mine ready to explode. I was silent because I didn't want to be the one to set it off.

   _____

   _____

   _____

   _____

2. Bill has enormous endurance. For example, the ability to lift weights for three hours and then play basketball all afternoon.

   _____

   _____

   _____

   _____

3. One of my greatest joys in life is eating desserts. Such as cherry cheesecake or vanilla cream puffs. Almond fudge cake makes me want to dance.

   _____

   _____

   _____

   _____

4. Andy used to have many bad eating habits. For instance, chewing with his mouth open. Another habit was touching food with his finger to see how cold or hot it was.

   _____

   _____

   _____

   _____

5. Clyde put potatoes in the oven without first punching holes in them. A half hour later, there were several explosions. With potatoes splattering all over the walls of the oven.

   _____

   _____

   _____

   _____

MISSING-SUBJECT FRAGMENTS

Underline the word group in which the subject is missing in each selection below.

1 One example of my father's generosity is that he visits sick friends in the hospital. And takes along get-well cards with a few dollars folded in them.

2 Sarah looked with admiration at the stunningly attractive model. And wondered how the model looked upon waking up in the morning.

How to Correct Missing-Subject Fragments

1 Attach the fragment to the preceding sentence. Selection 1 could read: "One example of my father's generosity is that he visits sick friends in the hospital and takes along get-well cards with a few dollars folded in them."

2 Add a subject (which can often be a pronoun standing for the subject in the preceding sentence). Selection 2 could read: "She wondered how the model looked upon waking up in the morning."

PRACTICE

Underline the missing-subject fragment in each selection. Then rewrite that part of the selection needed to correct the fragment. Use one of the two methods of correction described on page 21.

1. Tom went to the refrigerator to get milk for his breakfast cereal. And discovered about one tablespoon of milk left in the carton.

    _____

    _____

2. While sitting in class, she realized she had lost a ring. But happily found it in the women's room after class. The ring wasn't worth much money but had an enormous personal value to her.

    _____

    _____

3. Because they had a six-pack of beer with them, they were not allowed into the football game. Also, were asked to leave the parking lot as well. What angered them is that some adults carried beer into the game without being refused admission.

    _____

    _____

4. Sarah read that one of the first signs of aging is that the nose grows longer. She started checking her nose in the mirror each day. And even measured it with a ruler, so she'd have a figure to compare it with six months later.

    _____

    _____

    _____

5. Several teachers in my school embarrassed us with their sarcasm. Also, seated us in rows from the brightest student to the dumbest. I can imagine the pain the student in the last seat must have felt.

    _____

    _____

    _____

A REVIEW: How to Check for Sentence Fragments

1 Read your paper aloud from the *last* sentence to the *first*. You will be better able to see and hear whether each word group you read is a complete thought.

2 Ask yourself of any word group you think is a fragment: Does this contain a subject and a verb and express a complete thought?

3 More specifically, be on the lookout for the most common fragments:

- Dependent-word fragments (starting with words like *after, because, since, when,* and *before*)

- *-ing* and *to* fragments (*-ing* or *to* at or near the start of a word group)

- Added-detail fragments (starting with words like *for example, such as, also,* and *especially*)

- Missing-subject fragments (a verb is present but not the subject)

REVIEW TEST **1**

Underline the fragment in each selection. Then correct the fragment in the space provided.

Example   Sam received all kinds of junk mail. <u>Then complained to the post office</u>. Eventually, some of the mail stopped.

Then he complained to the post office.

1. After seeing an offensive mouthwash ad on television. I resolved never to buy that brand again.

2. A phone call warned me to be on the lookout for Joe Murdstone. Who just got back into town.

3. People worked together on the assembly line. Moving quickly and efficiently. They wanted to make as much money as possible.

4. Tony and Lola saw hundreds of lightning bugs flickering over the lake. While they were taking a midnight walk. They were also attacked by hundreds of man-of-war mosquitoes.

   _____

   _____

5. Hordock's furniture store just went out of business. The place where I worked as a stock boy. Now I'll have to look for another job.

   _____

   _____

6. One kind of defense mechanism is substitution. A form of self-deception in which we replace one goal with another. For example, if we cannot be an A-level student, we may try to be socially popular.

   _____

   _____

7. Italian food is mouth-watering. Especially pizza. Spaghetti is delicious, too.

   _____

   _____

8. Andy always wins at hide-and-seek. Peeking through his fingers as he counts to one hundred. Soon the other kids will catch on.

   _____

   _____

9. Margie has worked on the crossword puzzle all day. All the while, mumbling each clue out loud. I hope she finishes soon.

   _____

   _____

10. Our yard sale was an enormous success. We sold everything. Except for the self-portrait of my grandfather.

   _____

   _____

 REVIEW TEST 2

Turn each of the following word groups into a complete sentence. Use the space provided.

Example   Feeling very confident

Feeling very confident, I began my speech.

1. Bob, who is my best friend

   _____

2. Because I was short on cash

   _____

3. During my walk along the trail

   _____

4. The parking ticket that I forgot to pay

   _____

5. To get to the church on time

   _____

6. When the noise stopped

   _____

7. Was ready for a change

   _____

8. Forgetting to eat breakfast

   _____

9. Sue and several of her friends

   _____

10. After Tony hung up his shirt

    _____

REVIEW TEST 3

In the space provided, write *C* if a word group is a complete sentence; write *frag* if it is a fragment. The first two are done for you.

1. When I prepare for the beach.   *frag*

2. I first select a colorful bikini with a matching beach coat.   *C*

3. Second, gathering together a pair of large, dark sunglasses, a beach bag and beach towel, suntan lotion, and a very comfortable lounge chair.   _____

4. Also, a large rimmed hat in an unusual bright color.   _____

5. In addition, I take along my radio to listen to some popular music.   _____

6. Occasionally taking along a good book to read as well.   _____

7. I then make sure to tuck in my beach bag some fattening snacks.   _____

8. Such as potato chips, chocolate chip cookies, and a frozen candy bar insulated in aluminum foil.   _____

9. Before leaving, I check to make sure my fingernail polish matches my toenail polish.   _____

10. Then on my way to a great afternoon at the beach.   _____

Now correct the fragments you have found. Attach the fragments to sentences that come before or after them, or make whatever other change is needed to turn a fragment into a sentence. Use the space provided. The first one is corrected for you.

1. *When I prepare for the beach, I first select a colorful bikini with matching beach coat.*

2. _____

_____

3. _____

_____

4. _____

_____

5. _____

_____

6. _____

_____

REVIEW TEST 4

Write quickly for five minutes about what you like to do in your leisure time. Don't worry about spelling, punctuation, finding exact words, or organizing your thoughts. Just focus on writing as many words as you can without stopping.

After you have finished, go back and make whatever changes are needed to correct any fragments in your writing.

Run-on Sentences

A *run-on sentence* is two complete thoughts that are run together with no adequate sign given to mark the break between them.* Some run-on sentences have no punctuation at all to mark the break between the thoughts:

Rita decided to stop smoking she didn't want to die of lung cancer.
The exam was postponed the class was canceled as well.
I took lots of vitamin C however, I still came down with the flu.

In other run-on sentences, also known as *comma splices,* a comma is placed between the two complete thoughts. But the comma alone is ***not enough*** to join two complete thoughts:

Rita decided to stop smoking, she didn't want to die of lung cancer.
The exam was postponed, the class was canceled as well.
I took lots of vitamin C, however, I still came down with the flu.

There are three common ways of correcting run-on sentences:

1 Use a period and a capital letter to mark the break between the thoughts:

Rita decided to stop smoking. She didn't want to die of lung cancer.

The exam was postponed. The class was canceled as well.

I took lots of vitamin C. However, I still came down with the flu.

2 Use a comma plus a joining word (*and, but, for, or, nor, so, yet*) to connect the two complete thoughts:

Rita decided to stop smoking, for she didn't want to die of lung cancer.

The exam was postponed, and the class was canceled as well.

I took lots of vitamin C, but I still came down with the flu.

3 Use a semicolon (;) to connect the two complete thoughts:

Rita decided to stop smoking; she didn't want to die of lung cancer.
The exam was postponed; the class was canceled as well.
I took lots of vitamin C; however, I still came down with the flu.

* *Note:* Some instructors refer to each complete thought in a run-on sentence as an *independent clause.* A *clause* is simply a group of words having a subject and a verb. A clause may be *independent* (expressing a complete thought and able to stand alone) or *dependent* (not expressing a complete thought and not able to stand alone). A run-on sentence is two independent clauses that are run together with no adequate sign given to mark the break between them.

The following pages give you practice in the three most common methods of correcting run-on sentences. (A fourth method is introduced on page 35.)

METHOD 1: PERIOD AND A CAPITAL LETTER

One way of correcting a run-on sentence is to use a period and a capital letter at the break between the two complete thoughts. Use this method especially if the thoughts are not closely related or if another method would make the sentence too long.

PRACTICE

Locate the split in each of the following sentences. Reading each sentence aloud will help you "hear" where a major break or split in the thought occurs. At such a point, your voice will probably drop and pause.

Correct the run-on sentence by putting a period at the end of the first thought and a capital letter at the start of the next thought.

Example   Martha Grencher shuffled around the apartment in her slippers. Her husband couldn't stand their slapping sound on the floor.

1. No one swam in the lake that summer a little boy had dropped his pet piranhas into the water.

2. The window shade snapped up like a gunshot her cat leaped four feet off the floor.

3. Sue's doctor told her he was an astrology nut she did not feel good about learning that.

4. I always have bad luck with cotton jeans they shrink so much they end up around my ankles.

5. The heat was up to 80° in the apartment the air was so dry that her skin felt parched.

6. Lola didn't get into the bar the bouncer refused even to look at her fake I.D.

7. Lobsters are cannibalistic and will feed on each other this is one reason they are hard to raise in captivity.

8. All the chocolate candies had a purplish tinge as a result, she was afraid to eat any.

9. I brushed my teeth too hard as a child I actually wore away part of my gumline.

10. Fruit flies hovered around the kitchen sink the only way Clyde could kill them was by slapping them between his palms in midair.

A Warning: Words That Can Lead to Run-on Sentences

People often write run-on sentences when the second complete thought begins with one of the following words:

I	we	there	now
you	they	this	then
he, she, it		that	next

Remember to be on the alert for run-on sentences whenever you use one of these words in a paper.

PRACTICE

Write a second sentence to go with each of the sentences below. Start the second sentence with the word given in italics. Your sentences can be serious or playful.

Example   *then*   When the Wolfman came in the window, the first thing I did was pull a gun from under my pillow. *Then I said, "This gun shoots silver bullets, Buddy."*

he   1. The Wolfman did not hesitate. _____

_____

there   2. As we looked out of the tour bus, we saw all kinds of litter on the highway.

_____

then   3. The first thing I ate after the long hike was a bacon sandwich. _____

_____

it   4. I could not understand why my car would not start. _____

_____

she   5. Martha had never heard Fred use such language before. _____

_____

METHOD 2: COMMA AND A JOINING WORD

Another way of correcting a run-on sentence is to use a comma plus a joining word to connect the two complete thoughts. Joining words (also called *conjunctions*) include *and, but, for, or, nor, so,* and *yet*. Here is what the four most common joining words mean:

and: in addition to, along with

His feet hurt from the long hike, and his stomach was growling.

(*And* means *in addition:* His feet hurt from the long hike; *in addition,* his stomach was growling.)

but: however, except, on the other hand, just the opposite

I remembered to get the Kleenex, but I forgot to get the paper towels.

(*But* means *however:* I remembered to get the Kleenex; *however,* I forgot to get the paper towels.)

for: because, the reason why, the cause for something

She was afraid she would not do well in the course, for she had always had bad luck with English before.

(*For* means *because* or *the reason why:* She was afraid she would not do well in the course; *the reason why* was that she had always had bad luck with English before.)

If you are not comfortable using *for,* you may want to use *because* instead of *for* in the activities that follow. If you do use *because,* omit the comma before it.

so: as a result, therefore

The windshield wiper was broken, so she was in trouble when the rain started.

(*So* means *as a result:* The windshield wiper was broken; *as a result,* she was in trouble when the rain started.)

PRACTICE 1

Insert the joining word (*and, but, for, so*) that logically connects the two thoughts in each sentence.

1. A lot of men today get their hair styled, _____ they use perfume and other cosmetics as well.

2. Clyde asked his wife if she had any bandages, _____ he was dressed so sharply he was liable to cut himself to death.

3. I flunked Biology I and Introduction to Business, _____ I managed C's in Sociology and General Math.

4. She had trouble doing her homework, _____ her son was sick and kept distracting her.

5. He failed the vision part of his driver's test, _____ he did not get his driver's license that day.

PRACTICE 2

Add a complete and closely related thought to go with each of the following statements. Use a comma plus the italicized joining word when you write the second thought.

Example   *for*   Lola spent the day walking barefoot, *for the heel of one of her shoes came off.*

but   1. She wanted to go to the party _____

_____

and   2. Tony washed his car in the morning _____

_____

so   3. The day was dark and rainy _____

_____

for   4. I'm not going to eat in the school cafeteria anymore _____

_____

but   5. I asked my brother to get off the telephone _____

_____

PRACTICE 3

Place a slash mark at the break within each of the run-on sentences that follow. Remember that reading each sentence out loud (or "aloud" in your head) will help you hear the break. Then correct the run-on sentence by using either

1   a period and a capital letter

2   a comma and the logical joining word (*and, but, for, so*)

In general, use a period and a capital letter when the thoughts are not closely related in meaning. Use a comma and a joining word when the thoughts are closely related.

Examples Lola loves the velvety texture of cherry Jell-O/she also loves to squish it between her teeth.

Jello-O. She also

I can't study for the test this weekend, my boss wants me to work overtime.

weekend, for my boss

1. He used to fill up his tank with $10 worth of gas today the gas costs him $15.

2. I was a madman in my youth, I would do anything on a dare.

3. Lola missed her midsemester exam in Sociology 201 she had a flat tire while driving out on the Black Horse Pike.

4. Fred Grencher was surprised when he tasted his wife's homemade blueberry yogurt he didn't expect it to taste so good.

5. They planned to take a cruise for their summer vacation, they weren't able to save enough money.

6. He changes the baby's diapers he also prepares the formula.

7. Carol's hair is naturally oily, she has to wash it every morning.

8. David was angry at himself he had passed an old man sitting in a daze on the curb and had not stopped to help him.

9. Bill ate a ham and cheese on rye and half a pizza for supper then he had two ice cream bars and a big hunk of pound cake for dessert.

10. Clyde was angry at Charlotte and wanted to yell at her, he knew that was not going to solve anything.

METHOD 3: SEMICOLON

A third method of correcting a run-on sentence is to use a semicolon to mark the break between two thoughts. A *semicolon* (;) is made up of a period and a comma and is sometimes called a strong comma. The semicolon signals more of a pause than a comma alone but not quite the full pause of a period.

Here are some earlier sentences that were connected with a comma plus a joining word. Notice that a semicolon, unlike the comma alone, can be used to connect the two complete thoughts in each sentence:

A lot of men today get their hair styled; they use perfume and other cosmetics, too.

She had trouble doing her homework; her son was sick and kept distracting her.

I was a madman in my youth; I would do anything on a dare.

The use of the semicolon can add to sentence variety. For some people, however, the semicolon is a confusing mark of punctuation. Keep in mind that if you are not comfortable using it, you can and should use one of the first two methods of correcting a run-on sentence.

PRACTICE

Insert a semicolon where the break occurs between the two complete thoughts in each of the following sentences:

Example   She had a wig on; it looked more like a hat than a wig.

1. George robs banks for a living at age fifteen he wanted to be a banker.
2. Tony never goes to a certain gas station anymore he found out that the service manager overcharged him for a valve job.
3. I spent three months looking for an apartment I could not find anything decent for under $200 a month.
4. It rained all week parts of the highway were flooded.
5. A redheaded woodpecker tapped at the trunk of the cherry tree a conniving cat observed from a distance.

Semicolon with a Connecting Word

A semicolon is sometimes used with a connecting word and a comma to join two complete thoughts:

We were short of money; therefore, we decided not to eat out that weekend.

The roots of a geranium have to be crowded into a small pot; otherwise, the plants may not flower.

I had a paper to write; however, my brain had stopped working for the night.

Here is a list of common connecting words (also known as *adverbial conjunctions*). Brief meanings are given for most of the words.

however	means *but*
nevertheless	means *however*
on the other hand	means *however*
instead	means *as a substitute*
meanwhile	means *in the intervening time*
otherwise	means *under other conditions*
indeed	means *in fact*
in addition	
also	means *in addition*
moreover	means *in addition*
furthermore	means *in addition*
as a result	
thus	means *as a result*
consequently	means *as a result*
therefore	means *as a result*

PRACTICE

Choose a logical connecting word from the above group and write it in the space provided. In addition, put a semicolon *before* the connector and a comma *after* the connector.

Example Exams are over *; however,* I still feel tense and nervous.

1. I did not understand the teacher's point _____ I asked her to repeat it.

2. With his thumbnail, Clyde tried to split open the cellophane covering on the new record album _____ the cellophane refused to tear.

3. Fred Grencher worries about his hair thinning_____ he worries about developing a midriff bulge.

4.   They decided not to go to the movie _____ they went to play miniature golf.

5.   I decided to skip lunch _____ I would be late for class.

A Note on Subordination

A fourth method of joining together related thoughts is to use subordination. *Subordination* is a way of showing that one thought in a sentence is not as important as another thought. Here are three earlier sentences that have been recast so that one idea is subordinated to (made less important than) the other idea:

> When the window shade snapped up like a gunshot, her cat leaped four feet off the floor.

> Because it rained all week, parts of the highway were flooded.

> Although they planned to take a cruise for their summer vacation, they weren't able to save enough money.

Subordination is explained in full on pages 295 to 302.

A REVIEW: How to Check for Run-on Sentences

1   To see if a sentence is a run-on, read it aloud and listen for a break marking two complete thoughts. Your voice will probably drop and pause at the break.

2   To check an entire paper, read it aloud from the *last* sentence to the *first*. Doing so will help you hear and see each complete thought.

3   Be on the lookout for words that can lead to run-on sentences:

I	he, she, it	they	this	then
you	we	there	that	next

4   Correct run-on sentences by using one of the following methods:
   - A period and a capital letter
   - A comma and a joining word (*and, but, for, or, nor, so, yet*)
   - A semicolon
   - Subordination (as explained on pages 295–302)

REVIEW TEST **1**

Put a slash mark between the two complete thoughts in each of the sentences that follow. Then correct the run-on sentence in the space provided. Use either (1) a period and a capital letter or (2) a comma and the joining word *and, but, for,* or *so*. If the ideas seem closely related, you may want to use the joining word. Otherwise you may want to use a period and a capital letter.

Example   I moan and groan when I have to get up in the morning/

anyone hearing me would think I was crazy.   *morning. Anyone*

1. Flies were getting into the house, the window screen was torn. _____

2. She got A's in her math homework by using her pocket calculator she was not allowed to use the calculator at school. _____

3. I take a 250-milligram vitamin C tablet every morning I never get colds anymore. _____

4. He went down to the lake to take pictures of the Canadian geese it was raining and the geese had disappeared. _____

5. The Beatles sing "All You Need Is Love," Frank really believes this is true. _____

6. Clyde met Charlotte at McDonald's they shared a large order of fries. _____

7. I found the cat sleeping on the stove, the dog was eating the morning mail. _____

8. I lifted the empty Coke bottle above me, a few more drops fell out of it and into my thirsty mouth. _____

9. She had a twenty-mile drive to the school she sometimes arrived late for class. _____

10. These pants are guaranteed to wear like iron they also feel like iron. _____

REVIEW TEST 2

Correct each run-on sentence by using either (1) a period and a capital letter, (2) a comma and a joining word, or (3) a semicolon. Do not use one method of correction exclusively.

Example Tony hated going to a new barber. $\overset{H}{\cancel{he}}$ was afraid his hair would be butchered.

1. He took enormous bites of the roast beef sandwich it was the first decent thing he had eaten all day.

2. Sara leaped up screaming a black spider was on her leg.

3. My wet fingers stuck to the frosty ice cube tray, I had to pry them loose before they froze.

4. Four films were playing in town three were X-rated, and one was a Disney cartoon.

5. Clyde took his son to the children's zoo at the shopping center both of them enjoyed petting the goats, lambs, and fawns.

6. The fried crust on my veal cutlet was thicker than the cutlet therefore, I asked the waiter to take it back to the kitchen.

7. Tony got terry-cloth covers for his car the original vinyl material made his pants sweat.

8. She's very tired when she gets home from work she often sleeps for an hour before dinner.

9. I wanted badly to cry however, I remained cold and silent.

10. My freshman year in college was not a success I spent most of my time in the game room.

REVIEW TEST 3

On separate paper, write nine sentences, each of which has two complete thoughts. Use a period and a capital letter between the thoughts in three of the sentences. Use a comma and a joining word (*and, but, or, nor, for, so, yet*) to join the thoughts in another three sentences. Use a semicolon to join the thoughts in the final three sentences.

REVIEW TEST 4

Write quickly for five minutes about what you did this past weekend. Don't worry about spelling, punctuation, finding exact words, or organizing your thoughts. Just focus on writing as many words as you can without stopping.

After you have finished, go back and make whatever changes are needed to correct any run-on sentences in your writing.

Verb Endings

People at times have trouble with verb endings for the present tense (-s or -es) or the past tense (-ed). They may drop such endings when speaking and, as a result, also tend to drop them when writing. The activities in this section should help make the inclusion of verb endings a writing habit.

PRESENT TENSE ENDINGS

Following are examples of verbs in the present tense. Notice that in these cases no verb ending is needed:

I look at you.
You smile at me.
We enjoy each other.
People like us.
They respect us as well.

But a verb ending is needed when the subject is *he, she, it,* or any one person or thing:

He	He yells.
She	She throws things.
It	It really angers me.
One person	Their son John storms out of the house.
One person	Their daughter Sheila cries.
One thing	At night the house jumps.

Remember, then, to add -s or -es to the present form of any verb that follows *he, she, it,* or any one person or thing. Here are some other examples:

Clyde believes in looking good. (Add -s to *believe*)

He dresses as carefully as his wife. (Add -es to *dress*)

She tries to help him coordinate his outfits. (*Note:* For a word ending in a consonant plus *y*, always change the *y* to *i* before adding -es.)

PRACTICE 1

All but one of the ten sentences that follow need -s or -es verb endings. Cross out the incorrect verb forms and write the correct forms in the spaces provided. Mark the correct sentence with a *C*.

Example   Pat gossip about me all the time.   *gossips*

1. He tow away cars for a living and is ashamed of his job. _____
2. The book sell for $8 but is worth about $2. _____
3. Lola was please by Tony's thoughtful gift. _____
4. Whole wheat bread taste better to me than rye bread. _____
5. Bob weaken his lungs by smoking so much. _____
6. The sick baby cry whenever her mother puts her down. _____
7. You make me angry sometimes. _____
8. Clyde drive 25 miles to work each day. _____
9. She live in a rough section of town. _____
10. He feel that former convicts should be denied voting rights. _____

PRACTICE 2

Rewrite the short selection below, adding present tense -*s* verb endings wherever needed.

Charlotte react badly when she get caught in a traffic jam. She open the dashboard compartment and pull out an old pack of Marlboros that she keep for such occasions. She light up and drag heavily, sucking the smoke deep into her lungs. She get out of the car and look down the highway, trying to see where the delay is. Back in the car, she drum her fingers on the steering wheel. If the jam last long enough, she start talking to herself and angrily kick off her shoes.

_____
_____
_____
_____
_____
_____
_____
_____

PRACTICE 3

Write five sentences in the present tense about people you know. Use the verbs below.

Example love *My wife loves to read People magazine.*

work 1. _____

smile 2. _____

try 3. _____

dress 4. _____

carry 5. _____

PAST TENSE ENDINGS

Regular verbs form the past tense by adding *-d* or *-ed* to the present. Here are examples of verbs in the past tense:

At one time Clyde *smoked* two packs of cigarettes a day, but then he *started* sucking lollipops instead.
(Add *-d* to *smoke* and *-ed* to *start*.)

Sarah *hurried* to get to Safeway before closing time.
(For a word ending in a consonant plus *y*, always change the *y* to *i* before adding *-ed*. Thus, *hurry + ed = hurried*.)

When the bus *stopped* at my street, I was daydreaming and forgot to get off.
(Double a final consonant when adding *-ed* to a word that, first, has one syllable or is accented on the last syllable and, second, ends with a consonant preceded by a vowel. Thus, *stop + ed = stopped*.)

PRACTICE 1

Add *-d* or *-ed* verb endings where needed in the sentences that follow.

Example This morning I fail*ed* a chemistry quiz.

1. Jack always enjoy eating anchovy pizza, but one day it start doing a flaming sword dance in his stomach.

2. My mother warm up the meat loaf for me, and I gobble it hungrily.

3. I miss quite a few days of class early in the semester while getting my head together, but I have resolve to make up the work.

4. When my baby brother start crying, my father turn on the TV for him.

5. I pinch my finger in the door, and it swell to twice its size.

6. My father patch the ceiling, but it collapse this morning anyway.

7. I invited only members of the track team to the meeting, but Sid show up anyway.

8. As Alice was about to finish work last night, a man walk into the diner and order two dozen hamburgers.

9. Sam try to put out the candle flame with his finger; he end up burning himself.

10. The chili we prepared yesterday burn my insides.

PRACTICE 2

Rewrite the short selection below, adding past tense *-d* or *-ed* verb endings wherever needed.

Bill's boss shout at Bill. Feeling bad, Bill went home and curse his wife. Then his wife scream at their son. Angry himself, the son went out and cruelly tease a little girl who live next door until she cry. Bad feelings were pass on as one person wound the next with ugly words. No one manage to break the vicious cycle.

_____

_____

_____

_____

_____

_____

PRACTICE 3

Write five sentences in the past tense using the verbs at the top of the next page.

Example snore *You snored like a chain saw last night.*

laugh   1. _____

arrive 2. _____

hurry   3. _____

rob   4. _____

prepare 5. _____

REVIEW TEST 1

Decide on the correct *-s*, *-es*, *-d*, or *-ed* ending for each verb at the left and write the verb in the space provided. The context will show you whether present or past time is involved. In some cases, you can use either present or past tense.

Example   live   The bird that _____*lives*_____ under the rafters of my porch

add   _____*adds*_____ a few more twigs to her nest each day.

pull   1. When I _____ the blanket out of the spin drier, it crackled and

pop   _____ with static electricity.

wrap   2. The blanket _____ itself around my arm as I

try   _____ to fold it.

pick   3. When he _____ the morning newspaper off the front step, a

scurry   shiny brown bug _____ from under it, past his bare feet and into the house.

enjoy 4. He _____ watching *Star Trek* reruns when they play on tele-

watch   vision. However, he never _____ the series when it first played on television.

tell   5. Although Lola _____ Tony she loves him, she sometimes

like   _____ to go out with other men.

know   6. Tony _____ this and so doesn't feel guilty when he

flirt   _____ with other women.

tow   7. Yesterday my car was _____ away for illegal parking; a friend

charge   tells me the city _____ $50 to give it back.

hurry 8. She _____ to get the dishes done before the movie

start   _____ on television.

clean   9.   In the evening while Clyde _____ up the supper dishes, Char-

play   lotte _____ with her son in the backyard.

burn   10.   The cheese pizza _____ the roof of his mouth, and he quickly

swallow   _____ some cold water.

REVIEW TEST **2**

Use the spaces provided to write in the verbs and the dropped *-s*, *-es*, *-d*, or *-ed* endings in the following sentences. You can tell from the context of each sentence whether present or past time is involved. Put a *C* beside the one sentence with no verb-ending mistakes.

1. The most stubborn person Vonnie know is her boyfriend, James Fisher. _____

2. If James say "No" to something that is exactly what he mean. _____ _____

3. Once Vonnie ask him if she could use his car to go shopping, and he answer, "Not until you have more driving experience." _____ _____

4. Vonnie had been driving for almost two years and plead with him until she was almost blue in the face, but the answer was still "No." _____

5. Last Christmas James promise to spend the holidays with her family. _____

6. He stay for Christmas Day only, though she try to persuade him to stay for a few more days. _____ _____

7. He said, "I promise I would stay for Christmas, but that's all. My boss plan to work tomorrow, and I plan to be with him." _____ _____

8. He then explain that his boss had promise him extra pay. _____ _____

9. There was nothing Vonnie could do to stop him. _____

10. Once James make up his mind about something he really stand his ground. _____ _____

Irregular Verbs

Regular verbs form the past tense and the past participle (the form of the verb used with *have, has,* or *had*) simply by adding *-d* or *-ed* to the present. For example, the past tense of the regular verb *enjoy* is *enjoyed*; the past participle is *have, has,* or *had enjoyed*. However, other verbs have irregular forms in their past tense and past participle. For example, the past tense of the irregular verb *grow* is *grew*; the past participle is (*have, has,* or *had*) *grown*.

LIST OF IRREGULAR VERBS

Almost everyone has some degree of trouble with irregular verbs. When you are unsure about the form of a verb, you can check the list of irregular verbs on the following pages. Or you can check your dictionary, which gives the principal parts of irregular verbs (see page 152).

Present	Past	Past Participle
arise	arose	arisen
awake	awoke *or* awaked	awoken *or* awaked
be (am, are, is)	was (were)	been
become	became	become
begin	began	begun
bend	bent	bent
bite	bit	bitten
blow	blew	blown
break	broke	broken
bring	brought	brought
build	built	built
burst	burst	burst
buy	bought	bought
catch	caught	caught
choose	chose	chosen
come	came	come
cost	cost	cost
cut	cut	cut
do (does)	did	done
draw	drew	drawn
drink	drank	drunk
drive	drove	driven
eat	ate	eaten

fall	fell	fallen
feed	fed	fed
feel	felt	felt
fight	fought	fought
find	found	found
fly	flew	flown
freeze	froze	frozen
get	got	got *or* gotten
give	gave	given
go (goes)	went	gone
grow	grew	grown
have (has)	had	had
hear	heard	heard
hide	hid	hidden
hold	held	held
hurt	hurt	hurt
keep	kept	kept
know	knew	known
lay	laid	laid
lead	led	led
leave	left	left
lend	lent	lent
let	let	let
lie	lay	lain
light	lit	lit
lose	lost	lost
make	made	made
meet	met	met
pay	paid	paid
ride	rode	ridden
ring	rang	rung
run	ran	run
say	said	said
see	saw	seen
sell	sold	sold
send	sent	sent
shake	shook	shaken
shrink	shrank	shrunk
shut	shut	shut
sing	sang	sung
sit	sat	sat
sleep	slept	slept
speak	spoke	spoken
spend	spent	spent
stand	stood	stood

steal	stole	stolen
stick	stuck	stuck
sting	stung	stung
swear	swore	sworn
swim	swam	swum
take	took	taken
teach	taught	taught
tear	tore	torn
tell	told	told
think	thought	thought
wake	woke *or* waked	woken *or* waked
wear	wore	worn
win	won	won
write	wrote	written

PRACTICE 1

Cross out the incorrect verb form in the following sentences. Then write the correct form of the verb in the space provided.

Example   When the mud slide started, the whole neighborhood ~~begun~~ going downhill.   *began*

1. The game show contestant learned she had chose the box
   with a penny in it.   _____

2. The mechanic done an expensive valve job on my engine
   without getting my permission.   _____

3. Charlotte has wore that ring since the day Clyde bought
   it for her.   _____

4. She has wrote a paper that will make you roar with laughter. _____

5. The gas station attendant gived him the wrong change.   _____

6. My sister be at school when a stranger came asking for her
   at our home.   _____

7. The basketball team has broke the school record for most
   losses in a year.   _____

8. Because I had lended him the money, I had a natural
   concern about what he did with it.   _____

9. I seen that stray dog nosing around the yard yesterday.   _____

10. I knowed her face from somewhere, but I couldn't re-
    member just where.   _____

PRACTICE 2

For each of the italicized verbs, fill in the three missing forms in the following order:

(*a*) The present tense, which takes an -*s* ending when the subject is *he, she, it,* or any *one person* or *thing* (see page 38)

(*b*) The past tense

(*c*) The past participle—the form that goes with the helping verb *have, has,* or *had*

Example My uncle likes to *give* away certain things. He (*a*) __*gives*__ old, threadbare clothes to the Salvation Army. Last year he (*b*) __*gave*__ me a worthless television set in which the picture tube was burned out. He (*c*) has __*given*__ away stuff that a junk dealer would reject.

1. I like to *freeze* Hershey bars. A Hershey bar (*a*) _____ in half an hour. Once I (*b*) _____ a bottle of Yoo-Hoo. I put it in the freezer to chill and then forgot about it. Later I opened the freezer and discovered that it had (*c*) _____ and exploded.

2. I *know* the girl in the lavender bikini. She (*a*) _____ me, too. I (*b*) _____ her brother before I met her. I have (*c*) _____ him since boyhood.

3. My relatives like to *grow* things. For example, my grandmother (*a*) _____ poppies. Last year she (*b*) _____ Venus's-flytraps. She had (*c*) _____ mostly tobacco plants the year before.

4. I *go* to parties a lot. Often Camille (*a*) _____ with me. She (*b*) _____ with me just last week. I have (*c*) _____ to parties every Friday for the past month.

5. My brother likes to *throw* things. Sometimes he (*a*) _____ socks in his bureau drawer. In high school he (*b*) _____ footballs while quarterbacking the team. And he has (*c*) _____ Frisbees in our backyard for as long as I can remember.

6. I *see* her every weekend. She (a) _____ her other friends
    during the week. We first (b) _____ each other on a cold
    Saturday night last winter, when we went for supper at an Indian restau-
    rant. Since then we have (c) _____ each other every weekend
    except when my car has broken down.

7. I often *lie* down for a few minutes after a hard day's work. Sometimes my
    husband (a) _____ down with me. Yesterday was Saturday,
    so we (b) _____ in bed all morning. We probably would have
    (c) _____ in bed all afternoon, but we wanted to get some
    planting done in our vegetable garden.

8. I *do* not understand the assignment. It simply (a) _____ not
    make sense to me. I was surprised to learn that Shirley (b)
    _____ understand it. In fact, she had already (c)
    _____ the assignment.

9. I often find it hard to *begin* writing a paper. The assignment that I must do
    (a) _____ to worry me while I'm watching television, but I
    seldom turn off the set. Once I waited until the late movie had ended before
    I (b) _____ to write. If I had (c) _____ earlier,
    I would have gotten a decent night's sleep.

10. Martha likes to *eat*. She (a) _____ as continuously as some
    people smoke. Once she (b) _____ a large pack of cookies in
    half an hour. Even if she has (c) _____ a heavy meal, she
    often starts munching snacks right afterward.

TROUBLESOME IRREGULAR VERBS

Four common irregular verbs that often given people trouble are *be, do, have,*
and *go.* See page 53 for a discussion of these verbs. Three sets of other irregular
verbs that can lead to difficulties are *lie-lay, sit-set,* and *rise-raise.*

Lie-Lay

The principal parts of *lie* and *lay* are

Present	Past	Past Participle
lie	lay	lain
lay	laid	laid

To lie means *to recline* or *to rest. To lay* means *to put* or *to place something.*

To lie	To lay
Tony *lies* on the couch.	I *lay* the mail on the table.
This morning he *lay* in the tub.	Yesterday I *laid* the mail on the counter.
He has *lain* in bed all week with the flu.	I have *laid* the mail where everyone will see it.

PRACTICE

Underline the correct verb. Use a form of *lie* if you can substitute *recline*. Use a form of *lay* if you can substitute *place*.

1. Martha is the sort of person who (lies, lays) her cards on the table.
2. I am going to (lie, lay) another log on the fire.
3. (Lying, Laying) down for an hour after supper helps Fred regain his energy.
4. I have (lain, laid) all the visitors' coats in the master bedroom.
5. Frankenstein (lay, laid) on the table, waiting for lightning to recharge his batteries.

Sit-Set

The principal parts of *sit* and *set* are

Present	Past	Past Participle
sit	sat	sat
set	set	set

To sit means *to take a seat* or *to rest*. *To set* means *to put* or *to place*.

To sit	To set
I *sit* down during work breaks.	Tony *sets* out the knives, forks, and spoons.
I *sat* in the doctor's office for three hours.	His sister already *set* out the dishes.
I have always *sat* in the last desk.	They have just *set* out the dinnerware.

PRACTICE

Underline the correct form of the verb. Use a form of *sit* if you can substitute *rest*. Use a form of *set* if you can substitute *place*.

1. During family arguments I try to (sit, set) on the fence instead of taking sides.
2. I walked three blocks before (sitting, setting) down the heavy suitcases.

3.   Charlie (sat, set) the grapefruit on the teacher's desk.

4.   That poor man has not (sat, set) down once today.

5.   You can (sit, set) the laundry basket on top of the washer.

Rise-Raise

The principal parts of *rise* and *raise* are

Present	Past	Past Participle
rise	rose	risen
raise	raised	raised

To rise means *to get up* or *to move up*. *To raise* (which is a regular verb with simple *-ed* endings) means *to lift up*.

To rise	To raise
The soldiers *rise* at dawn.	I'm going to *raise* the stakes in the card game.
The crowd *rose* to applaud the batter.	I *raised* the shades to let in the sun.
Dracula has *risen* from the grave.	I would have quit if the company had not *raised* my salary.

PRACTICE

Underline the correct verb. Use a form of *rise* if you can substitute *get up*. Use a form of *raise* if you can substitute *lift up*.

1.   Even though I can sleep late on Sunday if I want to, I usually (rise, raise) early.

2.   Some dealers (rise, raise) rather than lower their prices before a sale.

3.   After five days of steady rain, the water in the dam had (risen, raised) to a dangerous level.

4.   The landlord (rose, raised) the rent in order to force the tenants out of the apartment.

5.   The cost of living (rises, raises) steadily from year to year.

REVIEW TEST 1

Cross out the incorrect verb form. Then write the correct form of the verb in the space provided.

1.   While I was kneading the meat loaf, someone rung the doorbell.   _____

2. My first grade teacher, Ms. Rickstein, teached me the meaning of fear. _____

3. Lola brang a sweatshirt with her, for she knew the mountains got cold at night. _____

4. We done the grocery shopping on Thursday evening. _____

5. She had went home early from the dance, for she didn't like any of the people she had seen there. _____

6. The police officer came with me when I drived home to get my owner's registration card. _____

7. The boy next door growed 6 inches in less than a year. _____

8. We had gave the landlord notice three times that our plumbing system needed repairs, and each time he failed to respond. _____

9. I had ate so much food at the buffet dinner that I went into the bathroom to loosen my belt. _____

10. Last summer I swum the width of that river and back again. _____

REVIEW TEST 2

Write short sentences that use the form requested for the following irregular verbs.

Example The past of *ride* _The Lone Ranger rode into the sunset._

1. The past of *break* _____
2. The past participle of *bring* _____
3. The past participle of *grow* _____
4. The past of *choose* _____
5. The present of *do* _____
6. The past of *drunk* _____
7. The past participle of *write* _____
8. The present of *give* _____
9. The past participle of *begin* _____
10. The present of *go* _____

Subject-Verb Agreement

A verb must agree with its subject in number.   A *singular subject* (one person or thing) takes a singular verb.   A *plural subject* (more than one person or thing) takes a plural verb.   Here are some examples of singular <u>subjects</u> and <u>verbs</u>:

Her weird <u>cat</u> <u>bites</u> people.
A diesel truck <u>driver</u> <u>makes</u> good money.
<u>He</u> <u>looks</u> as though <u>he</u> <u>wants</u> trouble.

Here are some examples of plural <u>subjects</u> and <u>verbs</u>:

Her weird <u>cats</u> <u>bite</u> people.
Diesel truck <u>drivers</u> <u>make</u> good money.
<u>They</u> <u>look</u> as though <u>they</u> <u>want</u> trouble.

Note: If a subject is *he, she, it,* or any one person or thing, the letter *-s* is added to the present verb.   (See also page 38.)

PRACTICE

Underline the correct word in the parentheses.

1.   The fan (needs, need) to be oiled.

2.   The snakes (slithers, slither).

3.   He (drives, drive) cautiously.

4.   The radio (blares, blare).

5.   My sister (loves, love) Donald Duck cartoons.

6.   His sneakers (squeaks, squeak).

7.   The sheet (looks, look) faded.

8.   The shirt (itches, itch) my arms.

9.   I bought some shrubs that (grows, grow) quickly.

10.   The book (appears, appear) well used.

AGREEMENT MISTAKES WITH FOUR COMMON IRREGULAR VERBS

Four common irregular verbs that may lead to agreement mistakes are *be, have, do,* and *go.* The principal parts of these verbs are

Present	Past	Past Participle
be	was	been
have	had	had
do	did	done
go	went	gone

You should know by heart the principal parts of these four verbs and also their present and past tense forms.

	Present		Past	
Be	I am	we are	I was	we were
	you are	you are	you were	you were
	he, she, it is	they are	he, she, it was	they were
Have	I have	we have	I had	we had
	you have	you have	you had	you had
	he, she, it has	they have	he, she, it had	they had
Do	I do	we do	I did	we did
	you do	you do	you did	you did
	he, she, it does	they do	he, she, it did	they did
Go	I go	we go	I went	we went
	you go	you go	you went	you went
	he, she, it goes	they go	he, she, it went	they went

PRACTICE

Cross out the incorrect verb form. Then write the correct form of the verb in the space provided. The number of spaces will tell you how many corrections to make in each sentence.

Example   Everyone has went home.   *gone* _____

1. Because I had a study hour before class, I were able to prepare for the quiz.   _____

2. Carol has a better typewriter than I does, so I is going to borrow it.   _____ _____

3. My television have to be fixed, for I does not want to miss the football game on Sunday.   _____   _____

4. My parents do so much for me that I be reluctant to ask them for a loan.   _____

5. They has decided to buy a VW, for it have everything they want in a car.   _____   _____

6. I were late for class because I only done my homework after getting up this morning.   _____   _____

7. It be frustrating to do your best and still have someone finish ahead of you.   _____

8. They be going to the dance, but I is staying home.   _____   _____

9. I were lightheaded and dizzy, so I gone to the coffee shop to eat.   _____   _____

10. Carol have to watch *60 Minutes* tonight, for her teacher have asked her to write a summary of the show.   _____   _____

Notes:

1 The verb *be* cannot by itself serve as a verb. You can use *be* only with another verb or the word *to*.

Incorrect	Correct
I be tired.	I am tired.
They be leaving soon.	They will be leaving soon.
You are going be late.	You are going to be late.

2 People sometimes make agreement mistakes with the following contractions. Think of the two words that each contraction stands for before using the contraction in a sentence.

doesn't (means *does not*)   don't (means *do not*)
wasn't (means *was not*)   weren't (means *were not*)

PRACTICE

Write a short sentence using correctly each of the verbs shown.

1. don't _____

2. wasn't _____

3. weren't _____

4. be _____

5. doesn't _____

OTHER SITUATIONS IN WHICH AGREEMENT MISTAKES ARE MADE

Mistakes in subject-verb agreement are sometimes made in the following situations:

- When words come between the subject and the verb
- When a verb comes before the subject
- With compound subjects
- With *who, which,* and *that*
- With special singular words

Each of these situations is explained on the following pages.

Words between the Subject and the Verb

Words that come between the subject and the verb do not change subject-verb agreement. In the following sentence,

The mean <u>cockroaches</u> behind my stove <u>get</u> high on Raid.

the subject (<u>cockroaches</u>) is plural and so the verb (<u>get</u>) is plural. The words *behind my stove* that come between the subject and the verb do not affect subject-verb agreement.

To help find the subject of certain sentences, you should cross out prepositional phrases (see page 7):

One ~~of the crooked politicians~~ was jailed ~~for a month~~.
Hamburger Helper, ~~along with other food supplements,~~ stretches my budget.

PRACTICE

Underline the subject and lightly cross out any words that come between the subject and the verb. Then double underline the verb choice in parentheses that you believe is correct.

Example The <u>price</u> ~~of the stereo speakers~~ (<u><u>is</u></u>, are) too high for my wallet.

1. The blue stain on the sheets (comes, come) from the cheap dish towel that I put in the washer with them.
2. The sport coat, along with the two pairs of pants, (sells, sell) for just $49.
3. The roots of the apple tree (is, are) very shallow.
4. Clyde's sisters, who wanted to be at his surprise party, (was, were) unable to come because of flooded roads.
5. The dust-covered books in the attic (belongs, belong) to my father.
6. The decisions of the judge (seems, seem) questionable.
7. Two cups of coffee in the morning (does, do) not make up a hearty breakfast.
8. The rust spots on the back bumpers of Emily's car (needs, need) to be cleaned off with a special polish.
9. The electric wiring in the apartments (is, are) dangerous and (needs, need) replacing.
10. Chapter Four of the psychology book, along with six weeks of class notes, (is, are) to be the basis of the test.

Verb before the Subject

A verb agrees with its subject even when the verb comes *before* the subject. Words that may precede the subject include *there, here,* and, in questions, *who, which, what,* and *where.*

<u>Waiting</u> for Martha Grencher at the streetcorner <u><u>were</u></u> two <u>panhandlers</u>.
There <u><u>are</u></u> many pizza <u>joints</u> in my town.
Here <u><u>is</u></u> your <u>receipt</u>.
Where <u><u>are</u></u> <u>they</u> <u>going</u> to sleep?

If you are unsure about the subject, ask *who* or *what* of the verb. With the first example above, you might ask, "*Who* were waiting at the streetcorner?" The answer, *two panhandlers,* is the subject.

PRACTICE

Write the correct form of the verb in the space provided.

(is, are)   1. There _____ long lines at the checkout counter.

(was, were)   2. Scampering to the door to greet Mrs. Grencher _____ her two little dogs.

(is, are)   3. Faster than speeding bullets _____ Superman.

(do, does)   4. Where _____ you go when you want to be alone?

(is, are)   5. Here _____ the site where the new gas station will be built.

(was, were) 6. At the end of the line, hoping to get seats into the movie, _____ Janet and Maureen.

(is, are)   7. There _____ too many people in this room for me to feel comfortable.

(is, are)   8. There _____ pretzels in the kitchen if you want something to go with your drinks.

(knows, know) 9. Who _____ the way out of this building?

(was, were) 10. I kept checking the mailbox because I forgot there _____ no mail delivered on a holiday.

Compound Subjects

Subjects joined by *and* generally take a plural verb.

Yoga and biking are Lola's ways of staying in shape.
Fear and ignorance have a lot to do with hatred.

When subjects are joined by *either . . . or, neither . . . nor, not only . . . but also,* the verb agrees with the subject closer to the verb.

Either the BeeGees or Stevie Wonder deserves the award for best album of the year.

The nearer subject, *Stevie Wonder,* is singular, and so the verb is singular.

PRACTICE

Write the correct form of the verb in the space provided.

(was, were) 1. Owning a car and having money in my pocket _____ the chief ambitions of my adolescence.

(has, have) 2. The kitchen and the bathroom _____ to be cleaned.

(is, are)   3. Going shopping and doing the laundry _____ two activities that take a good deal of my time.

(was, were) 4. Before they saw a marriage therapist, Peter and Jenny _____ planning to get divorced.

(is, are) 5. Not only the landlady's dog but also her children _____ very unfriendly to us.

(grows, grow) 6. Juicy strawberries and plump raspberries _____ in Mrs. Bland's backyard.

(has, have) 7. Jack Nicholson and Faye Dunaway _____ signed to co-star in the movie.

(is, are) 8. Watching birds through a telescope and restoring old furniture _____ two interests in my life.

(visits, visit) 9. My aunt and uncle from Canada _____ us every summer.

(is, are) 10. Light beer and white wine _____ the only alcoholic beverages the small café serves.

Who, Which, and That

When *who, which,* or *that* are used as subjects, they take singular verbs if the word they stand for is singular and plural verbs if the word they stand for is plural.

The bearded guy who is wearing the tight jeans is the soccer coach.

The verb is singular because *who* stands for *guy,* which is singular.

The guys who are wearing baggy pants are teachers.

The verb is plural because *who* stands for *guys,* which is plural.

PRACTICE

Write in the correct form of the verb in the space provided.

(lacks, lack) 1. He is a student who _____ the hunger to succeed.

(takes, take) 2. I dislike people who _____ advantage of me.

(is, are) 3. Carl took the recipes from a book which _____ very popular.

(was, were) 4. I removed the sheets that _____ jamming my washer.

(gives, give) 5. The Chevette is one of the small American cars that _____ good gasoline mileage.

(blares, blare)   6. The radio that _____ all night belongs to Mr. Finch.

(calls, call)   7. I resent a stranger who _____ me ''Honey.''

(braves, brave)   8. All the cheerleaders who _____ the weather deserve medals.

(scares, scare)   9. The noises that _____ us each night are being investigated.

(stumbles, stumble)   10. This job isn't for people who _____ over tough decisions.

Special Singular Subjects

The following words always take singular verbs:

one	anyone	everyone	someone	each
no one	anybody	everybody	somebody	either
nobody	anything	everything	something	neither
nothing				

Note: Both always takes a plural verb.

PRACTICE

Write in the correct form of the verb in the space provided.

(ignores, ignore)   1. Everyone in the neighborhood _____ Charlie Brown.

(dances, dance)   2. Nobody _____ like he does.

(deserves, deserve)   3. Either of our football team's guards _____ to be an all-state guard.

(was, were)   4. Both of the race drivers _____ injured.

(appears, appear)   5. Everyone who received an invitation _____ to be here.

(volunteers, volunteer)   6. No one ever _____ to work on that committee.

(owns, own)   7. One of my sisters _____ a car.

(has, have)   8. Somebody _____ been taking shopping carts from the super-market.

(thinks, think)   9. Everyone that I talked to _____ the curfew is a good idea.

(has, have)   10. Each of the candidates _____ talked about withdrawing from the race.

REVIEW TEST 1

Underline the correct word in the parentheses.

1. The carrots (was, were) moldy.
2. That ragged boy scrambling through the hedges (is, are) from the new family on the block.
3. The hamburger (does, do) not taste fresh.
4. There (is, are) five formulas we have to memorize for the test.
5. The comics in the newspaper (is, are) the first thing she reads.
6. Where (does, do) the McMurrays keep their new car?
7. The oily pizza and the watered-down coffee (was, were) hardly a memorable meal.
8. The rug and the wallpaper in that room (has, have) to be replaced.
9. Each of those breakfast cereals (contains, contain) a high proportion of sugar.
10. Vines that (winds, wind) heavily around trees sometimes kill them.

REVIEW TEST 2

Underline the correct word in the parentheses.

1. The old man standing under the park trees (does, do) not look happy.
2. The record (has, have) several deep scratches.
3. Skittering across the pond's surface (was, were) dozens of water bugs.
4. The price of the set of dishes you like so much (is, are) $84.
5. Mary's gentle voice and pleasant smile (attracts, attract) people to her.
6. Heavy snows and months of subfreezing temperatures (is, are) two reasons I moved to Florida.
7. What time in the morning (does, do) planes leave for Denver?
8. The serious look in that young girl's eyes (worries, worry) me.
9. I don't enjoy persons who (likes, like) to play pranks.
10. Everybody (agrees, agree) that the meeting was valuable.

Consistent Verb Tense

Do not shift verb tenses unnecessarily. If you begin writing a paper in the present tense, don't shift suddenly to the past. If you begin in the past, don't shift without reason to the present. Notice the inconsistent verb tenses in the following selection:

The shoplifter *walked* quickly toward the front of the store. When a clerk *shouts* at him, he *started* to run.

The verbs must be consistently in the present tense:

The shoplifter *walks* quickly toward the front of the store. When a clerk *shouts* at him, he *starts* to run.

Or the verbs must be consistently in the past tense:

The shoplifter *walked* quickly toward the front of the store. When a clerk *shouted* at him, he *started* to run.

PRACTICE

In each selection one verb must be changed so that it agrees in tense with the other verbs. Cross out the incorrect verb and write the correct form in the space at the right.

Example   Ted wanted to be someplace else when the dentist ~~carries~~ in a long needle.   *carried*

1. I played my stereo and watched television before I decide to do some homework.   _____

2. The hitchhiker stopped me as I walks from the turnpike rest station and said, "Are you on your way to San Jose?"   _____

3. I grabbed for the last bag of pretzels on the supermarket shelf. But when I pick them up, I discovered there was a tear in the cellophane bag.   _____

4. Ruby waits eagerly for the postman to arrive every day. Part of her hoped to get a letter in which someone declares he is madly in love with her and will cherish her forever.   _____

5. The first thing Jerry does every day is weigh himself. The scale informed him what he can eat that day.   _____

6. My sister sprinkles detergent flakes on my head and then ran around telling everyone that I had dandruff.   _____

7. Some students attend all their classes in school. They listen carefully during lectures but they don't take notes. As a result, they often failed tests.   _____

8. My father knocked on the bedroom door. When he asks me if he can come in, I said, "Not right now."   _____

9. His parents stayed together for his sake; only after he graduates from college were they divorced.   _____

10. In the movie, artillery shells exploded on the hide of the reptile monster. It just grinned, shrugs off the shells, and kept eating people.   _____

REVIEW TEST

Make the verbs in each selection consistent with the *first* verb used. Cross out each incorrect verb and write the correct form above it.

Example   I once walked for fifteen minutes in an underground subway system

spotted

before I ~~spot~~ an exit sign.

1. I walked through town yesterday, and a friend from grade school calls to me.

2. Sandy eats a nutritional breakfast, skipped lunch, and then enjoys a big dinner.

3. I settled back for a short nap and snore for the rest of the afternoon.

4. When we arrived at the theater, I suddenly remember that I had left the oven turned on at home.

5. Susan asked the grouchy bus driver for change and he counts out twenty-five pennies.

6. Little Andy loves fire, and his mother worried when matches are missing.

7. The coin collector informed me that my old penny wasn't worth much, but I found out later that he receives $50 for it.

8. After dinner my parents watched the news while the children clear the table.

9. I flunked parallel parking on my driver's test and learn it only a week later.

10. Every morning he starts the car, tuned in the radio, and adjusts the heat.

Additional Information about Verbs

The purpose of this special section is to provide additional information about verbs. Some people will find the grammar terms here a helpful reminder of earlier school learning about verbs. For them, the terms will increase their understanding of how verbs function in English. Other people may welcome more detailed information about terms used elsewhere in the text. In either case, remember that the most common mistakes that people make when writing verbs have been treated in earlier sections of the book.

THE PRINCIPAL PARTS OF VERBS

Every verb has three principal parts: the present, the past, and the past participle. These parts can be used to build all the verb tenses (the times shown by a verb).

A regular verb forms its past and past participle simply by adding *-ed* to the present. An irregular verb has irregular past and past participle forms. Here are the principal parts of the regular verb *laugh* and the irregular verb *take*.

Present	Past	Past Participle
laugh	laughed	laughed
take	took	taken

The principal parts of many irregular verbs are given on pages 44 to 46. You can also check a dictionary for the principal parts of irregular verbs.

VERB TENSE

Verbs tell us the time of an action. The time that a verb shows is usually called *tense*. The most common tenses are the simple present, past, and future. In addition, there are six other tenses that enable us to express more specific ideas about time than we could with the simple tenses alone. Given below are the nine verb tenses and examples of each tense. Read them over to increase your sense of the many different ways of expressing time in English.

Present	I *work*.
	Jill *works*.
Past	Howard *worked* on the lawn.

Future	You *will work* overtime this week.
Present Perfect	Gail *has worked* hard on the puzzle.
	They *have worked* well together.
Past Perfect	The pitcher *had worked* long hours on his slider.
Future Perfect	The volunteers *will have worked* many unpaid hours.
Present Progressive	I *am* not *working* today.
	You *are working* the second shift.
	The clothes dryer *is* not *working* properly.
Past Progressive	She *was working* outside.
	The plumbers *were working* here this morning.
Future Progressive	The sound system *will be working* by tonight.

The perfect tenses are formed by adding *have, has,* or *had* to the past participle (the form of the verb that ends, usually, in *-ed*). The progressive tenses are formed by adding *am, is, are, was,* or *were* to the present participle (the form of the verb that ends in *-ing*).

Most of the problems that people have with verbs involve verb endings in the present or past tense (see page 38) and the parts of irregular verbs (see page 44).

PRACTICE

On separate paper, write nine sentences using the nine verb tenses.

HELPING VERBS

There are three common verbs that can either stand alone or combine with (and "help") other verbs. Here are the verbs and their forms:

be (being, been, am, are, is, was, were)
have (has, having, had)
do (does, did)

Examples of the verbs:

Used Alone	Used As Helping Verbs
I *was* angry.	I *was growing* angry.
Sue *has* the key.	Sue *has forgotten* the key.
He *did* well in the test.	He *did fail* the previous test.

There are nine helping verbs (traditionally known as *modals,* or *modal auxiliaries*) that are always used in combination with other verbs. Here are the nine verbs and sentence examples of each.

can	I *can see* the rainbow.
could	I *could* not *find* a seat.
may	The game *may be postponed*.
might	Cindy *might resent* your advice.
shall	I *shall see* you tomorrow.
should	He *should get* his car serviced.
will	Tony *will want* to see you.
would	They *would* not *understand*.
must	You *must visit* us again.

Note from the examples that these verbs have only one form. They do not, for instance, add an *-s* when used with *he, she, it,* or any one person or thing.

PRACTICE

On separate paper, write nine sentences using the nine modals.

VERBALS

Verbals are special forms derived from verbs. The three kinds of verbals are infinitives, participles, and gerunds.

Infinitive

An infinitive is *to* plus the base form of the verb.

I started *to practice*.
Don't try *to lift* that table.
To become a millionaire is one of my goals in life.
I asked Russ *to drive* me home.

Participle

A participle is a verb form used as an adjective (a descriptive word). The present participle ends in *-ing*. The past participle ends in *-ed* or *-d*, *-t*, *-en*, or *-n*, or has internal vowel changes, as in *sung*.

Favoring his *cramped* leg, the *screaming* boy waded out of the pool.
The *laughing* child held up her *locked* piggy bank.
Using a shovel and bucket, I scooped water out of the *flooded* basement.

Gerund

A gerund is the *-ing* form of a verb used as a noun.

Studying wears me out.
Playing basketball is my main pleasure during the week.
Through *jogging,* you can get yourself in shape.

ACTIVE AND PASSIVE VERBS

When the subject of a sentence performs the action of a verb, the verb is in the *active voice*. When the subject of a sentence receives the action of a verb, the verb is in the *passive voice*. Active verbs are generally more effective than passive ones. Notice the difference between active and passive verbs in the following sentences.

Active	Passive
Lola ate the vanilla pudding.	The vanilla pudding was eaten by Lola.
(The subject, *Lola,* is the doer of the action.)	(The subject, *pudding,* does not act. Instead, something happens to it.)
The plumber replaced the hot water heater.	The hot water heater was replaced by the plumber.
(The subject, *plumber,* is the doer of the action.)	(The subject, *heater,* does not act. Instead, something happens to it.)

PRACTICE

Change the following sentences from the passive to the active voice. Note that you may have to add a subject in some cases.

Examples   The moped bicycle was ridden by Tony.

Tony rode the moped bicycle.

The basketball team was given a standing ovation.

The crowd gave the basketball team a standing ovation.

(Here a subject had to be added.)

1. The surprise party was organized by Charlotte.

2. Many people were offended by the comedian.

3. The old woman's groceries are paid for by the neighbors.

4. The horse chestnuts were knocked off the trees by the boys.

5. The devil was driven out of Regan by the exorcist.

Misplaced Modifiers

Misplaced modifiers are words that, because of awkward placement, do not describe the words the writer intended them to describe. Misplaced modifiers often confuse the meaning of a sentence. To avoid them, place words as close as possible to what they describe.

Misplaced Words	Correctly Placed Words
Tony bought an old car from a crooked dealer *with a faulty transmission.*	Tony bought an old car with a faulty transmission from a crooked dealer.
(The dealer had a faulty transmission?)	(The words describing the old car are now placed next to "car.")
I *nearly* earned a hundred dollars last week.	I earned nearly a hundred dollars last week.
(You just missed earning a hundred dollars, but in fact earned nothing?)	(The meaning—that you earned a little under a hundred dollars—is now clear.)
Bill yelled at the howling dog *in his underwear.*	Bill, in his underwear, yelled at the howling dog.
(The *dog* wore underwear?)	(The words describing Bill are placed next to him.)

PRACTICE

Underline the misplaced word or words in each sentence. Then rewrite the sentence, placing related words together and thereby making the meaning clear.

Examples   Charlotte returned the hamburger to the supermarket that was spoiled.

Charlotte returned the hamburger that was spoiled to the supermarket.

Our phone almost rang fifteen times last night.

Our phone rang almost fifteen times last night.

1. He swatted the wasp that stung him with a newspaper.

   _____

2. I almost had a dozen job interviews after I sent out my résumé.

   _____

   _____

3. Joanne decided to live with her grandparents when she attended college to save money.

    _____

4. I adopted a dog from a junkyard which is very close to my heart.

    _____

5. Tim and Rita decided to send their daughter to college on the day she was born.

    _____

6. We could see the football stadium driving across the bridge.

    _____

7. I glared at the man who slipped ahead of me in the ticket line angrily.

    _____

8. Clyde saw a three-car accident going to work.

    _____

    _____

9. I noticed a gray, furry nest in a corner of the apartment built by a gigantic spider.

    _____

10. The father ordered the meal for his family ranging from fried shrimp to chopped sirloin.

    _____

    _____

REVIEW TEST

Rewrite each sentence, adding the *italicized* words. Make sure that the intended meaning is clear and that two different interpretations are not possible.

Example   I borrowed a pen for the essay test. (Insert *that ran out of ink*)

I borrowed a pen that ran out of ink for the essay test.

or *For the essay test, I borrowed a pen that ran out of ink.*

1. Bill saw a kangaroo at the window. (Insert *under the influence of whiskey* to show that Bill was drunk.)

    _____

    _____

2. I've looked everywhere for an instruction book on how to play the guitar. (Insert *without success*.)

   _____

   _____

3. I told Albert he could raise Siamese cats. (Insert *over the phone*.)

   _____

   _____

4. We agreed to go out to dinner tonight. (Insert *in our science class*.)

   _____

   _____

5. The bird made me laugh. (Insert *while pecking at the blueberries*.)

   _____

   _____

6. Sam got stung by a bee. (Insert *playing tag*.)

   _____

   _____

7. Susie decided to hail a taxi. (Insert *weighed down with heavy packages*.)

   _____

   _____

8. We waited an hour before going on stage. (Insert *that seemed like an eternity* to show that the wait was a difficult one.)

   _____

   _____

9. He received a foreign sports car for his birthday. (Insert *which has a sun roof and steel radials*.)

   _____

   _____

10. Bob and I decided to get married. (Insert *on a rainy day in June* to show when the decision was made.)

   _____

   _____

Dangling Modifiers

A modifier that opens a sentence must be followed immediately by the word it is meant to describe. Otherwise, the modifier is said to be dangling, and the sentence takes on an unintended meaning. For example, in the sentence

While smoking a pipe, my dog sat with me by the crackling fire.

the unintended meaning is that the *dog* was smoking the pipe. What the writer meant, of course, was that *he,* the writer, was smoking the pipe. He should have said,

While smoking a pipe, *I* sat with my dog by the crackling fire.

The dangling modifier could also be corrected by placing the subject within the opening word group:

While *I* was smoking my pipe, my dog sat with me by the crackling fire.

Here are other sentences with dangling modifiers. Read the explanations of why they are dangling and look carefully at the ways they are corrected.

Dangling	Correct
Swimming at the lake, a rock cut Jim's foot.	Swimming at the lake, *Jim* cut his foot on a rock.
(*Who* was swimming at the lake? The answer is not *rock* but *Jim.* The subject *Jim* must be added.)	*or:* When *Jim* was swimming at the lake, he cut his foot on a rock.
While eating my sandwich, five mosquitoes bit me.	While *I* was eating my sandwich, five mosquitoes bit me.
(*Who* is eating the sandwich? The answer is not *five mosquitoes,* as it unintentionally seems to be, but *I.* The subject *I* must be added.)	*or:* While eating my sandwich, *I* was bitten by five mosquitoes.
Getting out of bed, the tile floor was so cold that Maria shivered all over.	Getting out of bed, *Maria* found the tile floor so cold that she shivered all over.
(*Who* got out of bed? The answer is not *tile floor* but *Maria.* The subject *Maria* must be added.)	*or:* When *Maria* got out of bed, the tile floor was so cold that she shivered all over.

To join the team, a C average or better is necessary.	To join the team, *you* must have a C average or better.
(*Who* is to join the team? The answer is not *C average* but *you*. The subject *you* must be added.)	*or:* For *you* to join the team, a C average or better is necessary.

The above examples make clear the two ways of correcting a dangling modifier. Decide on a logical subject and do one of the following:

1 Place the subject *within* the opening word group:

When *Jim* was swimming at the lake, he cut his foot on a rock.

Note: In some cases an appropriate subordinating word such as *When* must be added, and the verb may have to be changed slightly as well.

2 Place the subject right *after* the opening word group:

Swimming at the lake, *Jim* cut his foot on a rock.

PRACTICE 1

Ask *Who?* of the opening words in each sentence. The subject that answers the question should be near by in the sentence. If it is not, provide the logical subject by using either method of correction described above.

Example   While watching the late movie, sleep overcame me.

While I was watching the late movie, sleep overcame me.

or *While watching the late movie, I was overcome by sleep.*

1. Eating the hot dog, mustard dropped onto my blouse.

_____

_____

2. After putting on a corduroy shirt, the room didn't seem as cold.

_____

_____

3. Flunking out of school, my parents demanded that I get a job.

   _____

4. Confused about which road to take, my CB was used to get directions.

   _____

   _____

5. Joining the Glee Club, the social life of Mike became more active.

   _____

   _____

6. While visiting the Jungle Park Safari, a baboon scrambled onto the hood of their car.

   _____

   _____

7. Under attack by beetles, Charlotte sprayed her roses with insecticide.

   _____

   _____

8. Standing at the ocean's edge, the wind coated my glasses with a salty film.

   _____

   _____

9. To pass Dr. Stein's course, regular class attendance is necessary.

   _____

   _____

10. Braking the car suddenly, my shopping bags tumbled off the seat.

    _____

    _____

PRACTICE 2

Complete the following sentences. In each case, a logical subject should follow the opening words.

Example   Checking the oil stick, *I saw that my car was a quart low.*

1. Since failing the first test, _____

2. Before learning how to dance, _____

3. While flying the kite, _____

4. After taking my coffee break, _____

5. Though very tired, _____

REVIEW TEST

Place a *D* for *Dangling* or a *C* for *Correct* in front of each sentence. Remember that the opening words are a dangling modifier if they have no logical subject to modify.

_____ 1. Containing dangerous chemicals, people are not swimming in the lake.

_____ 2. Containing dangerous chemicals, the lake is not open for swimming.

_____ 3. Having eaten several spicy tacos, my stomach began an Indian war dance.

_____ 4. Having eaten several spicy tacos, I began to feel my stomach doing an Indian war dance.

_____ 5. Hitching a ride, I was picked up by a Mack truck.

_____ 6. Hitching a ride, a Mack truck picked me up.

_____ 7. While waiting for the bus, rain began to fall.

_____ 8. While waiting for the bus, it began to rain.

_____ 9. While I was waiting for the bus, rain began to fall.

_____ 10. Frustrated by piles of homework, she was tempted to watch television.

_____ 11. Frustrated by piles of homework, her temptation was to watch television.

_____ 12. Riding my bike, the cocker spaniel bit my ankle.

_____ 13. While I was riding my bike, the cocker spaniel bit my ankle.

_____ 14. Riding my bike, I was bitten on the ankle by a cocker spaniel.

_____ 15. Sweating in the suffocating summer heat, the frosty Coke made Sue's mouth water.

_____ 16. Because Sue was sweating in the suffocating summer heat, the frosty Coke made her mouth water.

_____ 17. Falling heavily, Dan broke his arm.

_____ 18. Falling heavily, Dan's arm was broken.

_____ 19. Just before finishing the book, the power failed.

_____ 20. Just before I finished the book, the power failed.

Faulty Parallelism

Words in a pair or a series should have a parallel structure. By balancing the items in a pair or a series so that they have the same kind of structure, you will make the sentence clearer and easier to read. Notice how the parallel sentences that follow read more smoothly than the nonparallel ones.

Nonparallel (Not Balanced)	Parallel (Balanced)
In the evening Clyde likes playing with his son, *to read the newspaper,* and watching television.	In the evening Clyde likes playing with his son, reading the newspaper, and watching television.
	(A balanced series of *-ing* words: *playing, reading, watching*)
After the camping trip I was exhausted, irritable, and *wanted to eat.*	After the camping trip I was exhausted, irritable, and hungry.
	(A balanced series of descriptive words: *exhausted, irritable, hungry*)
Lola likes to wear soft sweaters, to eat exotic foods, and *bathing* in Calgon bath oil.	Lola likes to wear soft sweaters, to eat exotic foods, and to bathe in Calgon bath oil.
	(A balanced series of *to* verbs: *to wear, to eat, to bathe*)
The single life offers more freedom of choice; *more security is offered by marriage.*	The single life offers more freedom of choice; marriage offers more security.
	(Balanced verbs and word order: *single life offers . . .; marriage offers . . .*)

Balanced sentences are not a skill you need worry about when writing first drafts. But when you rewrite, you should try to put matching words and ideas into matching structures. Such parallelism will improve your writing style.

PRACTICE 1

The unbalanced part of each of the following sentences is *italicized.* Rewrite the unbalanced part so that it matches the rest of the sentence.

Example   In the afternoon, I changed two diapers, ironed several shirts, and *was watching* soap operas. *watched*

1.   Mrs. Grencher likes to water her garden, *to walking her fox terrier,* and to yell at her husband.

2.   Filled with talent and *ambitious,* Charlie plugged away at his sales job.

3.   Lola plans to become a model, lawyer, or *to go into nursing.*

4.   When I saw my roommate with my girl friend, I felt worried, angry, and *embarrassment* as well.

5.   On Saturday many supermarkets have crowded parking lots and *there are long lines for checkout.*

6.   My cat likes sleeping in the dryer, lying in the bathtub, and *to chase squirrels.*

7.   The bacon was fatty, *grease was on the potatoes,* and the eggs were cold.

8.   With her *eyes that were green* and pale skin, she appeared ghostly in the moonlight.

9.   During the holidays I enjoy stuffing myself, watching television, and *rides around town with friends.*

10. To us, the employees, the customers are rude, ignorant, and *are handled with difficulty.*

PRACTICE 2

Combine each group of short sentences into one sentence. Omit unnecessary words and express parallel ideas in parallel form.

Example   The auto shop foreman is a tall man. He is mustached and is turning bald.

The auto shop foreman is a tall, mustached, balding man.

1. Gail is a sweet woman. In addition, she is attractive. And there is an engaging quality about her.

    _____

    _____

    _____

2. My first grade teacher was an elderly woman. She was tall. And she had a friendly manner.

    _____

    _____

    _____

3. Instead of studying he listens to his stereo. Sometimes he flies paper airplanes. Other times he likes to shoot darts.

    _____

    _____

    _____

4. People in the lobby munched popcorn. They had sodas they were sipping. And they shuffled their feet impatiently.

    _____

    _____

    _____

5. One by one the dry brown leaves fell from the plant. They went scattering on the floor.

    _____

    _____

    _____

6. I like Dan's easy manner. His humor is good. And he has a sense of class.

_____

_____

_____

7. Our city buses are frequently crowded. They are often dirty. And they run late.

_____

_____

_____

8. I headed for the pool. I had a magazine to read. I also carried with me a Pepsi and a lounge chair.

_____

_____

_____

9. To deal with my cold, my first purchase was Kleenex. I also bought vitamin C and, in addition, several cans of fruit juice.

_____

_____

_____

10. While watching television, Lana likes to paint. Sometimes she plays solitaire during this time. Another television pastime is preparing delicious desserts.

_____

_____

_____

 REVIEW TEST 1

Draw a line under the unbalanced part of each sentence on the next page. Then rewrite the unbalanced part so that it matches the other item or items in the sentence.

Example   I enjoy watering the grass and <u>to work</u> in the garden.
   *working*_____

1. After going to class, reading the text, and the study of her notes, she failed the test.

    _____

2. They shopped on Saturday morning, went to a football game in the afternoon, and were watching television in the evening.

    _____

3. Frances enjoys shopping for new clothes, to try different cosmetics, and reading beauty magazines.

    _____

4. My car needed the brakes replaced, the front wheels aligned, and the recharging of the battery.

    _____

5. While waiting for supper, he munched some pretzels, was eating some cheese and crackers, and drank a Coke.

    _____

6. Having a headache, my stomach being upset, and a bad case of sunburn did not put me in a good mood for the evening.

    _____

7. The neighborhood group asked the town council to repair the potholes and that a traffic light be installed.

    _____

8. Cooking three meals, to clean the house, and caring for three small children leave them exhausted at the end of the day.

    _____

9. Last week I finished my term paper, took all my final exams, and an interview for a summer job.

    _____

10. My duties as a nurse's aid included serving juice and cookies, to make the beds, and sterilizing all the water pitchers and bedpans.

    _____

 REVIEW TEST 2

On separate paper, write five sentences of your own that use parallel structure.

Pronoun Agreement, Reference, and Point of View

Pronouns are words that take the place of nouns (persons, places, or things). In fact, the word pronoun means *for a noun*. Pronouns are shortcuts that keep you from unnecessarily repeating words in writing. Here are some examples of pronouns:

Shirley had not finished *her* paper. (*Her* is a pronoun that takes the place of *Shirley's*.)

Tony swung so heavily on the tree branch that *it* snapped. (*It* replaces *branch*.)

When the three little pigs saw the wolf, *they* pulled out cans of Mace. (*They* is a pronoun that takes the place of *pigs*.)

This section presents rules that will help you avoid three common mistakes people make with pronouns. The rules are as follows:

1 A pronoun must agree in number with the word or words it replaces.
2 A pronoun must refer clearly to the word it replaces.
3 Pronouns should not shift unnecessarily in point of view.

PRONOUN AGREEMENT

A pronoun must agree in number with the word or words it replaces. If the word a pronoun refers to is singular, the pronoun must be singular; if that word is plural, the pronoun must be plural. (Note that the word a pronoun refers to is also known as the *antecedent*.)

Barbara agreed to lend me *her* disco albums.

People walking the trail must watch *their* step because of snakes.

In the first example, the pronoun *her* refers back to the singular word *Barbara*; in the second example, the pronoun *their* refers back to the plural word *People*.

PRACTICE

Write the appropriate pronoun (*their, they, them, it*) into the blank space in each of the following sentences.

Example The quarterback and center got _____*their*_____ signals mixed.

1. The value that people receive for _____ dollars these days is rapidly diminishing.

2. Fred never misses his daily workout; he believes _____ keeps him healthy.

3. Sometimes in marriage, partners expect too much from _____ mates.

4. For some students, college is often their first experience with an undisciplined learning situation, and _____ are not always ready to accept the responsibility.

5. The polyester shirt did not shrink or wrinkle with washing, but _____ was uncomfortable to wear.

Special Singular Words

The following group of words (also known as *indefinite pronouns*) are always singular.

one	no one	nobody
each	anyone	anybody
either	someone	somebody
neither	everyone	everybody

If a pronoun in a sentence refers to one of the above singular words, the pronoun should be singular.

Nobody dances the way he does.

One of the women could not find her purse.

Everyone must be in his seat before the teacher takes the roll.

In each example, the pronoun is singular because it refers back to one of the special singular words.

Note: In the last example, if everyone in the class was a woman, the pronoun would be *her.* If the class was a mixed group of women and men, the pronoun form would be *his or her:*

Everyone must be in his or her seat before the teacher takes the roll.

Some writers follow the traditional practice of using *his* to refer to both women and men. Some now use *his or her* to avoid an implied sexual bias. To avoid using *his* or the somewhat awkward *his or her,* a sentence can often be rewritten in the plural:

Students must be in their seats before the teacher takes the roll.

PRACTICE

Underline the correct pronoun.

1. What somebody doesn't know won't hurt (him, them).
2. Everybody must pay (her, their) tuition at the time of registration.
3. Before we have a discussion, each person must decide on one question that (he, they) wants to ask.
4. Each of my sisters has (her, their) own room.
5. Everyone should plan on devoting a couple of (his, their) hours for volunteer work.
6. Someone has blocked the driveway with (her, their) car.
7. Either of the travel routes has (their, its) share of places to see.
8. None of the boys remembered to bring (his, their) radio.
9. Nobody I have asked wants to donate (her, their) time.
10. Anybody who purchases stock in that company probably lost all (his, their) money.

PRONOUN REFERENCE

A sentence may be confusing and unclear if a pronoun appears to refer to more than one word, or if the pronoun does not refer to any specific word. Look at this sentence:

Joe almost dropped out of school, for he felt *they* emphasized discipline too much.

Who emphasized discipline too much? There is no specific word that *they* refers to. Be clear:

Joe almost dropped out of school, for he felt *the teachers* emphasized discipline too much.

Here are sentences with other kinds of faulty pronoun references. Read the explanations of why they are faulty and look carefully at the ways they are corrected.

Faulty	Clear
Jane told Margie that *she* lacked self-confidence. (*Who* lacked self-confidence: Jane or Margie? Be clear.)	Jane told Margie, ''You lack self-confidence.'' (Quotation marks, which can sometimes be used to correct an unclear reference, are explained on page 124.)
Nancy's mother is a hairdresser, but Nancy is not interested in *it*. (There is no specific word that *it* refers to. It would not make sense to say, ''Nancy is not interested in hairdresser.'')	Nancy's mother is a hairdresser, but Nancy is not interested in becoming one.
Ron blamed the police officer for the ticket, *which* was foolish. (Does *which* mean that the officer's giving the ticket was foolish, or that Ron's blaming the officer was foolish? Be clear.)	Foolishly, Ron blamed the police officer for the ticket.

PRACTICE

Rewrite each of the following sentences to make clear the vague pronoun reference. Add, change, or omit words as necessary.

Example Our cat was friends with our bird until he bit him.

Until the cat bit the bird, the two were friends.

1. Sarah never lets her aggressive children play with the neighbor's cats, for she knows they scratch and bite.

    _____

    _____

2. I love Parmesan cheese on veal, but it does not always agree with me.

    _____

    _____

3. An editorial in today's paper says they believe the chief of police is accepting bribes.

    _____

    _____

4. She wanted to go downstairs and say something to her arguing parents so that it would make things better.

    _____

    _____

5. When I asked why I had failed my driver's test, he said I had driven too slowly.

    _____

    _____

6. Angry at striking out, Tony hurled the baseball bat at the fence and broke it.

    _____

    _____

7. The teachers at the high school always tell the students how well they are doing.

    _____

    _____

8. Dad ordered my brother to paint the garage doors because he didn't want to do it.

    _____

    _____

9. Craig is quitting the basketball team because he feels they emphasize winning too much.

    _____

    _____

10. He got a tutor to help him with psychology and began to enjoy the course. This led to a B on his next test.

_____

_____

_____

PRONOUN POINT OF VIEW

Pronouns should not shift their point of view unnecessarily. Always write a paper using a consistent point of view. It may be a first-, second-, or third-person point of view.

First person	I (my, mine, me)	we (our, us)
Second person	you (your)	you (your)
Third person	he (his, him)	they (their, them)
	she (her)	
	it (its)	
	one, a person	

For instance, if you start writing in the third person *she,* don't jump suddenly to the second person *you.* Or if you are writing in the first person *I,* don't shift unexpectedly to *one.* Look at the examples.

Inconsistent	Consistent
She enjoys movies like *The Return of the Vampire* that frighten *you.*	She enjoys movies like *The Return of the Vampire* that frighten *her.*
(The most common mistake people make is to let a *you* slip into their writing after they start another pronoun.)	
As soon as a person walks into Helen's apartment, *you* can tell that Helen owns a cat.	As soon as a person walks into Helen's apartment, *he* can tell that Helen owns a cat.
(Again, the *you* is a shift in point of view.)	(Words like *a person* or *someone* or *anyone* can be used along with other third-person words like *he.* See also the note on sexual references on page 81.)

PRACTICE

Cross out inconsistent pronouns in the following sentences and write the correct form of the pronoun above each crossed-out word.

Example   From where we stood, ~~you~~ *we* could see three states.

1. In our society, we often need a diploma before you are hired for a job.
2. One reason that I like living in the city is that you always have a wide choice of sports events and movies to attend.
3. I work at a shop where you do not get paid for all the holidays one should.
4. Even though I was doing well in the course, I could not be sure that a poor test score would not ruin your grade.
5. In our campsite, you had only a radio as a contact with the outside world.
6. If you think you're coming down with cold symptoms, one should take precautions right away.
7. A person dieting should have the encouragement of friends; you should also have lots of willpower.
8. If anyone got near Rex, you got snapped at viciously.
9. On the night the heat went off, no one could get warm, no matter how many blankets you used.
10. A worker can take a break only after a relief person comes to take your place.

 REVIEW TEST 1

Underline the correct word in the parentheses.

1. When the moon and stars come out, (it, the night) is beautiful.
2. If a person is going to write a composition, (he, you, they) should prepare at least one rough draft.
3. Hitting the wall with her skateboard, she chipped (it, the skateboard).
4. Persons wanting old furniture should check the newspaper classified section; also, (they, you) might stop at yard sales.
5. We drove for hours and (we, you) got scared by the heavy fog.

6. Cindy is the kind of woman that you can always count on to do (their, her) best.

7. Although we had a delightful vacation, (you, we) are always glad to get home.

8. I've always loved butterfly exhibits, so I decided to start collecting (them, butterflies).

9. When Sally asked why she was being given a ticket, (he, the officer) said she ran a stop sign.

10. I buy my clothes at the outlet store because (it has, they have) the best prices.

REVIEW TEST 2

Cross out the pronoun error in each sentence and write the correction above the error.

Examples   No one except me is going to be late with ~~their~~ *her* term paper.

When Clyde takes his son Paul to the park, ~~he~~ *Paul* enjoys himself.

I work much better when the boss doesn't hover over ~~you~~ *me* and tell you what to do.

1. After throwing the dog a stick, I took it home.

2. Everyone on the team was in the locker room packing their travel bag.

3. Ralph walks the dog so he won't get fat.

4. One of the children forgot to put on their rubbers.

5. I've been taking cold medicine and now it's better.

6. When people face a common problem, your personal relationship often becomes stronger.

7. Everyone who was at the dance has their own memories of the sudden fire.

8. Sometimes our teacher has Ted write on the board because chalk dust makes him sneeze.

9. Even though I closed the bedroom door, you could still hear the television downstairs.

10. If a person walks through those woods, you will see at least ten kinds of nesting birds.

Pronoun Types

This section describes some common types of pronouns: subject and object pronouns, demonstrative pronouns, possessive pronouns, and reflexive pronouns.

SUBJECT AND OBJECT PRONOUNS

Pronouns change their form depending upon the place that they occupy in a sentence.

Subject pronouns include:	Object pronouns include:
I	me
he	him
she	her
we	us
they	them

Subject Pronouns

The subject pronouns are subjects of verbs.

They are getting tired. (*They* is the subject of the verb *are getting*.)
She will decide tomorrow. (*She* is the subject of the verb *will decide*.)
We women organized the game. (*We* is the subject of the verb *organized*.)

Several kinds of mistakes that people sometimes make with subject pronouns are explained starting below.

1 Use a subject pronoun in spots where you have a compound (more than one) subject.

Incorrect	Correct
Nate and *me* went shopping yesterday.	Nate and *I* went shopping yesterday.
Him and *me* spent lots of money.	*He* and *I* spent lots of money.

Hint: If you are not sure what pronoun to use, try each pronoun by itself in the sentence. The correct pronoun will be the one that sounds right. For example, "*Me* went shopping yesterday" does not sound right; "*I* went shopping yesterday" does.

2 Use a subject pronoun after forms of the verb *be*. Forms of *be* include *am, are, is, was, were, has been, have been,* and others.

It was *I* who telephoned.
It may be *they* at the door.
It is *she*.

The sentences above may sound strange and stilted to you since they are seldom used in conversation. When we speak with one another, forms such as "It was me," "It may be them," and "It is her" are widely accepted. In formal writing, however, the grammatically "correct" forms are still preferred.

Hint: Avoid having to use the pronoun form after *be* by simply rewording a sentence. Here is how the preceding examples could be reworded:

I was the one who telephoned.
They may be at the door.
She is here.

3 Use subject pronouns after *than* or *as*. The subject pronoun is used because a verb is understood after the pronoun.

You read faster than I (read). (The verb *read* is understood after *I*.)

Tom is as stubborn as I (am). (The verb *am* is understood after *I*.)

We don't go out as much as they (do). (The verb *do* is understood after *they*.)

Hint: Avoid mistakes by simply adding the "missing" verb at the end of the sentence.

Object Pronouns

The object pronouns (*me, him, her, us, them*) are the objects of verbs or prepositions. (Prepositions are connecting words like *for, at, about, to, before, by, with,* and *of*. See also page 7.)

Lola chose *me*. (*Me* is the object of the verb *chose*.)

We met *them* at the theater. (*Them* is the object of the verb *met*.)

Don't mention UFOs to *us* skeptics. (*Us* is the object of the preposition *to*.)

Tony ran by *them*. (*Them* is the object of the preposition *by*.)

People are sometimes uncertain about what pronoun to use when two objects follow the verb.

Incorrect	Correct
I spoke to George and *he*.	I spoke to George and *him*.
She pointed her finger at Linda and *I*.	She pointed her finger at Linda and *me*.

Hint: If you are not sure what pronoun to use, try each pronoun by itself in the sentence. The correct pronoun will be the one that sounds right. For example, "I spoke to he" doesn't sound right; "I spoke to him" does.

PRACTICE 1

Underline the correct subject or object pronoun in each of the following sentences. Then show whether your answer is a subject or object pronoun by circling the S or O in the margin. The first one is done for you as an example.

S Ⓞ 1. I left the decision to (<u>her</u>, she).

S O 2. My sister and (I, me) decided to combine funds to buy our parents' Christmas present.

S O 3. He arrived sooner than (they, them).

S O 4. Give more spaghetti to Hal and (her, she).

S O 5. Marge and (she, her) gave the car an oil change.

S O 6. The two people failed for cheating on the test were Mary and (he, him).

S O 7. (She, Her) and Barbara are jealous of my success.

S O 8. (We, Us) fellows decided to get up a football game.

S O 9. I don't feel he is a better volleyball player than (me, I).

S O 10. (Her, She) and (I, me) are not talking to each other.

PRACTICE 2

Write in a subject or object pronoun that fits in the space provided. Try to use as many different pronouns as possible. The first one is done for you as an example.

1. Lola ran after Sue and ____*me*____ to return the suntan lotion she had borrowed.

2. Mr. Spud, our football coach, asked Gary and _____ to play on both offense and defense.

3. Pull the map out of the glove compartment and give it to_____.

4. The bowling team presented _____ with a bronze trophy.

5. The teacher caught Ted and _____ whispering together during the exam.

6. No one was dressed up as much as _____ was.

7. My sister and _____ decided to care for the stray puppy.

8. I'm tired of _____ and their polite artificial smiles.

9. The block party was organized by _____ and our neighbors.

10. My uncle entertained _____ kids with his John Wayne imitation.

DEMONSTRATIVE PRONOUNS

Demonstrative pronouns point to or single out a person or thing. There are four demonstrative pronouns:

Singular	Plural
this, that	these, those

Generally speaking, *this* and *these* refer to things close at hand; *that* and *those* refer to things farther away.

Is anyone using *this* spoon?
I am going to throw away *these* magazines.
I just bought *that* white Volvo at the curb.
Pick up *those* toys in the corner.

Note: Do not use *them, this here, that there, these here,* or *those there* to point out. Use only *this, that, these,* or *those.*

Incorrect	Correct
Them tires are badly worn.	*Those* tires are badly worn.
This here book looks hard to read.	*This* book looks hard to read.
That there candy is delicious.	*That* candy is delicious.
Those there squirrels are pests.	*Those* squirrels are pests.

PRACTICE 1

Cross out the incorrect form of the demonstrative pronoun and write the correct form in the space provided.

Example ~~Them~~ clothes need washing. *Those*

1. That there dog will bite you if she gets a chance. _____

2. This here fingernail is not growing straight. _____

3. Them girls cannot be trusted. _____

4. Carry in those there shopping bags if you want to help. _____

5. The place where I'd like to live is that there corner house. _____

PRACTICE 2

Write four sentences using *this, that, these,* and *those.*

_____

_____

_____

_____

POSSESSIVE PRONOUNS

Possessive pronouns show ownership or possession.

Clyde revved up *his* motorcycle and blasted off.
The keys are *mine.*

In these sentences, *his* shows that the motorcycle belongs to Clyde; *mine* shows that the keys belong to the speaker. Following is a list of possessive pronouns:

my, mine   their, theirs
you, your   our, ours
his, her, hers

Notes:
1 A possessive pronoun *never* uses an apostrophe. (See also page 120.)

Incorrect	Correct
That coat is *hers'*.	That coat is *hers.*
The card table is *theirs'*.	The card table is *theirs.*

2 Do not use any of the following nonstandard forms to show possession.

Incorrect	Correct
I met a friend of *him*.	I met a friend of *his*.
Can I use *you* car?	Can I use *your* car?
Me sister is in the hospital.	*My* sister is in the hospital.
Whatever is left over is *yourn*.	Whatever is left over is *yours*.
That magazine is *mines*.	That magazine is *mine*.

PRACTICE

Cross out the incorrect pronoun form in each of the sentences that follow. Write the correct form in the space at the right.

Example ~~Me~~ car has broken down again.   _____My_____

1. That car won't be safe until you get its' brakes fixed.   _____

2. If you are a friend of him, you're welcome to stay with us.   _____

3. The seat you are sitting on is mines.   _____

4. The neighbors called they dogs to chase the cat off the lawn.   _____

5. The coffeepot is ours'.   _____

REFLEXIVE PRONOUNS

Reflexive pronouns are ones that refer back to the subject of a sentence. Following is a list of reflexive pronouns:

Singular		Plural
myself	himself	ourselves
yourself	herself	yourselves
	itself	themselves

Note: In the plural, *self* becomes *selves*.

Lola washes *herself* in Calgon bath oil.
Bob had only *himself* to blame.
They treated *themselves* to a Bermuda vacation.

Sometimes the reflexive pronoun is used for emphasis:

You will have to wash the dishes *yourself*.
We *ourselves* are willing to forget the matter.
The President *himself* keeps down his living room thermostat.

Note: Be careful that you do not use any of the following incorrect forms as reflexive pronouns.

Incorrect	Correct
He believes in *hisself.*	He believes in *himself.*
We drove the children *ourself.*	We drove the children *ourselves.*
They saw *themself* in the fun house mirror.	They saw *themselves* in the fun house mirror.
I'll do it *meself.*	I'll do it *myself.*

PRACTICE

Cross out the incorrect form of the reflexive pronoun and write the correct form in the space at the right.

Example She believes that God helps those who help ~~themself~~ *themselves*

1. Tony considers hisself the strongest wrestler in the class. _____

2. They are only making theirselves look foolish. _____

3. You must carry your luggage yourselfs. _____

4. Many firefighters themself do not have smoke detectors in their homes. _____

5. We decided to finish the basement by ourself. _____

REVIEW TEST **1**

Underline the correct word in the parentheses.

1. I'm going to leave if (that, that there) waiter doesn't come over here soon.
2. Though secured by a chain, the snarling German shepherd still terrified Lee and (I, me).
3. That FM radio is (mine, mines).
4. Watching Alan and (I, me) dancing made him grit his teeth.
5. My aunts promised (us, we) girls a trip to Canada for graduation.
6. The service manager (hisself, himself) will fix the carburetor for you.
7. I think (those, those there) people should be kicked out of the theater for talking.
8. The giggling boys only made (themself, themselves) look foolish.

9. If the decision were up to (they, them), my position in the company would be as pencil sharpener.

10. If (she, her) and Sandy had reported the leak, the cellar would not have flooded.

REVIEW TEST 2

Cross out the pronoun error in each sentence and write the correct form above it.

Example   Terry and ~~he~~ ^I^ have already seen the movie.

1. Our friends have gotten theirselves into debt by overusing credit cards.

2. This here heat pump will save on your energy bill.

3. Watching the football game, us fans soon realized that our team would lose.

4. If you and her get confused about directions, stop and check at a service station.

5. These here walls badly need painting.

6. Before he took a foul shot, the basketball player crossed hisself for good luck.

7. Jane and me refused to join the union.

8. The parents theirselfs must share the blame for their child's failure in school.

9. Our class painted a better wall mural than them.

10. You and me have got to have a talk.

REVIEW TEST 3

On separate paper, write sentences that use correctly each of the following words or word groups.

Example   Peter and him   *The coach suspended Peter and him.*

1. those
2. Sue and she
3. faster than I
4. ours
5. Lola and me

6. David and them
7. yourselves
8. with Linda and him
9. you and I
10. the neighbors and us

Adjectives and Adverbs

Adjectives and adverbs are descriptive words. Their purpose is to make the meanings of the words they describe more specific.

ADJECTIVES

Adjectives describe nouns (names of persons, places, or things) or pronouns.

Charlotte is a *kind* woman. (The adjective *kind* describes the noun *woman*.)
He is *tired*. (The adjective *tired* describes the pronoun *he*.)

Adjectives usually come before the word they describe (as in *kind woman*). But they also come after forms of the verb *be* (*is, are, was, were*, and so on). Less often, they follow verbs such as *feel, look, smell, sound, taste, appear, become*, and *seem*.

That bureau is *heavy*. (The adjective *heavy* describes the bureau.)
The children are *restless*. (The adjective *restless* describes the children.)
These pants are *itchy*. (The adjective *itchy* describes the pants.)

ADVERBS

Adverbs describe verbs, adjectives, or other adverbs. Adverbs usually end in *-ly*.

Charlotte spoke *kindly* to the confused man. (The adverb *kindly* describes the verb *spoke*.)
The man said he was *completely* alone in the world. (The adverb *completely* describes the adjective *alone*.)
Charlotte listened *very* sympathetically to his story. (The adverb *very* describes the adverb *sympathetically*.)

A Common Mistake with Adjectives and Adverbs

Perhaps the most common mistake that people make with adjectives and adverbs is to use an adjective instead of an adverb after a verb.

95

	Incorrect	Correct

<table>
<tr><td></td><td align="center">Incorrect</td><td align="center">Correct</td></tr>
</table>

Tony breathed *heavy*.
I rest *comfortable* in that chair.
She learned *quick*.

Tony breathed *heavily*.
I rest *comfortably* in that chair.
She learned *quickly*.

PRACTICE

Underline the adjective or adverb needed.

1. Her pink-striped top clashed (violent, violently) with her orange-checkered skirt.
2. If I had not run (quick, quickly), the dog would have caught me.
3. The crowd pushed (angry, angrily) toward the box office window.
4. Sam peered with (considerable, considerably) effort through the grimy cellar window.
5. The trees swayed (gentle, gently) in the wind.
6. I was (real, really) tired.
7. I exercise (regular, regularly) and my eating habits are also (regular, regularly).
8. Sarah sat very (quiet, quietly) on the stairs, listening to her parents quarrel (angry, angrily) in the kitchen.
9. I listened (careful, carefully) to the doctor's (exact, exactly) instructions.
10. (Slow, Slowly) but (sure, surely), I improved my grades in school.

Well and Good

Two words often confused are *well* and *good*. *Good* is an adjective; it describes nouns. *Well* is usually an adverb; it describes verbs. *Well* (rather than *good*) is also used when referring to a person's health.

I became a *good* swimmer. (*Good* is an adjective describing the noun *swimmer*.)
Howard did *well* on that exam. (*Well* is an adverb describing the verb *did*.)
I explained that I wasn't feeling *well*. (*Well* is used in reference to health.)

PRACTICE

Write *well* or *good* in the sentences that follow.

1. He writes _____ enough to pass the course.
2. We always have a _____ time at the county fair.

3. The mayor and district attorney know each other very _____.

4. Jim has not been feeling _____ lately.

5. I did not do _____ when I took the typing test.

REVIEW TEST **1**

Underline the correct word in the parentheses.

1. My boss (frequent, frequently) tells me what a good job I do.

2. I (bad, badly) need a rest.

3. Tony didn't feel (good, well) after eating diced eggplant in clam sauce.

4. I was so (high, highly) qualified for the job that they could not afford to hire me.

5. I slept (light, lightly), for the stereo blared (noisy, noisily) upstairs.

6. He was found (innocent, innocently) of the charges but the judge lectured him (harsh, harshly).

7. My mother was in an (extreme, extremely) bad mood today.

8. Hal swam (effortless, effortlessly) through the water, not making a single (awkward, awkwardly) movement.

9. I ran (quick, quickly) to open the door for it was raining (fierce, fiercely) outside.

10. The lecturer spoke (slow, slowly), so I was able to take (good, well) notes.

REVIEW TEST **2**

Write a sentence that uses correctly each of the following adjectives and adverbs.

1. nervous _____

2. nervously _____

3. good _____

4. well _____

5. careful _____

6. carefully _____

Comparisons

For most **short** words, add *-er* when comparing two things and *-est* when comparing three or more things.

I am *taller* than my brother, but my father is the *tallest* person in the house.

The farm market sells *fresher* vegetables than the corner store, but the *freshest* vegetables are the ones grown in my own garden.

For most **longer** words (two or more syllables), add *more* when comparing two things and *most* when comparing three or more things.

Backgammon is *more enjoyable* to me than checkers, but chess is the *most enjoyable* game of all.

My mother is *more talkative* than my father, but my grandfather is the *most talkative* person in the house.

PRACTICE

Fill in the comparative or superlative forms for the following words. Two are done for you as examples.

	Comparative (Two)	Superlative (Three or More)
fast	*faster*	*fastest*
timid	*more timid*	*most timid*
kind		
ambitious		
generous		
fine		
likable		

Notes:

1 Be careful that you do not use both an *-er* ending plus *more*, or an *-est* ending plus *most*.

Incorrect	Correct
Football is a *more livelier* game than baseball.	Football is a *livelier* game than baseball.
Tod Traynor was voted the *most likeliest* to succeed in our high school class.	Tod Traynor was voted the *most likely* to succeed in our high school class.

2   Pay special attention to the following four words, each of which has irregular forms.

	Comparative (Two)	Superlative (Three or More)
bad	worse	worst
good, well	better	best
little	less	least
much, many	more	most

PRACTICE

Add to each sentence the correct form of the word in the margin.

Example   bad   The _____*worst*_____ day of my life was when my house caught fire.

comfortable   1.   My jeans are the _____ pants I own.

difficult   2.   My biology exam was the _____ of my five exams.

easy   3.   The _____ way to get a good grade in the class is to take effective notes.

little   4.   I made _____ money in my job as a delivery boy than I did as a golf caddy.

good   5.   The _____ pay I ever made was as a drill press operator in a machine shop.

long   6.   The ticket lines for the rock concert were the _____ I have ever seen.

memorable   7.   The _____ days of my childhood are the ones I spent on trips with my grandfather.

experienced   8.   I am a _____ driver than my sister, but my brother is the _____ driver in the family.

bad   9. This year's drought is _____ than last year's; forecasters are

saying that next year's drought may be the _____ of this century.

good 10. I like the diner's cheesecake _____ than its custard pie.

REVIEW TEST 1

Cross out the errors in comparison and write in the correct forms where needed.

Examples   For me, the country is a ~~more~~ harder place to live than the city.

worse
My car runs ~~badder~~ than ever before.

1. His eyes are his most attractivest feature.

2. Accounting has been the usefulest course that I have taken.

3. I am the taller of the five children in my family.

4. My coach said I had the most good chance of any person on the team of becoming a professional ballplayer.

5. *The Night of the Living Dead* is the most scariest movie I have ever seen.

6. At this time it is importanter to be in school than to have a full-time job.

7. Your cotton jeans are more softer than mine.

8. Despite reforms, conditions at the prison are more worse than before.

9. Mr. Scott is the helpfulest of my teachers.

10. Sandra's hair is more blonder than mine because hers comes from a bottle.

REVIEW TEST 2

Write five sentences using any five of the words or word groups that follow.

| most honest | best | more harmful | most entertaining |
| easier | quieter | loudest | more useful |

1. _____

2. _____

3. _____

4. _____

5. _____

Paper Format

Here are guidelines to follow in preparing a paper for an instructor.

1 Use full-sized theme or typewriter paper, 8½ by 11 inches.

2 Keep wide margins (1 to 1½ inches) all around the paper. In particular, do not crowd the right-hand or bottom margins. The white space makes your paper more readable; also, the instructor has room for comments.

3 If you write by hand,

    a Use a blue or black pen (*not* a pencil).

    b Be careful not to overlap letters or to make decorative loops on letters. On narrow-ruled paper, write on every other line.

    c Make all your letters distinct. Pay special attention to *a, e, i, o,* and *u*—five letters that people sometimes write illegibly.

    d Keep your capital letters clearly distinct from small letters. You may even want to print all capital letters.

4 Center the title of your paper on the first line of page one. Do not put quotation marks around the title or underline the title. Capitalize all the major words in a title, including the first word. Small connecting words within a title like *of, for, the, in,* and *to* are not capitalized.

5 Skip a line between the title and the first line of your text. Indent the first line of each paragraph about five spaces (half an inch) from the left-hand margin.

6 Make commas, periods, and other punctuation marks firm and clear. Leave a slight space after each period. When you type, leave a double space after a period.

7 If you break a word at the end of a line, break only between syllables (see page 145). Do not break words of one syllable.

8 Put your name, date, and course number where your instructor asks for them.

Also keep in mind these important points about the title and the first sentence of your paper:

• The title should be several words that tell what the paper is about. The title should usually *not* be a complete sentence.

• Do not rely on the title to help explain the first sentence of your paper. The first sentence must stand independent of the title.

PRACTICE 1

Identify the mistakes in format in the following lines from a student theme. Explain the mistakes in the spaces provided. One mistake is described for you as an example.

	"The generation gap in our house"
	When I was a girl, I never argued with my paren-
	ts about differences between their attitude and mine.
	My father would deliver his judgment on an issue
	and that was the end of the matter. There was no

1. *Hyphenate only between syllables (par-ents)*
2. _____
3. _____
4. _____
5. _____
6. _____

PRACTICE 2

As already stated, a title should tell in several words what a paper is about. Often a title can be based on the sentence that expresses the main idea of a paper.

Following are five main idea sentences from student papers. Write a suitable and specific title for each paper, basing the title on the main idea.

Example *"Aging Americans as Outcasts"*

Our society treats aging Americans as outcasts in many ways.

1. Title _____

Selfishness is a common trait in young children.

2. Title _____

 Exercising every morning has had positive effects on my health.

3. Title _____

 My teenage son is a stubborn person.

4. Title _____

 To survive in college, a person must learn certain essential study skills.

5. Title _____

 Only after I was married did I fully realize the drawbacks and values of single life.

PRACTICE 3

In four of the five sentences that follow, the writer has mistakenly used the title to help explain the first sentence. But as has already been stated, you must *not* rely on the title to help explain your first sentence.

Rewrite the sentences so that they stand independent of the title. Put *Correct* under the one sentence that is independent of the title.

Example   Title: Flunking an Exam
 First Sentence: I managed to do this because of several bad habits.

 Rewritten: *I managed to flunk an exam because of several bad habits.*

1. Title: The Worst Day of My Life
 First Sentence: It began when my supervisor at work gave me a message to call home.

 Rewritten: _____

 _____

2. Title: Catholic Church Services
 First Sentence: They have undergone many changes in the last few years.

 Rewritten: _____

 _____

3. Title: An Embarrassing Moment
   First Sentence: This happened to me when I was working as a waitress at the Stanton Hotel.

   Rewritten: _____

   _____

4. Title: The Inability to Share
   First Sentence: The inability to share can cause great strains in a relationship.

   Rewritten: _____

   _____

5. Title: Offensive Television Commercials
   First Sentence: Many that I watch are degrading to human dignity.

   Rewritten: _____

   _____

REVIEW TEST

Use the space provided to rewrite the following sentences from a student paper, correcting the mistakes in format.

	"my husband's Grandfather"
	He was seventy-four when I first met him, but
	in many ways he was the youngest person I ever
	knew, I couldn't help being impressed with the
	strength of his handshake, the tightness of the

Capital Letters

MAIN USES OF CAPITAL LETTERS

Capitalize the following:

First Word in a Sentence and the First Word in a Direct Quotation

The panhandler touched me and asked, "Do you have any change?"
(Capitalize the first word in the   (Capitalize the first word in the
sentence.)   direct quotation.)

"If you want a ride," said Brenda, "get ready now. Otherwise, I'm going alone."

(*If* and *Otherwise* are capitalized because they are the first words of sentences within a direct quotation. But *get* is not capitalized because it is part of the first sentence within the quotation.)

Names of Persons and the Word *I*

Last night I ran into Tony Curry and Lola Morrison.

Names of Particular Places

Charlotte graduated from Fargone High School in Orlando, Florida. She then moved with her parents to Bakersfield, California, and worked for a time there at Alexander's Gift House. Eventually she married and moved with her husband to the Naval Reserve Center in Atlantic County, New Jersey. She takes courses two nights a week at Stockton State College. On weekends she and her family often visit the nearby Wharton State Park and go canoeing on the Mullica River. She does volunteer work at Atlantic City Hospital in connection with the First Christian Church. In addition, she works during the summer as a hostess at Convention Hall and the Holiday Inn.

But: Use small letters if the specific name of a place is not given.

Charlotte sometimes remembers her unhappy days in high school and at the gift shop where she worked after graduation. She did not imagine then that she would one day be going to college and doing volunteer work for a church and hospital in the community where she and her husband live.

Names of Days of the Week, Months, and Holidays

Clyde was angry at himself for forgetting that Sunday was Mother's Day.

During July and August, Fred's company works a four-day week, and he has Mondays off.

Bill still has a scar on his ankle from a cherry bomb that exploded near him on a Fourth of July and a scar on his arm where he stabbed himself with a fishhook on a Labor Day weekend.

But: Use small letters for the seasons—summer, fall, winter, spring.

Names of Commercial Products

Clyde uses Scope mouthwash, Certs mints, and Dentyne gum to drive away the taste of the Marlboro cigarettes and White Owl cigars that he always smokes.

My sister likes to play Monopoly and Sorry; I like chess and poker; my brother likes Scrabble, baseball, and table tennis.

But: Use small letters for the *type* of product (mouthwash, mints, gum, cigarettes, and so on).

Names of Organizations such as Religious and Political Groups, Associations, Companies, Unions, and Clubs

Fred Grencher was a Lutheran for many years but converted to Catholicism when he married. Both he and his wife, Martha, are members of the Democratic Party. Both belong to the American Automobile Association. Martha works part time as a refrigerator salesperson at Sears. Fred is a mail carrier and belongs to the Postal Clerks Union.

Tony met Lola when he was a Boy Scout and she was a Campfire Girl; she asked him to light her fire.

Titles of Books, Magazines, Newspapers, Articles, Stories, Poems, Films, Television Shows, Songs, Papers That You Write, and the Like

On Sunday Lola read the first chapter of *I Know Why the Caged Bird Sings*, a book required for her writing course. She looked through *The New York Times* that her parents had gotten. She then read an article titled ''Thinking about a Change in Your Career'' and a poem titled ''Some Moments Alone'' in *Cosmopolitan* magazine. At the same time she played an old Beatles album, *Abbey Road*. In the evening she watched *Wild Kingdom* on television and a movie, *Magnum Force,* starring Clint Eastwood. Then from 11 P.M. to midnight she worked on a paper titled ''Uses of Leisure Time in Today's Culture'' for her sociology class.

But: Unless they are in the first words in titles, do not capitalize small connecting words like *in, the, and, of,* and *for.* (Note the words within titles in the preceding selection that are *not* capitalized.)

PRACTICE 1

Cross out the words that need capitals in the following sentences. Then write the capitalized form of the word in the spaces provided. The number of spaces tells you how many corrections to make in each case.

Example   He brushes with ~~crest~~ toothpaste but gets cavities all the time.

    Crest _____

1. The exterminating job was too big for raid, so she got on the phone to ratner pest control.

   _____   _____   _____   _____

2. In january I wish for spring, but in august I wish for winter again.

   _____   _____

3. The mild-mannered reporter named clark kent said to the Wolfman, "you better think twice before you mess with me, Buddy."

   _____   _____   _____   _____

4. While watching television, he drank four pepsis, ate an entire pack of ritz crackers, and finished up a bag of oreo cookies.

   _____   _____   _____

5. While riding his yamaha from his parents' home in florida to his sister's home in New Mexico, he was almost run over by a greyhound bus.

   _____   _____   _____

6. Lamont said to his father, "you're a bigot, Dad." His father replied, "watch your lip, Son, or i'll put my foot in it."

   _____   _____   _____

7. Last friday George took his entire paycheck, went to morton's, a discount store, and bought himself a 19-inch zenith color television.

   _____   _____   _____

8. On their first trip to New York City, Fred and Martha visited the empire State Building, Times square, and the Church of St. Peter and Paul. They also attended a play, *A Chorus Line,* at the Shubert Theatre and saw the New York mets play at shea Stadium.

   _____   _____   _____

9. Clyde was listening to Ike and Tina Turner's recording of "Proud mary," Paul was watching *sesame Street,* and Charlotte was reading an article in the *Reader's digest* titled, "let's Stop Peddling Sex."

   _____   _____   _____   _____

10. They are relentless comparison shoppers and will drive five miles if they can get kellogg's Special K or dial soap for three cents less at pathmark than at safeway.

   _____   _____   _____   _____

PRACTICE 2

Many errors in capitalization are caused by adding capitals where they are not needed. Cross out the incorrectly capitalized letters in the following sentences and write the correct forms in the spaces provided. The number of spaces tells you how many corrections to make in each sentence.

1. During the Summer I like to sit in my backyard, Sun bathe, and read Magazines.

   _____   _____   _____

2. Every Week I seem to be humming another Tune. Lately I have been humming the Melody for a Gum commercial on Television.

   _____   _____   _____   _____   _____

3. My Main object in High School was to travel through all the fifty States in our Country and then to get married and have a family. But my Goal now is to become a Lawyer and work for the good of others.

   _____   _____   _____   _____   _____   _____   _____

4. The Title of my Paper was, "The End of the Civil War." My Teacher did not give me a good Grade for it.

   _____   _____   _____   _____

5. My Friend Roger said, "People no longer have to go to College and get a Degree in order to find a good Job and succeed in Life."

   _____   _____   _____   _____   _____

OTHER USES OF CAPITAL LETTERS

Capitalize the following:

Relatives

I got Mother to babysit for me.
I went with Grandfather to the church service.
Uncle Carl and Aunt Lucy always enclose five dollars with birthday cards.

But: Do not capitalize words like *mother, father, grandmother, grandfather, uncle, aunt,* and so on when they are preceded by a possessive word (*my, your, his, her, our, their*).

I got my mother to babysit for me.
I went with my grandfather to the church service.
My uncle and aunt always enclose five dollars with birthday cards.

Titles

I wrote to Senator Grabbel and Congresswoman Punchie.
Professor Snorrel sent me to Chairperson Ruck, who sent me to Dean Rappern.
He drove to Dr. Helen Thompson's office after the cat bit him.
The speaker at the military academy commencement was Chaplain Devine.

But: Use small letters when titles appear by themselves, without specific names.

I wrote to my senator and congresswoman.

The professor sent me to the chairperson, who sent me to the dean.

He drove to his doctor's office after the cat bit him.

The speaker at the commencement exercises was a chaplain who had served in Southeast Asia.

Geographic Locations

Johnny Carson grew up in the Midwest. He worked in the East for a number of years and then moved to the West Coast.

But: Use small letters when giving directions.

Ms. Chiquita Banana lives south of the border.

Because I have a compass in my car, I know that I won't be going east or west when I want to go north.

Historical Periods and Events

Hector did well answering an essay question about the Second World War, but he lost points on a question about the Great Depression.

Opening and Closing of a Letter

Dear Sir: Sincerely yours,
Dear Madam: Truly yours,

Note: Capitalize only the first word in a closing.

Races, Nationalities, Languages

The research study centered on low-income Caucasians and Negroes.

They have German knives and Danish glassware in the kitchen, an Indian wallhanging in the bedroom, African sculptures in the study, and an Oriental rug in the living room.

She knows German, and Spanish, but she speaks mostly American slang.

Religious Writings, Groups, and the Deity

He wondered whether God would punish him if he didn't read the New Testament every day.

Her mother was a Protestant, and her father was a Roman Catholic; she herself eventually converted to Judaism.

Buddha, Allah, Jehovah, God—people have called Him many names.

Specific School Courses

I got A's in Accounting I and Small Business Management, but I got C's in Human Behavior and Spanish.

But: Use small letters for general subject areas.

I earned good grades in business courses, but I did not do so well in my psychology or language courses.

REVIEW TEST 1

Add capitals where needed in the following sentences.

Example At the end of ̷fairview ̷avenue I said to Linda, "̷turn left."

1. School begins after labor day and carries straight through with no holidays until thanksgiving.

2. I asked my dad, "when's uncle Bill getting his toupee?"

3. I'm doing well in English Composition and Human Behavior, but I'm flunking Western civilization.

4. The only thing I enjoyed about spring valley high school was marching in the band.

5. Henry borrows suspense novels from the library, but Sarah buys them at reilly's, a bookstore on second street.

6. "to get to the haunted house," said the gas station attendant, "you have to drive five blocks south on woodhaven road."

7. After serving in vietnam, Sam returned home and got a job in sales at glidden paint.

8. My sister is addicted to maxwell house coffee and winston cigarettes.

9. After reading betty rollins' book, *first you cry,* I got an appointment at shore memorial hospital to have a checkup for breast cancer.

10. It rained and hailed on tuesday, the day they planned to visit walt disney world in anaheim, california.

 REVIEW TEST 2

On separate paper, write:

- Seven sentences demonstrating the seven main uses of capital letters
- Eight sentences demonstrating the eight other uses of capital letters

Numbers

1 Spell out numbers that take no more than two words. Otherwise, use the numbers themselves.

During the past five years, over twenty-five barracuda have been caught in the lake.
The parking fine was ten dollars.
In my grandmother's attic are eighty-four pairs of old shoes.

But:

Each year about 250 baby trout are added to the lake.
My costs after contesting a parking fine in court were $135.
Grandmother has 382 back copies of the *Reader's Digest* in her attic.

2 Be consistent when you use a series of numbers. If some numbers in a sentence or paragraph require more than two words, then use numbers themselves throughout the selection:

> During his election campaign, State Senator Mel Grabble went to 3 county fairs, 16 parades, 45 cookouts, and 112 club dinners, and delivered the same speech 176 times.

3 Use numbers to show dates, times, addresses, percentages, and parts of a book.

> The letter was dated April 3, 1872.
>
> My appointment was at 6:15. (*But:* Spell out numbers before *o'clock*. For example: The doctor didn't see me until seven o'clock.)
>
> He lives at 212 West 19 Street.
>
> About 20 percent of our class have dropped out of school.
>
> Turn to page 179 in Chapter 8 and answer questions 1–10.

PRACTICE

Use the above rules to make the corrections needed in these sentences.

1. 3 boys were arrested.

2. Rich was born on February fifteenth, nineteen fifty-two.

3. I made eight-hundred-and-fifty dollars waitressing this past summer.

4. For tomorrow's class, we must do activity four on page 74 of the book.

5. By the time I was eight I owned three cats, two dogs, and 4 rabbits.

6. Crimes in that district last year included 322 store thefts, 74 muggings, and twenty-five cases of aggravated assault.

7. I see a 2 dollar bill about once every 3 months.

8. I have gotten A's in 4 courses, B's in six courses, and C's in fifteen courses.

9. The game begins at 7 o'clock.

10. Virginia does fifteen push-ups, thirty sit-ups, and 350 running steps every morning.

Abbreviations

While abbreviations are a helpful time-saver in note-taking, you should avoid most abbreviations in formal writing. Listed below are some of the few abbreviations that can acceptably be used in compositions. Note that a period is used after most abbreviations.

1   Mr., Mrs., Ms., Jr., Sr., Dr. when used with proper names:

   Mr. Tibble   Dr. Stein   Ms. O'Reilly

2   Time references:

   A.M. or a.m.   P.M. or p.m.   B.C. or A.D.

3   First or middle name in a signature:

   R. Anthony Curry   Otis T. Redding   J. Alfred Prufrock

4   Organizations, technical words, and trade names known primarily by their initials:

   FBI   UN   CBS   FM   STP

PRACTICE

Cross out the words that should not be abbreviated and correct them in the spaces provided.

1.   For six yrs. I lived at First Av. and Gordon St.

   _____   _____   _____

2.   When we arrived in San Fran., Calif., I had to enter Riverview Hosp.

   _____   _____   _____

3.   Dec. 5, 1975, is a Sat. morning I will never forget.

   _____   _____

4.   I came downstairs at ten min. after eight and discovered that my new Sony color telev. had been stolen.

   _____   _____

5.   Before her biol. and Eng. exams, Linda was so nervous that her doc. gave her a tranq.

   _____   _____   _____   _____

End Marks

A sentence always begins with a capital letter. It always ends with a period, a question mark, or an exclamation point.

PERIOD (.)

Use a period after a sentence that makes a statement.

More single parents are adopting children.
It has rained for most of the week.

Use a period after most abbreviations.

Mr. Thoms	B.A.	Dr. Ballard
Ms. Howar	a.m.	Tom Ricci, Jr.

QUESTION MARK (?)

Use a question mark after a *direct* question.

When is your paper due?
How is your cold?
Tom asked, "When are you leaving?"
Rosa suggested, "Why doesn't everyone take a break?"

Do not use a question mark after an *in*direct question (a question where no immediate reply is called for).

He asked how my cold was.
She asked when the paper was due.
Tom asked when I was leaving.
Rosa suggested that everyone take a break.

EXCLAMATION POINT (!)

Use an exclamation point after a word or sentence that expresses strong feeling.

Come here!
Ouch! This pizza is hot!
That truck just missed us!

Note: Be careful not to overuse exclamation points.

PRACTICE

Add a period, question mark, or exclamation point, as needed, to each of the following sentences.

1. How long will the store sale continue
2. Watch out for that bump in the road
3. The copper bracelet on her arm helps her arthritis
4. Does Barbara's room always look like a hurricane came for a visit
5. Dr. Kirby specializes in acupuncture of the wallet
6. Manny, Moe, and Jack are always working on their cars
7. Watch out or you'll step on my sunglasses
8. He asked if I had read Tolkien's *The Lord of the Rings*
9. "It will take hours to clean up this mess " Ellen cried.
10. Little Alan asked his uncle, "Is your mustache a wig "

Apostrophe

The two main uses of the apostrophe are:

1 to show the omission of one or more letters in a contraction
2 to show ownership or possession

Each use is explained on the pages that follow.

APOSTROPHE IN CONTRACTIONS

A contraction is formed when two words are combined to make one word. An apostrophe is used to show where letters are omitted in forming the contraction. Here are two contractions:

have + not = haven't (the *o* in *not* has been omitted)
I + will = I'll (the *wi* in *will* has been omitted)

The following are some other common contractions:

I + am = I'm	it + is = it's
I + have = I've	it + has = it's
I + had = I'd	is + not = isn't
who + is = who's	could + not = couldn't
do + not = don't	I + would = I'd
did + not = didn't	they + are = they're

Note: will + not has an unusual contraction: won't

PRACTICE 1

Combine the following words into contractions. One is done for you.

we + are = __*we're*__   you + have = _____

are + not = _____   has + not = _____

you + are = _____   who + is = _____

they + have = _____   does + not = _____

would + not = _____   there + is = _____

PRACTICE 2

Write the contraction for the words in parentheses.

Example He (could not) __*couldn't*__ come.

1. (I will) _____ be with you shortly if (you will)

    _____ just wait a minute.

2. (It is) _____ such a long drive to the ball park that Clyde (would not) _____ go there if you paid him.

3. You (should not) _____ drink any more if (you are) _____ hoping to get home safely.

4. Alice's husband (is not) _____ the aggressive type, and her former husbands (were not) _____ either.

5. (I would) _____ like to know (who is) _____ in charge of the cash register and why (it is) _____ taking so long for this line to move.

Note: Even though contractions are common in everyday speech and in written dialogue, usually it is best to avoid them in formal writing.

PRACTICE 3

Write five sentences using the apostrophe in different contractions.

1. _____
2. _____
3. _____
4. _____
5 _____

Four Contractions to Note Carefully

Four contractions that deserve special attention are *they're, it's, you're,* and *who's.* Sometimes these contractions are confused with the possessive words *their, its, your,* and *whose.* The following chart shows the difference in meaning between the contractions and the possessive words.

Contractions	Possessive Words
they're (means *they are*)	their (means *belonging to them*)
it's (means *it is* or *it has*)	its (means *belonging to it*)
you're (means *you are*)	your (means *belonging to you*)
who's (means *who is*)	whose (means *belonging to whom*)

Note: Possessive words are explained further on pages 120–121.

PRACTICE

Underline the correct form (the contraction or the possessive word) in each of the following sentences. Use the contraction whenever the two words of the contraction (*they are, it is, you are, who is*) would also fit.

1. (They're, Their) going to hold the party in (they're, their) family room.
2. (You're, Your) not going to be invited if you insist on bringing (you're, your) accordion.
3. (Who's, Whose) going with us and (who's, whose) car are we taking?
4. (It's, Its) too early to go to bed and (it's, its) too late in the day to take a nap.
5. If (you, you're) not going to drive by (they're, their) house, (it's, its) going to be impossible for them to get home tonight.

APOSTROPHE TO SHOW OWNERSHIP OR POSSESSION

To show ownership or possession, we can use such words as *belongs to, possessed by, owned by,* or (most commonly) *of.*

the television set that *belongs to* Tony
the gas station *owned by* our cousin
the backyard *possessed by* my neighbor
the footprints *of* the animal

But the apostrophe plus *s* (if the word does not end in *s*) is often the quickest and easiest way to show possession. Thus we can say:

Tony's television set   my neighbor's backyard
our cousin's gas station   the animal's footprints

Points to Remember

1   The *'s* goes with the owner or possessor (in the examples given, *Tony, cousin, the neighbor, the animal*). What follows is the person or thing possessed (in the examples given, *the television set, gas station, backyard, footprints*).

2   There should always be a break between the word and the *'s.*

Tony's   not   *Tonys*

Yes   No

PRACTICE 1

Rewrite the italicized part of each of the sentences listed below, using the *'s* to show possession. Remember that the *'s* goes with the owner or possessor.

Examples   *The motorcycle owned by Clyde* is a monster of a machine.
              Clyde's motorcycle
              The roommate of my brother is a sweet and friendly person.
              My brother's roommate

1. *The sneakers owned by Lola* were stolen.
   _____

2. As a joke, he put on *the lipstick that belongs to Veronica.*
   _____

3. *The house of his brother* was burglarized.
   _____

4. *The tires belonging to the car* are badly worn.
   _____

5. *The bicycle owned by Fran* was stolen from the bike rack outside of school.
   _____

6. I discovered the *nest of the blue jay* while pruning the tree.
   _____

7. I don't like *the title of my paper.*
   _____

8. *The arthritis of my mother* gets progressively worse.
   _____

9. *The boyfriend belonging to my sister* is a gorgeous hunk of man.
   _____

10. *The energy level possessed by the little boy* is much higher than hers.
    _____

PRACTICE 2

Underline the word in each sentence that needs an *'s*. Then write the word correctly in the space at the right. One is done for you as an example.

1. The <u>children</u> voices carried downstairs.   *children's*

2. Georgia husband is not a take-charge guy.   _____

3. My friend video game requires skill to play.   _____

4. When the teacher anger became apparent, the class quickly
    grew quiet.   _____

5. His girl friend apple pie made his stomach rebel.   _____

6. Albert dog looks like a porcupine without its quills.   _____

7. Under the couch were several of our daughter toys.   _____

8. The manager secretary is going to retire.   _____

9. That wine tastes like last night rain.   _____

10. The dentist charged fifty dollars to fix their son tooth.   _____

PRACTICE 3

Add an *'s* to each of the following words to make them the possessors or owners of something. Then write sentences using the words. Your sentences can be serious or playful. One is done for you as an example.

1. Grandmother *Grandmother's*   *Grandmother's shotgun is used to shoot crows and gophers.*

2. Lola _____   _____

3. teacher _____   _____

4. car _____   _____

5. dentist _____   _____

6. brother _____   _____

The Apostrophe versus Possessive Pronouns

Do not use an apostrophe with possessive pronouns. They already show ownership. Possessive pronouns include *his, hers, its, yours, our,* and *theirs.*

The bookstore lost its lease.	*not*	The bookstore lost its' lease.
The racing bikes were theirs.	*not*	The racing bikes were theirs'.
The change is yours.	*not*	The change is yours'.
His problems are ours, too.	*not*	His' problems are ours', too.
His skin is more sunburned than hers.	*not*	His' skin is more sunburned than hers'.

The Apostrophe versus Simple Plurals

When you want to make words plural, just add an *s* at the end of a word. Do *not* add an apostrophe. For example, the plural of the word *movie* is *movies,* not *movie's* or *movies'.* Look at this sentence:

Lola adores Tony's broad shoulders, rippling muscles, and warm eyes.

The words *shoulders, muscles,* and *eyes* are simple plurals, meaning more than one shoulder, more than one muscle, more than one eye. The plural is shown by adding *s* only. (Plurals are explained starting on page 157.) On the other hand, the *'s* after Tony shows possession—that Tony owns the shoulders, muscles, and eyes.

PRACTICE

Insert **'** or **'s** where needed to show possession in the following sentences. Write *plural* above words where the *s* ending simply means more than one thing.

Example The coils in Stan Morrow's air conditioner always freeze up on hot days.

(The *'s* shows that Stan Morrow is the owner of the air conditioner; *coils* and *days* are simple plurals, meaning more than one coil, more than one day.)

1. Tony favorite breakfast is five strips of bacon and fried potatoes.

2. My father influence on his brothers has been enormous.

3. When I walked into the doctor office, there were eight persons waiting there who also had appointments.

4. Bill job of slaughtering pigs was enough to make him a vegetarian.

5. When the teacher voice trembled, the students looked up, startled.

6. As Rick skill at guessing the essay questions on a test increased, his grades improved.

7.   My friends cooking is not the greatest: she made spaghetti for us and the noodles were so tightly stuck together that I had to cut them with a knife.

8.   His wife habit of taking the hangers from his closet really bothers him.

9.   I asked the record clerk for several blank cassette tapes and Carly Simon latest album.

10. After six weeks without rain, the nearby streams started drying up and the lakes water level fell sharply.

The Apostrophe with Words Ending in -s

If a word ends in *-s*, show possession by adding only an apostrophe. Most plurals end in *-s*, and so show possession simply by adding the apostrophe.

Charles' suede shirt   my parents' station wagon
Doris' car   the Beatles' last album
Ms. Rogers' briefcase   the students' class rings

PRACTICE

Add an apostrophe where needed.

1.   Did you hear that Jones wife wants a divorce?
2.   The transit workers strike continued until their demands were negotiated.
3.   When the students gripes about the cafeteria were ignored, many of them started to bring their own lunches.
4.   Lois dog gets his exercise by biting people.
5.   The two little boys father looks very tired.

 REVIEW TEST 1

Cross out each word that needs an ' or an *'s*. Then write the word correctly in the space provided. The number of spaces shows you the number of corrections needed in each sentence.

1.   Youre right and Im wrong, though I hate to admit it.   _____   _____

2.   Clyde quick hands reached out to break his son fall.   _____   _____

3. My mothers recipe for potato filling is famous among our family's relatives and friends. _____

4. The kites string broke when it got caught in the branches of a tree. _____

5. On windy days Linda wig must be pinned on securely so that it wont blow off. _____   _____

6. That dogs bite is worse than his bark. _____

7. We met two guys after Sundays football game and went with them to the movies that night. _____

8. My neighbor yard is full of trash and is populated by rabbits, squirrels, and gophers. _____

9. On Sunday she and her boys went to a barbecue at her daughters house. _____

10. Martha dog, Fang, barks on nights when theres a full moon. _____   _____

 REVIEW TEST 2

Insert an ' or an 's where needed. One sentence is correct.

1. Tonys Uncle Ralph had to take several stiff exams before he qualified for his morticians license.

2. Some researchers have found that peoples attitudes about sexual behavior have changed significantly in recent years.

3. The power company lost its good reputation when its chief officers were convicted of taking bribes.

4. Woody Allens humor is no more a lightweight affair than was Muhammad Alis boxing.

5. Carlas plane arrived on time but her suitcases were delayed.

6. Freds car wouldnt start until the baby-faced mechanic replaced its spark plugs and points.

7. The books cover was torn off, and many of its pages were smudged and crumpled.

8. Bobs eyes expanded when he saw that the snarling dogs chain was ready to snap.

9. The rock festivals first performers were Gladys Knight and the Pips.

10. If youre selling anything, Im not home.

Quotation Marks

The two main uses of quotation marks are:

1 To set off the exact words of a speaker or writer
2 To set off the titles of short works

Each use is explained on the pages that follow.

QUOTES TO SET OFF THE WORDS OF A SPEAKER OR WRITER

Use quotation marks when you want to show the exact words of a speaker or writer.

"Say something tender to me," whispered Lola to Tony.
(Quotation marks set off the exact words that Lola spoke to Tony.)

Mark Twain once wrote, "The more I know about human beings, the more I like my dog."
(Quotation marks set off the exact words that Mark Twain wrote.)

"The best part of my job," Bill said, "is that there's plenty of overtime."
(Two pairs of quotes are used to enclose Bill's exact words.)

Sharon complained, "I worked so hard on this paper. I spent two days getting information in the library and two days writing it. And guess what grade I got on it?"
(Note that the end quotes do not come until the end of Sharon's speech. Place quotation marks before the first quoted word of a speech and after the last quoted word. As long as no interruption occurs in the speech, do not use quotation marks for each new sentence.)

Punctuation hint: In the four examples above, notice that a comma sets off the quoted part from the rest of the sentence. Also observe that commas and periods at the end of a quote always go *inside* quotation marks.
Complete the following statements that explain how capital letters, commas, and periods are used in quotations. Refer to the four examples as guides.

1   Every quotation begins with a _____ letter.

2   When a quotation is split (as in the sentence about Bill), the second part does not begin with a capital letter unless it is a _____ sentence.

3   _____ are used to separate the quoted part of a sentence from the rest of the sentence.

4   Commas and periods that come at the end of a quote go

_____ quotation marks.

The answers are *capital, new, Commas,* and *inside.*

PRACTICE 1

Insert quotation marks where needed in the sentences that follow.

1.   Don't shout at me, Lola said to her mother.
2.   The teacher asked Sharon, Why are your eyes closed?
3.   Christ said, I come that you may have life, and have it more abundantly.
4.   I refuse to wear those itchy wool pants! Ralph shouted at his parents.
5.   His father replied, We should give all the clothes you never wear to the Salvation Army.
6.   The nervous boy whispered hoarsely over the telephone, Is Linda home?
7.   When I was ten, Lola said, I spent my entire summer playing Monopoly.
8.   Tony said, When I was ten, I spent my whole summer playing basketball.
9.   The critic wrote about the play, It runs the gamut of emotions from A to B.
10.   The best way to tell if a mushroom is poisonous, the doctor solemnly explained, is if you find it in the stomach of a dead person.

PRACTICE 2

Rewrite the following sentences, adding quotation marks where needed. Use a capital letter to begin a quote and use a comma to set off a quoted part from the rest of the sentence.

Example   I'm getting tired Sally said.

"I'm getting tired," Sally said.

1. Fred said I'm going with you.

   _____

2. Everyone passed the test the teacher informed them.

   _____

3. My parents asked where were you?

   _____

4. I hate that commercial he muttered.

   _____

5. If you don't leave soon, he warned, you'll be late for work.

   _____

PRACTICE 3

1. Write three quotations that appear in the first part of a sentence.

   Example <u>"Let's go shopping," I suggested.</u>

   a. _____

   b. _____

   c. _____

2. Write three quotations that appear at the end of a sentence.

   Example <u>Bob asked, "Have you had lunch yet?"</u>

   a. _____

   b. _____

   c. _____

3. Write three quotations that appear at the beginning and end of a sentence.

   Example <u>"If the bus doesn't come soon," Mary said,</u>
   <u>"we'll freeze."</u>

   a. _____

   b. _____

   c. _____

Indirect Quotations

An indirect quotation is a rewording of someone else's comments, rather than a word-for-word direct quotation. The word *that* often signals an indirect quotation.

Direct Quote	Indirect Quote
Fred said, "The distributor cap on my car is cracked."	Fred said that the distributor cap on his car is cracked.
(Fred's exact spoken words are given, so quotation marks are used.)	(We learn Fred's words *in*directly, so no quotation marks are used.)
Sally's note to Jay read, "I'll be working late. Don't wait up for me."	Sally left a note for Jay that said she would be working late and that he shouldn't wait up for her.
(The exact words that Sally wrote in the note are given, so quotation marks are used.)	(We learn Sally's words indirectly, so no quotation marks are used.)

PRACTICE 1

Rewrite the following sentences, changing words as necessary to convert the sentences into direct quotations. The first one is done for you as an example.

1. Fred asked Martha if he could turn on the football game.

   Fred asked, "Martha, can I turn on the football game?"

2. Martha said that he could listen to the game on the radio.

   _____

3. Fred replied he was tired of being told what to do.

   _____

4. Martha said that as long as she was bigger and stronger, she would make the rules.

   _____

   _____

5. Fred said that the day would come when the tables would be turned.

   _____

PRACTICE 2

Rewrite the following sentences, converting each direct quotation into an indirect statement. In each case you will have to add the word *that* or *if* and change other words as well.

Example   The barber asked Fred, "Have you noticed how your hair is thinning?"

The barber asked Fred if he had noticed how his hair was thinning.

1. He said, "As the plane went higher, my heart sank lower."

    _____

2. The designer said, "Shag rugs are back in style."

    _____

3. The foreman asked Jake, "Have you ever operated a lift truck?"

    _____

4. My nosy neighbor asked, "Were Ed and Ellen fighting?"

    _____

5. Martha complained, "I married a man who eats Tweeties cereal for breakfast."

    _____

QUOTES TO SET OFF THE TITLES OF SHORT WORKS

Short works are usually set off by quotation marks while long works are underlined. Use quotes to set off the titles of such short works as articles in books, newspapers, or magazines; chapters in a book; short stories, poems, and songs.

On the other hand, you should underline the titles of books, newspapers, magazines, plays, movies, record albums, and television shows.

Note: In printed works such titles are set off by italics—slanted type that looks *like this.*

Quotation Marks	Underlines
the article "The Mystique of Law-yers"	in the book <u>Verdicts on Lawyers</u>
the article "Getting a Fix on Re-pairs"	in the newspaper <u>The New York Times</u>
the article "Animal Facts and Fal-lacies"	in the magazine <u>Reader's Digest</u>
the chapter "Why Do Men Marry?"	in the book <u>Passages</u>

the story ''The Night the Bed Fell''	in the book <u>A Thurber Carnival</u>
the poem ''A Prayer for My Daughter''	in the book <u>Poems of W. B. Yeats</u>
the song ''Winds of the Old Days''	in the album <u>Diamonds and Rust</u>
	the television show <u>Family</u>
	the movie <u>Gone With the Wind</u>

PRACTICE

Use quotation marks or underlines as needed.

1. Edgar Allan Poe's short story The Murders in the Rue Morgue and his poem The Raven are in a paperback titled Great Tales and Poems of Edgar Allan Poe.

2. My assignment is to research an article titled A New Treatment for Hypertension in the latest issue of Newsweek.

3. States of Consciousness, the sixth chapter of Linda Davidoff's Introduction to Psychology, will be the basis for our next test.

4. Tony's favorite television show is Star Trek, and his favorite movie is Star Wars.

5. He bought the Ladies' Home Journal because he wanted to read the cover article titled Secrets Men Never Tell You.

6. The assignment was to read the chapter titled A Kite in James Herndon's How to Survive in Your Native Land.

7. When she got her new TV Guide, she read an article titled The New Comedians and then thumbed through the listings to see who would be the guests that week on the Tonight Show.

8. The night before his exam, he discovered with horror that the chapter Becoming Mature was missing from Childhood and Adolescence, the psychology text that he had bought secondhand.

9. In Dr. Hickory's new book, Black Walnuts and You, there is a chapter titled How to Make Walnut Peanut Butter.

10. Every holiday season our family watches the movie A Christmas Carol on television.

OTHER USES OF QUOTATION MARKS

1 To set off special words or phrases from the rest of a sentence:

Many people spell the words ''a lot'' as *one* word, ''alot,'' instead of correctly spelling them as two words.

I have trouble telling the difference between ''their'' and ''there.''

2 To mark off a quote within a quote:

The instructor said, ''Know the chapter titled 'Status Symbols' in *Adolescent Development* if you expect to pass the test.''

Lola said, ''One of my favorite Mae West lines is, 'I used to be Snow White, but I drifted.' ''

Note: Quotes within a quote are indicated by a *single* quotation mark.

REVIEW TEST **1**

Place quotation marks around the exact words of a speaker or writer in the sentences that follow.

1. Is something wrong with your car again? the mechanic asked Fred.
2. Muhammad Ali once said, I'm so fast I could hit you before God gets the news.
3. The sign read, Be careful how you drive. You may meet a fool.
4. One of Moms Mabley's favorite lines was, The only thing an old man can do for me is to bring me a message from a young one.
5. In the course of a discussion with some students, Katherine Anne Porter observed, Loneliness and misunderstanding are the fundamental facts of the human condition.
6. John Kennedy once said, Ask not what your country can do for you; ask what you can do for your country.
7. A passenger in the car ahead of Clyde threw a food wrapper and empty cups out of the window. That man, said Clyde to his son, is a human pig.
8. Fred asked the struggling old lady on the street if he could help with her heavy bag. Go to blazes, you masher, she said.
9. A woman who was one of Winston Churchill's political enemies once remarked, If Churchill were my husband, I would put poison in his coffee. Churchill's reply was, Madam, if I were your husband, I would drink it.
10. In his autobiography, Dick Cavett describes his first meeting with Groucho Marx. Cavett approached Groucho at a street corner and said, Hello, Groucho, I'm a big fan of yours. Groucho's response was, If it gets any hotter I could use a big fan.

REVIEW TEST **2**

1. Write a sentence in which you quote a favorite expression of someone you know. Identify the relationship of the person to you.

Example   *My brother Sam often says after a meal,*
         "That wasn't bad at all."

2.   Write a quotation that contains the words *Tony asked Lola.*   Write a second
     quotation that includes the words *Lola replied.*

3.   Write down a sentence that interests you from a book.   Identify the title and
     author of the book.

Example   *Thoreau writes in Walden, "What a man*
         thinks of himself, that is what determines, or
         rather indicates, his fate."

4.   Write down a sentence that interests you from a newspaper.   Identify the title
     and the author (if given) of the article.

5.   Write down a sentence that interests you from a magazine.   Identify the title
     and the author of the article.

REVIEW TEST 3

   Go through the comics section of a newspaper to find a comic strip that amuses
you. Be sure to choose a strip where two or more characters are speaking to each
other. Write a full description that will enable people who have not read the comic
strip to visualize it clearly and appreciate its humor. Describe the setting and action
in each panel and enclose the words of the speakers in quotation marks.

Comma

SIX MAIN USES OF THE COMMA

Commas are used mainly as follows:

1 To separate items in a series
2 To set off introductory material
3 On both sides of words that interrupt the flow of thought in a sentence
4 Between two complete thoughts connected by *and, but, for, or, nor, so, yet*
5 To set off a direct quotation from the rest of a sentence
6 For certain everyday material

You may find it helpful to remember that the comma often marks a slight pause or break in a sentence. Read aloud the sentence examples given for each rule and listen for the minor pauses or breaks that are signaled by commas.

Comma between Items in a Series

Use a comma to separate items in a series.

Magazines, paperback novels, and textbooks crowded the shelves.
Hard-luck Sam needs a loan, a good-paying job, and a close friend.
The television game shows enraged him so much he did not know whether to laugh, cry, or throw up.
Eve bit into the ripe, juicy apple.
More and more people entered the crowded, noisy stadium.

Notes:
a The final comma in a series is optional, but often it is used.
b. A comma is used between two descriptive words in a series only if *and* inserted between the words sounds natural. You could say:

Eve bit into the ripe *and* juicy apple.
More and more people entered the crowded *and* noisy stadium.

But notice in the following sentences that the descriptive words do not sound natural when *and* is inserted between them. In such cases, no comma is used.

She drove a bright red Corvette. (A bright *and* red Corvette doesn't sound right, so no comma is used.)

Dr. Van Helsing noticed two tiny puncture marks on his patient's neck. (Two *and* tiny puncture marks doesn't sound right, so no comma is used.)

PRACTICE

Place a comma between items in a series.

1. Wild Bill relaxes by reading Donald Duck Archie and Bugs Bunny comic books.
2. Cold eggs burned bacon and watery orange juice are the reasons I've never returned to that diner for breakfast.
3. She was sure that the rich tangy mellow beer in the glass was Lowenbrau.
4. Tony makes Big Macs by putting two all-beef patties special sauce lettuce cheese pickles and onions on a sesame seed bun.
5. Kevin did the laundry helped clean the apartment waxed the car and watched ABC's *Wide World of Sports.*

Comma after Introductory Material

Use a comma to set off introductory material.

Looking up in the sky, I saw a man who was flying faster than a speeding bullet.

Although I have a black belt in karate, I decided to go easy on the demented bully who kicked sand in my face.

Holding a baited trap, Clyde cautiously approached the gigantic mousehole.

In addition, he held a broom in his hand.

Also, he wore a football helmet in case a creature should leap out at his head.

Note: If the introductory material is brief, the comma is sometimes omitted. In the activities here, you should include the comma.

PRACTICE

Place commas after introductory material.

1. Even though she had an upset stomach she went bowling with her husband. In turn he cleaned up the supper dishes when they got home later.
2. Looking back over the last ten years I can see several decisions I made that really changed my life.
3. Since I needed the money I told my boss I would be willing to work overtime all weekend. Also I agreed to work for time-and-a-half without any double time. However I intend never to volunteer to do this again.

4. After seeing the accident Susan wanted to stop driving forever. Even so she went driving to the shopping mall over ice-covered roads.

5. To get her hair done she drives to a beauty salon several miles away. Once there she enjoys listening to the gossip in the beauty shop. Also she likes looking through *Playgirl, Cosmopolitan,* and other magazines in the shop.

Comma around Words Interrupting the Flow of Thought

Use a comma on both sides of words that interrupt the flow of thought in a sentence.

That game show, at long last, has been canceled.

You, my man, are going to get yours.

Martha, our new neighbor, used to work as a bouncer at Rexy's Tavern.

The children used the old Buick, rusted from disuse, as a backyard clubhouse.

Usually you can "hear" words that interrupt the flow of thought in a sentence. However, if you are not sure if certain words are interrupters, remove them from the sentence. If it still makes sense without the words, you know the words are interrupters and that the information they give is nonessential. Such nonessential information is set off with commas. In the following sentence,

Dody Thompson, who lives next door, won the javelin-throwing competition.

the words *who lives next door* are extra information, not needed to identify the subject of the sentence, Dody Thompson. Put commas around such nonessential information. On the other hand, in the sentence

The woman who lives next door won the javelin-throwing competition.

the words *who lives next door* supply essential information, information needed for us to identify the woman being spoken of. If the words were removed from the sentence, we would no longer know who won the competition. Commas are not used around such essential information.

Here is another example:

Wilson Hall, which the tornado destroyed, was ninety years old.

The subject of the sentence, *Wilson Hall,* is identified. Commas are used around *which the tornado destroyed,* the extra information about the building. On the other hand, in the sentence

The building which the tornado destroyed was ninety years old.

the words *which the tornado destroyed* are needed to identify the building. Commas are not used around such nonessential information.

Most of the time you will be able to "hear" words that interrupt the flow of thought in a sentence and will not have to think about whether the words are essential or nonessential.

PRACTICE

Use commas to set off interrupting words.

1. Friday is the deadline the absolute final deadline for your papers to be turned in.
2. The nursery rhyme told how the cow a weird creature jumped over the moon. The rhyme also related how the dish who must also have been strange ran away with a spoon.
3. Dody Thompson's husband a mild man who works as a bookkeeper attended the track meet. People say that he strange as it seems is the real boss in the family.
4. This cheese to be sure has an odor as powerful as a skunk's.
5. Tod voted the most likely to succeed in our high school graduating class recently made the front page of our newspaper. He was arrested with other members of the King Kongs a local motorcycle gang for creating a disturbance in the park.

Comma between Complete Thoughts Connected by a Joining Word

Use a comma between two complete thoughts connected by *and, but, for, or, nor, so, yet.*

The polyester bed sheets had a gorgeous design on them, but they didn't feel as comfortable as plain white cotton sheets.

We could always tell when our teacher felt disorganized, for his shirt would not be tucked in.

The teenage girls walked the hot summer streets trying to attract boys, and the teenage boys drove by in their shined-up cars hoping to attract girls.

Notes:
a The comma is optional when the complete thoughts are short ones.

Grace's skin tans and Mark's skin freckles.
Her soda turned watery for the ice melted quickly.
The day was overcast so they didn't go swimming.

b Be careful not to use a comma in sentences having *one* subject and a *double* verb. The comma is used only in sentences made up of two complete thoughts (two subjects and two verbs). In this sentence

Bill will go partying tonight and forget all about tomorrow's exam.

there is only one subject (*Bill*) and a double verb (*will go* and *forget*). No comma is needed. Likewise, the following sentence

Rita was a waitress at the Holiday Inn last summer and probably will work there this summer.

has only one subject (*Rita*) and a double verb (*was* and *will work*); therefore, no comma is needed.

PRACTICE

Place a comma before a joining word that connects two complete thoughts (two subjects and two verbs). Remember, do *not* place a comma within sentences that have only one subject and a double verb.

1. I spent all of Saturday morning trying to fix my car but I still wound up taking it to a garage in the afternoon.
2. She felt like shouting but didn't dare open her mouth.
3. He's making $20,000 a year selling cosmetics to beauty shops but he still has regrets about not having gone to college.
4. Bill often goes into bars and asks people to buy him a drink.
5. He decided not to take the course in advanced math for he wanted to have time for a social life during the semester.
6. He left the dentist's office with his mouth still numb from Novocain and he talked with a lisp for two hours.
7. With a sigh of relief, Charlotte unbuttoned her pants and kicked off her shoes.
8. The dancers in the go-go bar moved like wound-up Barbie dolls and the men in the audience sat as motionless as stones.
9. She realized that she was going to have to cut back on her drinking but she wasn't able to discipline herself to do so.
10. Her throat became very dry during the long speech and beads of perspiration began to appear on her forehead.

Comma with Direct Quotations

Use a comma to set off a direct quotation from the rest of a sentence.

His father shouted, "Why don't you go out and get a job?"

"Our modern world has lost a sense of the sacredness of life," the speaker said.

"No," said Celia to Jerry. "I won't go to the roller derby with you."

"Can anyone remember," wrote Emerson, "when the times were not hard and money not scarce?"

Note: Commas and periods at the end of a quote go inside quotation marks. See also page 124.

PRACTICE

Use commas to set off quotes from the rest of the sentence.

1. "I can't wait to have a fishburger and french fries" said Lola to Tony as they pulled into the drive-in restaurant.
2. Tony asked "What would you like to drink?"
3. "Wait a minute" said Lola. "For a change, you stay in the car and let me get the goodies. What do you want?"
4. "Two quarter-pounders with cheese, two large fries, and a large birch beer" said Tony.
5. "Good grief" said Lola. "It's hard to believe you don't weigh three hundred pounds."

Comma with Everyday Material

Use a comma with certain everyday material.

Persons Spoken To

I think, Sally, that you should go to bed.
Cindy, where did you put my shoes?
Are you coming with us, Bob?

Dates

March 4, 1972, is when Martha buried her third husband.

Addresses

Tony's grandparents live at 183 Roxborough Avenue, Cleveland, Ohio 44112.

Note: No comma is used to mark off the zip code.

Openings and Closings of Letters

Dear Santa,	Sincerely yours,
Dear Larry,	Truly yours,

Note: In formal letters, a colon is used after the opening: Dear Sir: *or* Dear Madam:

Numbers

Sarah swears that at least 50,000 beetles attacked her roses last summer.

PRACTICE

Place commas where needed.

1. I am sorry Sir but you cannot sit at this table.
2. I expected you Mike and you Susan to set a better example for the others.
3. The movie stars Kitty Litter and Dredge Rivers were married on September 12 1978 and lived at 3865 Sunset Boulevard Los Angeles California for one month.
4. They received 75000 congratulatory fan letters and were given picture contracts worth $900000 in the first week of their marriage.
5. Kitty left Dredge on October 12 1978 and ran off with their marriage counselor.

UNNECESSARY USE OF COMMAS

Commas are far more often overused than underused.   You should not use a comma unless a given comma rule applies or unless a comma is otherwise needed to help a sentence read clearly.   And remember that "when in doubt" about whether to use a comma, it is usually best to "leave it out." Following are some typical examples of unnecessary commas.

Sharon told me, that my socks were different colors.
(A comma is not used before *that* unless the flow of thought is interrupted.)

The union negotiations, dragged on for three days.
(Do not use a comma between a simple subject and verb.)

I waxed all the furniture, and cleaned the windows.
(Use a comma before *and* only with more than two items in a series or when *and* joins two complete thoughts.)

Sharon carried, the baby into the house.
(Do not use a comma between a verb and its object.)

PRACTICE

Cross out commas that do not belong. Some commas are correct. Do not add any commas.

1. Frank said to me, that the work was already done.
2. Eggs must then be added, to the recipe.
3. As the heavy Caterpillar tractor, rumbled up the street, our house windows rattled.
4. I am allergic to wool rugs, and cat fur.
5. The short, chubby blonde with the grin on her face is, my sister.
6. The club members asked me whether, I had ever taken karate lessons.
7. Las Vegas, Miami Beach, and Atlantic City, are the three places where he has worked as a bartender.
8. The brown cotton shirt that Jay has worn, for two years is threadbare and faded.
9. Thomas Farley, the handsome young man, who just took off his trousers, is an escaped mental patient.
10. Because, Mary is single, her married friends do not invite her, to their parties.

 REVIEW TEST 1

Insert commas where needed. In the space provided under each sentence, summarize briefly the rule that explains the use of the comma(s).

1. After I fell and fractured my wrist I decided to sell my skateboard.

   _____

2. She asked her son "Are you going to church with me tomorrow?"

   _____

3. The weather bureau predicts that sleet fire or brimstone will fall on Washington today.

   _____

4. The ignition system in his car as well as the generator was not working properly.

_____

5. Tony asked Lola "Have you ever had nightmares in which some kind of monster was ready to swallow you?"

_____

6. They attacked their bathroom with Lysol Comet and Fantastik.

_____

7. The pan of bacon fat heating on the stove burst into flame and he quickly set a lid on the pan to put out the fire.

_____

8. Clyde's bad cough which he had had for almost a week began to subside.

_____

9. I wear thick socks while hiking but I still return from a trip with blistered feet.

_____

10. When they found pencil shavings in the soup the guests decided they were not hungry.

_____

REVIEW TEST 2

1. Write a sentence telling of three items you want to get the next time you go to the store. _____

_____

2. Write a sentence that describes three things you would like to get done this week. _____

_____

3. Write two sentences, starting the first one with *If a prowler came into my bedroom* and the second one with *Also.* _____

_____

_____

_____

4. Write two sentences describing how you relax after getting home from school or work. Start the first sentence with *After* or *When*. Start the second sentence with *Next.*_____

_____

_____

_____

5. Write a sentence about a selfish or generous person you know. Use the words *a selfish person* or *a generous person* right after his or her name.

_____

_____

6. Write a sentence that tells something about your favorite magazine or television show. Use the words *which is my favorite magazine* or *which is my favorite television show* after the name of the magazine or show.

_____

_____

7. Write two complete thoughts about foods you enjoy. Use *and* to join the two complete thoughts. _____

_____

8. Write two complete thoughts about a person you know. The first thought should tell of something you like about the person. The second thought should tell of something you don't like. Join the thoughts with *but*.

_____

_____

_____

9. Invent a line that Lola might say to Tony. Use the words *Lola said* in the sentence._____

_____

10. Write a remark that you made to someone today. Use the words *I said* somewhere in the middle of the sentence. _____

_____

 REVIEW TEST 3

On separate paper, write six sentences, each sentence demonstrating one of the six main comma rules.

Other Punctuation Marks

COLON (:)

The colon is a mark of introduction. Use the colon at the end of a complete statement to do the following:

1   Introduce a list

The following were my worst jobs: truck loader in an apple plant, assembler in a battery factory, and attendant in a state mental hospital.

Note: *The following were my worst jobs* is a complete statement, and so a colon is used before the list. But look at this sentence:

My worst jobs were as a truck loader in an apple plant, an assembler in a battery factory, and an attendant in a state mental hospital.

In this sentence *My worst jobs were* is not a complete statement, and so no colon is used before the list.

2   Introduce a long quotation

Thoreau explains in *Walden:* "I went to the woods because I wished to live deliberately, to front only the essential facts of life, and see if I could not learn what it had to teach, and not, when I came to die, discover that I had not lived."

3   Introduce an explanation

There are two softball leagues in our town: the fast-pitch league and the lob-pitch league.

Two minor uses of the colon are after the opening in a formal letter (*Dear Sir or Madam:*) and between the hour and the minute when writing the time (*The plane is due in at 9:20*).

PRACTICE

Place colons where needed.

1. I have owned three cars a '68 Chevy, a '71 Buick, and a '78 Rabbit.
2. All the signs of the flu were present hot and cold spells, heavy drainage from the sinuses, a bad cough, and an ache through the entire body.
3. The teacher announced to his class "Call me 'Professor' at all times, smile and nod your heads as you listen to me, take down as gospel all of my golden words, and submit your assignments to me promptly and humbly."
4. For the test, remember the importance of these men Francis Bacon, John Donne, and Andrew Marvell.
5. The dream I had last night involved the weirdest situation a flock of chickens watching television in my living room.

SEMICOLON (;)

The semicolon signals more of a pause than the comma alone but not quite the full pause of a period.   Use a semicolon to do the following:

1 Join two complete thoughts that are not already joined by a connecting word such as *and, but, for,* or *so*

The chemistry lab blew up; Professor Thomas was fired.

I once stabbed myself with a pencil; a black mark has been under my skin ever since.

2 Join two complete thoughts that include a connecting word such as *however, otherwise, moreover, furthermore, therefore,* or *consequently*

I cut and raked the grass; moreover, I weeded the lawn.

Sally finished typing the paper; however, she forgot to bring it with her to class.

3 Mark off items in a series when the items themselves contain commas:

Winning prizes at the national flower show were Roberta Collins, Alabama, azaleas; Sally Hunt, Kentucky, roses; and Sue Kelly, Rhode Island, Shasta daisies.

The books that must be read for the course are *Report from Fire Engine No. 82,* by Dennis Smith; *Manchild in the Promised Land,* by Claude Brown; and *Man's Search for Meaning,* by Viktor Frankl.

PRACTICE

Place semicolons where needed.

1. Some people felt the glass was half-full others saw the glass as half-empty.
2. I would never apply for a job at that place starting salaries are very low.
3. Today Sandy has ignored me yesterday she was smiling at me.
4. No wonder I couldn't find ''Dear Abby'' the newspaper dropped her column.
5. My doctor advised me to start smoking cigarettes he said my body wasn't getting enough tar.

DASH (—)

A dash signals a degree of pause longer than a comma but not as complete as a period. Use the dash to do the following:

1 Set off words for dramatic effect

I didn't go out with him a second time—once was more than enough.
Some of you—I won't mention you by name—cheated on the test.
It was so windy that the VW passed him on the highway—overhead.

2 Set off a series of items

All our snacks—Triscuits, pretzels, crackers—were stolen from the car.
A meaningful job, a loving wife, and a car that wouldn't break down all the time—these are the things he wanted in life.

Notes:
a The dash is formed on the typewriter by striking the hyphen twice (--). In handwriting, the dash is as long as two letters would be.
b Be careful not to overuse dashes.

PRACTICE

Place dashes where needed.

1. The car is in excellent condition except that the brakes don't always work.
2. Riding my bike I get plenty of exercise especially when I am chased by dogs.
3. I'm advising you in fact, I'm telling you not to bother me again.
4. The package finally arrived badly damaged.
5. Chopping wood, building things, fishing these are the activities I enjoy.

HYPHEN (-)

Use a hyphen in the following ways:

1 With two or more words that act as a single unit describing a noun

The fast-talking salesman was so good that he went into politics.

When the driver removed his blue-tinted sunglasses, Lonnell saw the far-off look in his eyes.

Note: Look in your dictionary when you are unsure whether to use a hyphen between words.

2 To divide a word at the end of a line of writing or typing

When Alexander lifted up the hood of his car, he realized that one of the radiator hoses had broken.

Notes:

a Always divide a word between syllables. Use your dictionary (see page 149) to be sure of correct syllable divisions.

b Do not divide words of one syllable.

c Do not divide a word if you can avoid it.

PRACTICE

Place hyphens where needed.

1. High flying jets and gear grinding trucks are constant sources of noise pollution in our neighborhood.
2. I both admire and envy his well rounded personality.
3. When Anita turned on the kitchen light, ten legged creatures scurried everywhere over the crumb filled floor.
4. He had seventy two dollars in his pocket when he left for the local supermarket, and he had twenty two dollars when he got back.
5. The ten year old girl was remarkably self confident when she was giving her speech.

PARENTHESES ( )

Use parentheses to do the following:

1 Set off extra or incidental information from the rest of a sentence

The section of that book on the medical dangers of abortion (pages 35–72) is outdated.

Yesterday at Hamburger House (my favorite place to eat) the guy who makes french fries asked me to go out with him.

2 Enclose letters or numbers that signal items in a series

Three steps to follow in previewing a textbook are to (1) study the title, (2) read the first and last paragraphs, and (3) study the headings and subheadings.

Note: Do not use parentheses too often in your writing.

PRACTICE

Add parentheses where needed.

1. Certain sections of the novel especially Chapter Five made my heart race with suspense.
2. Did you hear that George Amy's first husband just got remarried?
3. Sigmund Freud 1856–1939 was the founder of psychoanalysis.
4. To make better use of your time, you should prepare 1 a daily list of things to do and 2 a weekly study schedule.
5. For the test we must know everything in the third chapter pages 72–96 of our biology text.

REVIEW TEST 1

At the appropriate spot, place the punctuation mark shown in the margin.

Example ; The singles dance was a success. I met several people I liked.

:
1. Before you go anywhere, finish your chores the laundry, the dishes, and the vacuuming.

—
2. The Easter Bunny, Santa Claus, and the Tooth Fairy these were the idols of my youth.

-
3. Tom's self important manner makes him boring to be with.

( )
4. The two most important steps in writing an effective paper are 1 to make a point of some kind and 2 to provide specific evidence to support that point.

:
5. Albert Einstein once said "It is in fact nothing short of a miracle that the modern methods of instruction have not yet entirely strangled the holy curiosity of inquiry; for this delicate little plant, aside from stimulation stands

mainly in need of freedom; without this it goes to wrack and ruin without fail.''

;   6. Clyde bought a remote control unit for his television set as a result, he can switch off the sound during commercials.

—   7. I asked the waiter to return the steak which seemed to consist of more fat than meat to the kitchen.

-    8. Fred always brings a pair of wide angle binoculars to the football games.

( )   9. The television set is relatively new having been bought only a year ago but has been to the repair shop three times.

;   10. Susan's job has made her very anxious she has begun to grind her teeth at night.

 REVIEW TEST 2

Add colons, semicolons, dashes, hyphens, or parentheses as needed. Each sentence requires only one of the five kinds of punctuation marks.

1. Bargain hunters swarmed around the entrance to the store the manager quickly opened the doors.

2. The diagram of the reproductive cycle pages 24–25 must also be studied for the test.

3. Self centered people are often very insecure individuals.

4. There is one sure way to get in trouble with that teacher ask too many questions.

5. Tarzan, Superman, the Lone Ranger these were the heroes of his boyhood.

6. George Orwell has written ''On the whole, human beings want to be good, but not too good, and not quite all the time. . . . Society has always to demand a little more from human beings than it will get in practice.''

7. Two squirrels there they are on top of the fence are building a nest in the storage shed.

8. The three required books on our psychology reading list are *Towards a Psychology of Being,* by Abraham Maslow *On Becoming a Person,* by Carl Rogers and *Love and Will,* by Rollo May.

9. I don't know why the door to the gas station rest room is locked perhaps the owner is afraid someone will get inside to clean it.

10. This do it yourself repair book will save homeowners a lot of money.

 REVIEW TEST 3

On separate paper, write two sentences for each of the following punctuation marks: colon, semicolon, dash, hyphen, parentheses.

Dictionary Use

The dictionary is a valuable tool. To take advantage of it, you need to understand the main kinds of information that a dictionary gives about a word. Look at the information provided for the word *disillusion* in the following entry from the *American Heritage Dictionary,* paperback edition.[1]

Spelling and syllabication   Pronunciation   Part of speech

dis·il·lu·sion (dĭs'ĭ-lōō'zhən) *v.* To free or deprive of illusion; disenchant. —*n* **1.** The act of disenchanting. **2.** The condition of being disenchanted —**dis'il·lu'sion·ment** *a*.

Meanings

Other form of the word

SPELLING

The first bit of information, in the boldface (heavy type) entry itself, is the spelling of *disillusion*. Get into the habit of using the dictionary for spelling. When you write a paper, allow yourself time to look up the spelling of all those words you are unsure about.

Use your dictionary to correct the spelling of the following words:

alright _____   elavater _____

assosiation _____   plesure _____

awkwerd _____   balence _____

diferent _____   beleiving _____

omited _____   libary _____

opinyon _____   apetite _____

critikal _____   happyness _____

embarasment _____   usualy _____

probaly _____   suprise _____

[1] © 1969, 1970, 1973, 1976, Houghton Mifflin Company. Reprinted by permission from the *American Heritage Dictionary of the English Language,* paperback edition.

SYLLABICATION

The second bit of information that the dictionary gives, also in the boldface entry, is the syllabication of **dis·il·lu·sion.** Note that a dot separates each syllable (or part) in the word.

Use your dictionary to mark the syllable divisions in the following words. Also indicate how many syllables are in each word.

b e l i e v e   (_____ syllables)

t r e a c h e r o u s   (_____ syllables)

d i s s a t i s f i e d   (_____ syllables)

u n p r e c e d e n t e d   (_____ syllables)

Noting syllable divisions will enable you to *hyphenate* a word: divide it at the end of one line of writing and complete it at the beginning of the next line. You can correctly hyphenate a word only at a syllable division, and you may have to check your dictionary to make sure of a particular word's syllable divisions.

PRONUNCIATION

The third bit of information in the dictionary entry is the pronunciation of *disillusion:* (dĭs′ĭ-lōō′zhən). You probably already know how to pronounce *disillusion,* but if you didn't, the information within the parentheses would serve as your guide.

To learn how to pronounce *disillusion,* you would have to do three things:

1 look at the letters given in parentheses
2 interpret the letters by using the pronunciation key at the bottom of the page (or elsewhere) in your dictionary
3 use the accent marks to know what syllables to stress in the word

The pronunciation key is made up of letter sounds and common words in which the sounds appear. You will probably use the key mainly as a guide to pronounce different vowel sounds (vowels are the letters *a, e, i, o,* and *u*). Here is part of the pronunciation key in the *American Heritage Dictionary:*

ă pat / ā ate / ĭ pit / ī pie / ŏ pot / ō go / ŏŏ took / ōō coo / ŭ cut

According to this key, how is each of the following letters in *disillusion* pronounced?

ĭ is pronounced like the *i* in the common word _____

ōō is pronounced like the *oo* in the common word _____

Most of the time, people are able to pronounce the consonant sounds (all the letters of the alphabet except the vowels) in words without using the pronunciation key. But if you are ever unsure about how to pronounce a consonant, use the key. It tells you, for instance, that the *zh* in (dĭs'ĭ-lōo'zhən) is pronounced like the *s* in the common word *vision*.

To complete your pronunciation of (dĭs'ĭ-lōo'zhən), look for the accent marks that show you what sounds to stress in the word. In this case, a light stress is placed on the first syllable (dis') and a heavy stress is placed on the third syllable (lōo').

Use your dictionary to complete the following exercises that relate to pronunciation.

Vowel Sounds

Look in the pronunciation key in your dictionary for the common word that tells you how to pronounce each of the following vowel sounds:

ē _____   ō _____   ī _____

ĕ _____   ŏ _____   ĭ _____

Note: The long vowel always has the sound of its own name.

The Schwa (ə)

The symbol ə in (dĭs'ĭ-lōo'zhən) looks like an upside down ə. It is called a *schwa,* and it stands for the unaccented sound in such words as *ago, item, edible, gallop,* and *circus.* More approximately, it stands for the sound *uh*—like the *uh* that speakers sometimes make when they hesitate in their speech. Perhaps it would help to remember that *uh,* as well as ə, could be used to represent the schwa sound.

Here are some of the many words in which the sound appears: *recollect* (rĕk'ə-lekt' or rĕk'uh-lekt'); *hesitate* (hĕz'ə·tāt or hĕz'uh-tāt); *courtesy* (kûr'tə-sē or kûr'tuh-sē). Open your dictionary to any page and you will almost surely be able to find three words that use the schwa in the pronunciation in parentheses after the main entry. Write three such words and their pronunciations in the following spaces:

1. _____   (_____)

2. _____   (_____)

3. _____   (_____)

Accent Marks

Some words contain both a primary accent, shown by a heavy stroke ('), and a secondary accent, shown by a lighter stroke ('). For example, in the word *discriminate* (dĭs-krĭm'ə-nat'), the strees or accent goes chiefly on the second syllable (krĭm'), and to a lesser extent, on the last syllable (nāt').

Use your dictionary to add stress marks to the following words:

soliloquy (sə lĭl ə kwē)
diatribe (dī ə trīb)
rheumatism (rōō mə tĭz əm)
representation (rĕp rĭ zĕn tā shən)

Full Pronunciation

Use your dictionary to write out the full pronunciation (the information given in parentheses) for each of the following words:

1. enigma _____
2. inveigle _____
3. tenacious _____
4. salient _____
5. permeate _____
6. epitome _____
7. cognizant _____
8. indigenous _____
9. insouciant _____
10. neuralgia _____
11. ethereal _____
12. capricious _____
13. fastidious _____
14. pejorative _____
15. vicissitude _____

PARTS OF SPEECH

The next bit of information that the dictionary gives about *disillusion* is *v.* This abbreviation means that the meanings of *disillusion* as a verb will follow.

At the front of your dictionary, you will probably find a key that will explain the meanings of abbreviations used in the dictionary. Use the key to fill in the meanings of the following abbreviations:

n. = _____   adj. = _____

pl. = _____   sing. = _____

PRINCIPAL PARTS OF IRREGULAR VERBS

Disillusion is a regular verb and forms its principal parts by adding *-ed*, *-ed*, and *-ing* to the stem of the verb. When a verb is irregular, the dictionary lists its principal parts. For example, with *begin* the present tense comes first (the entry itself, *begin*). Next comes the past tense (*began*), and then the past participle (*begun*)—the form of the verb used with such helping words as *have, had,* and *was.* Then comes the present participle (*beginning*)—the *-ing* form of the word.

Look up the principal parts of the following irregular verbs and write them in the spaces provided. The first one has been done for you.

Present	Past	Past Participle	Present Participle
see	saw	seen	seeing
go	_____	_____	_____
ride	_____	_____	_____
speak	_____	_____	_____

PLURAL FORMS OF IRREGULAR NOUNS

The dictionary supplies the plural forms of all irregular nouns (regular nouns form the plural by adding *-s* or *-es*). Give the plurals of the following nouns:

cemetery _____

knife _____

veto _____

neurosis _____

Note: See page 157 for more information about plurals.

MEANINGS

When there is more than one meaning to a word, the meanings are numbered in the dictionary, as with *disillusion*. In many dictionaries, the most common meanings are presented first. The introductory pages of your dictionary will explain the order in which meanings are presented.

Use your dictionary to write five separate meanings of the noun *ground:*

1. _____

2. _____

3. _____

4. _____

5. _____

Many dictionaries also provide information about etymology (the history of a word), usage (if a word is not standard English, it may have a usage label such as *slang, informal,* or *nonstandard*), and synonyms (words close in meaning to a given word).

Spelling Improvement

Poor spelling often results from bad habits developed in early school years. With work, such habits can be corrected. If you can write your name without misspelling it, there is no reason why you can't do the same with almost any word in the English language.

Following are four steps you can take to improve your spelling.

STEP 1: USING THE DICTIONARY

Get into the habit of using the dictionary. When you write a paper, allow yourself time to look up the spelling of all those words you are unsure about. Do not overlook the value of this step just because it is such a simple one. Just by using the dictionary, you can probably make yourself a 95 percent better speller.

STEP 2: KEEPING A PERSONAL SPELLING LIST

Keep a list of words you misspell and study the words regularly. Use the following space as a starter. When you accumulate additional words, you may want to use a back page of this book or your English notebook.

Incorrect Spelling	Correct Spelling	Points to Remember
alot	*a lot*	*two words*
writting	*writing*	*one "t"*

Hint: When you have trouble spelling long words, try to break the word down into syllables and see whether you can spell the syllables. For example, *misdemeanor* can be spelled easily if you can hear and spell in turn its four syllables: *mis de mean or.* Or, the word *formidable* can be spelled easily if you hear and spell in turn its four syllables: *for mid a ble.* Remember, then: Try to see, hear, and spell long words in terms of their syllable parts.

STEP 3: MASTERING COMMONLY CONFUSED WORDS

Master the meanings and spellings of the commonly confused words on pages 162 to 183. Your instructor may assign twenty words for you to study at a time and give you a series of quizzes until you have mastered them.

STEP 4: MASTERING A BASIC WORD LIST

Make sure you can spell all the words in the following list. They are some of the most-often-used words in English. Again, your instructor may assign twenty words for you to study at a time and give you a series of quizzes until you have mastered them.

ability	animal	been	children
absent	20 another	before	church
accident	answer	begin	cigarette
across	anxious	40 being	clothing
address	apply	believe	collect
advertise	approve	between	60 color
advice	argue	bottom	comfortable
after	around	breathe	company
again	attempt	building	condition
against	attention	business	conversation
all right	awful	came	daily
almost	awkward	careful	danger
a lot	back	careless	daughter
also	balance	cereal	decide
always	bargain	certain	death
although	beautiful	change	deposit
among	because	cheap	describe
angry	become	chief	different

direction	kindergarten	original	state
distance	kitchen	ought	200 straight
doubt	knowledge	pain	street
dozen	labor	160 paper	strong
during	language	pencil	student
each	120 laugh	people	studying
early	leave	perfect	suffer
80 earth	length	period	summer
easy	lesson	personal	sweet
education	letter	picture	teach
either	listen	place	telephone
English	loneliness	pocket	theory
enough	making	possible	thousand
entrance	marry	potato	ticket
everything	match	president	tired
examine	matter	pretty	today
exercise	measure	promise	together
expect	medicine	psychology	tomorrow
family	middle	public	tonight
flower	might	quick	tongue
foreign	million	raise	touch
friend	minute	ready	220 travel
from	mistake	really	truly
garden	money	180 reason	understand
general	month	receive	unity
grocery	140 morning	recognize	until
grow	mountain	remember	upon
100 guess	much	repeat	usual
handkerchief	needle	restaurant	value
happy	neglect	ridiculous	vegetable
heard	newspaper	said	view
heavy	noise	same	visitor
himself	none	sandwich	voice
holiday	nothing	sentence	warning
house	number	several	watch
however	ocean	shoes	welcome
hundred	offer	should	window
hungry	often	since	without
instead	omit	sleep	would
intelligence	only	smoke	writing
interest	operate	something	written
interfere	opportunity	soul	240 yesterday

Plurals

REGULAR PLURALS

Plural means more than one; *singular* means one. The plural of most words is formed by adding *-s* to the singular.

Singular	Plural
blanket	blankets
pencil	pencils
street	streets

IRREGULAR PLURALS

Following are rules that explain the function of certain irregular plurals.

1 Words ending in *s*, *ss*, *z*, *x*, *sh*, or *ch* usually form the plural by adding *-es*.

kiss	kisses	inch	inches
box	boxes	dish	dishes

Write the plurals of the following words.

sandwich _____   crash _____   fox _____

match _____   dress _____   pass _____

2 Words ending in a consonant plus *y* form the plural by changing *y* to *i* and adding *-es*.

party	parties	county	counties
baby	babies	city	cities

Note: If a vowel (*a, e, i, o, u*) comes before the *y*, add only *-s*.

toy	toys	turkey	turkeys

Write the plurals of the following words.

body _____   fallacy _____   donkey _____

country _____   penny _____   twenty _____

3 Some words ending in *f* change to *v* and add *-es* in the plural.

leaf   leaves   life   lives
wife   wives   ourself   ourselves

4 Some words ending in *o* form their plural by adding *-es*.

potato   potatoes   mosquito   mosquitoes
hero   heroes   tomato   tomatoes

5 Some words of foreign origin have irregular plurals. When in doubt, check your dictionary.

antenna   antennae   crisis   crises
criterion   criteria   medium   media

6 Some words form their plural by changing letters within the word.

man   men   foot   feet
tooth   teeth   goose   geese

7 Combined words (words made up of two or more words) form their plural by adding *-s* to the main word.

brother-in-law   brothers-in-law
passer-by   passers-by

PRACTICE

Complete the following sentences by filling in the plural of the word in the margin.

grocery   1. I carried six bags of _____ into the house.

town   2. How many _____ did you visit during the tour?

supply   3. While the Lone Ranger waited at the campsite, Tonto rode into town to get some _____ .

body   4. Because the gravediggers were on strike, _____ piled up in the morgue.

lottery   5. She plays two state _____ in hopes of winning a million dollars.

pass   6. Hank caught six _____ in a losing cause.

tragedy 7. That woman has had to endure many _____ in her life.

watch 8. I have found that cheap _____ work better for me than expensive ones.

suit 9. To help himself feel better, he went out and bought two _____.

boss 10. I have not one but two _____ to worry about every day.

THE OMITTED -S ENDING

One common mistake with plurals is dropping the -s ending. People who drop the ending from plurals when speaking also tend to do it when writing. This tendency is especially noticeable when the meaning of the sentence shows that a word is plural.

Ed and Mary pay two hundred dollar a month for an apartment that has only two room.

The -s has been omitted from *dollars* and *rooms*.

The activities that follow will help you correct the habit of omitting -s endings from plurals.

PRACTICE 1

Add -s endings where needed.

Example   Bill beat me at several game of dart.

1. When Rita's two boyfriend met each other last night, they almost came to blow.
2. My brother let out a choice selection of curse when he dropped his watch in the sand.
3. We were expected to write an essay of several paragraph on key event leading up to the Civil War.
4. Sunlight reflected off the windshield of the many car in the parking lot.
5. A number of house along the elevated subway route have been torn down to make room for two new highway that are being built.
6. Rainy day depress me, especially during those time when I am depressed already.
7. Our drive along the shoreline was marred by the billboard that seem to have popped up everywhere.

8. There were no folding chair in the room; instead, people were asked to sit on pillow spread around the floor.

9. From the top of either of those watchtower, you can see four different state.

10. Motorist waited restlessly as several tow truck worked to remove the tractor trailer spread-eagled across the highway.

PRACTICE 2

Write sentences that use plural forms of the following pairs of words.

Example   girls/bikes   *The little girls raced their bikes down the street.*

1. paper/grade _____

_____

2. pillow/bed _____

_____

3. sock/shoe _____

_____

4. day/night _____

_____

5. game/loss _____

_____

Note: People who drop the *-s* ending on nouns also tend to omit endings on verbs. Pages 38 to 43 will help you correct the habit of dropping endings on verbs. The guided composition activity on page 221 and editing activities on pages 283–289 give you practice in proofreading carefully for omitted noun and verb endings. In addition, the section that follows provides practice in a related problem—the omission of small connecting words in a sentence.

Omitted Words

Be careful not to leave out words when you write. Sometimes people omit small connecting words like *a, an, of, to,* or *the.* At times they leave out even larger words as well. The omission of any words in your writing may confuse and irritate your readers. They may not want to read what they regard as careless work.

Finding omitted words, like finding many other sentence-skills mistakes, is a matter of careful proofreading. You must develop your ability to look carefully at a page to find places where mistakes may exist.

The exercises here will give you practice in finding omitted words. Other sections of this book will give you practice with omitted word endings (see pages 38 and 159). Also, you will work extensively at proofing papers for omitted words when you do the passages in Part 2 of the book.

PRACTICE

Add *a, an, the, of, and,* or *to* as needed.

Example Some people regard television as ∧ tranquilizer, providing people with
temporary relief from ∧ pain and anxiety ∧ modern life.

1. When I began eating box of chicken I bought at the fast-food restaurant, I found several pieces that consisted of lot crust covering nothing but chicken bones.

2. Sally had teacher who tried light a piece chalk, thinking it was cigarette.

3. In his dream, Harry committed perfect crime: he killed his enemy with icicle, so murder weapon was never found.

4. Dr. Yutzer told me not worry about sore on my foot, but I decided to get second opinion.

5. As little girl ate vanilla sugar cone, ice cream dripped out hole at the bottom onto her pants.

6. When thick black clouds began form and we felt several drops rain, we knew picnic would be canceled.

7. After spending most her salary on new clothes, Susan looks like something out of fashion magazine.

8. As wasps buzzed around room, I ran for can of Raid.

9. Sam put pair wet socks in oven, for he wanted dry them out quickly.

10. Because weather got hot and stayed hot for weeks, my flower garden started look like dry flower arrangement.

Commonly Confused Words

HOMONYMS

The commonly confused words (also known as *homonyms*) on the following pages have the same sounds but different meanings and spellings. Complete the activities for each set of words, and check off and study the ones that give you trouble.

all ready   completely prepared
already   previously; before

We were *all ready* to go for we had eaten and packed *already* that morning.

Fill in the blanks with *all ready* or *already*.

1. I was _____ to start ordering breakfast when I found out that

the restaurant had _____ shifted to its luncheon menu.

2. A week ago, Sam was _____ to join the navy.

3. I've _____ practiced the tune a hundred times, and I think I'm

_____ to play my first band solo.

Write sentences using *all ready* and *already*.

_____

_____

brake stop
break come apart

His car bumper has a sticker reading, ''I *brake* for animals.''
''I am going to *break* up with Bill if he keeps seeing other women,'' said Rita.

Fill in the blanks with the correct form of *brake* or *break*.

1. When my car's emergency _____ slipped, the car rolled back

    and demolished my neighbor's rose garden, causing a _____ in our good relations with each other.

2. Linda told Peter she would _____ his nose if he refused to apply

    the _____ at all stop signs.

3. Instead of _____*ing* things to work off steam, why don't you try

    fixing something, like the _____<u>s</u> on your car.

Write sentences using *brake* and *break*.

_____

_____

course part of a meal; a school subject; direction; certainly
coarse rough

By the time the waitress served the customers the second *course* of the meal, she was aware of their *coarse* eating habits.

Fill in the blanks with *course* or *coarse*.

1. He felt the health teacher's humor was too _____ for his taste

    and was glad when he finished the _____.

2. If your boat goes off _____, you can get lost very quickly.

3. Of _____ Albert realized the _____ wood was
    not suitable for my sister's dollhouse.

Write sentences using *course* and *coarse*.

_____

_____

hear   perceive with the ear
here   in this place

"The salespeople act as though they don't see or *hear* me, even though I've been standing *here* for fifteen minutes," the woman complained.

Fill in the blanks with *hear* or *here*.

1.   "Did you _____ about the distinguished visitor who just came

     into town and is staying _____ at this very hotel."

2.   My mother always says, "Come _____ if you can't

     _____ what I'm saying."

3.   _____ at the top of the canyon, you can speak as softly as you

     can and still _____ an echo.

Write sentences using *hear* and *here*.

_____

_____

hole   an empty spot
whole   entire

"I can't believe I ate the *whole* pizza," moaned Ralph. "I think it's going to make a *hole* in my stomach lining."

Fill in the blanks with *hole* or *whole*.

1.   The _____ time I was at the party I tried to conceal the

     _____ I had in my trousers.

2.   Jed has a _____ brain, but he usually thinks with a

     _____ in his logic.

3.   I saved for that copper watering can for a _____ month and

     then bought one with a _____ in it.

Write sentences using *hole* and *whole*.

_____

_____

its belonging to it
it's the shortened form for "it is" or "it has"

The car blew *its* transmission (the transmission belonging to it, the car).
It's (it has) been raining all week and *it's* (it is) raining now.

Fill in the blanks with *its* or *it's*.

1. In the restaurant where I work, _____ always hot in the kitchen.

2. _____ unsanitary there, too, with roaches crawling all over the walls.

3. I don't think the restaurant deserves _____ reputation, and I don't think much of _____ wealthy, snobbish clientele.

Write sentences using *its* and *it's*.

_____

_____

knew past form of *know*
new not old

"I got *new* wallpaper put up," said Sarah.
"I *knew* there was some reason the place looked good for a change," said Bill.

Fill in the blanks with *knew* or *new*.

1. Lola _____ that getting her hair cut would give her face a _____ look.

2. Everyone but Eddie _____ that his _____ girl friend was after his money.

3. We _____ that the _____ television comedy would be canceled quickly.

Write sentences using *knew* and *new*.

_____

_____

know   to understand
no   a negative

"I don't *know* why my dog Fang likes to attack certain people," said Martha. "There's *no* one thing the people have in common."

Fill in the blanks with *know* or *no*.

1. I _____ of _____ way of telling whether that politician is honest.

2. I don't _____ why I sometimes get so depressed; there is _____ single reason why I should feel as blue as I do.

3. When that spoiled boy's parents say _____ to him, we all _____ a temper tantrum is likely to result.

Write sentences using *know* and *no*.

_____

_____

pair   a set of two
pear   a fruit

"What a great *pair* of legs Tony has," said Lola to Vonnie. Tony didn't hear her, for he was feeling very sick after munching on a green *pear*.

Fill in the blanks with *pair* or *pear*.

1. In his lunch box were a _____ of _____.

2. The _____ grove is one of the places where the _____ of escaped convicts were spotted last week.

3. The teacher asked our class to break up into _____.

Write sentences using *pair* and *pear*.

_____

_____

passed   went by; succeeded in; handed to
past   a time before the present; by, as in ''I drove past the house''

I *passed* him the wine bottle; it was the only way he could forget his unhappy *past*.

Fill in the blanks with *passed* or *past*.

1. I walked _____ the teacher's office but was afraid to ask her whether or not I had _____ the test.

2. In the _____ three weeks, I've _____ out hundreds of perfume samples in my job as an Avon representative.

3. This _____ summer, Tom _____ up a chance to go to school.

Write sentences using *passed* and *past*.

_____

_____

peace   calm
piece   a part

Nations often risk world *peace* by fighting over a *piece* of land.

Fill in the blanks with the correct form of *peace* or *piece*.

1. Martha did not have any _____ until she gave her pet dog Fang a _____ of her meat loaf.

2. A _____ of dust in your eye will give you no _____ until you remove it.

3. My cocker spaniel will rest in _____ if you give him a _____ of dog biscuit and an old towel.

Write sentences using *peace* and *piece*.

_____

_____

plain   simple
plane   aircraft

The *plain*, unassuming young man on the *plane* suddenly jumped up with a grenade in his hand and announced, "This plane is going to Tibet."

Fill in the blanks with *plain* or *plane*.

1. The game-show contestant opened the small box wrapped in _____ brown paper and found inside the keys to his own jet _____ .

2. The man in the bright red jacket and _____ gray pants is the owner of the World War II fighter _____ .

3. Susan has a _____ face according to her girl friends, but her five boyfriends don't seem to think so.

Write sentences using *plain* and *plane*.

_____

_____

principal   main; a person in charge of a school
principle   a law or standard

Note: It might help to remember that the *a* in *principal* is in *main* and in *man* or *woman*—the two meanings of *principal*.

Pete's high school *principal* had one *principal* problem: Pete.   This was because there were only two *principles* in Pete's life: rest and relaxation.

Fill in the blanks with *principal* or *principle*.

1. The _____ reason she dropped out of school was that she disliked her high school _____ .

2. Our high school _____ plans to stick to her _____ about bringing pets to school.

3. The reporter followed his _____s and refused to reveal his source.

Write sentences using *principal* and *principle*.

_____

_____

right   correct; opposite of "left"
write   what you do in English

If you have the *right* course card, I'll *write* your name on the class roster.

Fill in the blanks with *right* or *write*.

1. If I tell you where I asked Paul Newman to _____ his autograph
   for me, you'll think that I'm not _____ in the head.

2. Ellen wanted to _____ and thank Allan for his flowers, but she
   didn't think it _____ to keep leading him on.

3. Eddie thinks that I'm weird since I _____ with both my
   _____ and left hands.

Write sentences using *right* and *write*.

_____

_____

than (thăn)   used in comparisons
then (thĕn)   at that time

Note: It might help to remember that the *a* in *th<u>a</u>n* is also in *comp<u>a</u>re,* a meaning
of *than,* and that the *e* in *th<u>e</u>n* is also in *tim<u>e</u>,* a meaning of *then.*

When we were kids, my friend Elaine had prettier clothes *than* I did.   I really
envied her *then.*

Fill in the blanks with *than* or *then.*

1. I went to the front porch to get my newspaper, and _____ I
   made my breakfast. The news on the front page was no more cheerful
   _____ it had been the day before.

2. Marge thought she was better _____ the rest of us, but
   _____ she got the lowest grade in the history test.

3. I know more about hockey _____ my brother does, but
   _____ his main interest is playing basketball.

Write sentences using *than* and *then.*

_____

_____

their   belonging to them

there   at that place; a neutral word used with verbs like *is, are, was, were, have,* and *had*

they're   the shortened form of "they are"

Two people own that van over *there* (at that place). *They're* (they are) going to move out of *their* apartment (the apartment belonging to them) and into the van, in order to save money.

Fill in the blanks with *their, there,* or *they're.*

1. _____ will be a party at Ellen's house. She and Glenn are celebrating _____ graduation from Oakmont Community College.

2. They have been planning the party for three weeks, and _____ inviting a lot of people.

3. Ellen's parents will be away for the evening, so _____ will be nobody _____ to dampen the occasion.

Write sentences using *their, there,* and *they're.*

_____

_____

_____

threw   past form of *throw*

through   from one side to the other; finished

The fans *threw* so much litter on the field that the teams could not go *through* with the game.

Fill in the blanks with *threw* or *through.*

1. When Mr. Jefferson was _____ screaming about too much violence on television, he _____ the paper at his dog.

2. He couldn't see _____ the foggy windshield.

3. My favorite sweat socks went _____ hundreds of washings before they started to disintegrate and my mother _____ them away.

    Write sentences using *threw* and *through*.

    _____

    _____

to   a verb part, as in *to smile;* toward, as in "I'm going *to* heaven"

too overly, as in "The pizza was *too* hot"; also, as in "The coffee was hot, *too*."

two the number 2

Tony drove *to* the park *to* be alone with Lola. (The first *to* means "toward"; the second *to* is a verb part that goes with *be*.)

Tony's shirt is *too* tight; his pants are tight, *too*. (The first *too* means "overly"; the second *too* means "also.")

You need *two* hands (2 hands) to handle a Whopper.

Fill in the blanks with *to, too,* or *two*.

1. Tony met _____ girls at the party.

2. He went _____ the bathroom eight times because he was drinking _____ much.

3. Eventually neighbors complained, and so the police ended up coming _____ the party, _____ .

    Write sentences using *to, too,* and *two*.

    _____

    _____

    _____

your   belonging to you
you're   the shortened form of "you are"

> *You're* (meaning "you are") not going to the fair unless *your* brother (the brother belonging to you) goes with you.

Fill in the blanks with *your* or *you're*.

1. _____ always going to worry about having enough gas for _____ sports car, for _____ only able to get eight miles a gallon.

2. If you want _____ nerves and _____ pocket-book to stop taking a beating, _____ better off with an economy car.

3. _____ going to have less leg room and trunk space, but _____ less likely to get speeding tickets.

Write sentences using *your* and *you're*.

_____

_____

wear   to have on
where   in what place

> Fred wanted to *wear* his light pants on the hot day, but he didn't know *where* he had put them.

Fill in the blanks with *wear* or *where*.

1. Sara's friends always comment when Sara _____s___ her mother's old clothes.

2. _____ did you _____ your plaid flannel shirt and striped pants?

3. Does anyone know _____ the house keys are?

Write sentences using *wear* and *where*.

_____

_____

weather   atmospheric conditions
whether   if it happens that; in case; if

Some people go on holidays *whether* or not the *weather* is good.

Fill in the blanks with *weather* or *whether.*

1. The _____ is glorious, but I don't know _____ the water is warm enough for swimming.

2. _____ there's pouring rain or sweltering heat, I go jogging.

3. I always ask Bill _____ or not we're in for a storm, because he can feel bad _____ approaching in his bad knee.

Write sentences using *weather* and *whether.*

_____

_____

whose   belonging to whom
who's   the shortened form for "who is" and "who has"

Who's the teacher *whose* students are complaining?

Fill in the blanks with *whose* or *who's.*

1. _____ the guy _____ car I saw you in?

2. Elizabeth Taylor and Richard Burton starred in the movie _____ *Afraid of Virginia Woolf?*

3. _____ turn is it to water the grass?

Write sentences using *whose* or *who's.*

_____

_____

OTHER WORDS FREQUENTLY CONFUSED

Following is a list of other words that people frequently confuse. Complete the activities for each set of words, and check off and study the ones that give you trouble. (*Note:* This section also provides a list of incorrect word forms that sometimes appear in writing. See pages 181–183.)

a, an Both *a* and *an* are used before other words to mean, approximately, "one."

Generally you should use *an* before words starting with a vowel (*a, e, i, o, u*):

an ache   an experiment   an elephant   an idiot   an ox

Generally you should use *a* before words starting with a consonant (all other letters):

a Coke   a brain   a cheat   a television   a gambler

Fill in the blanks with *a* or *an*.

1. I need _____ pot of coffee to keep me awake, for I have

    _____ paper to write and _____ exam to study
    for.

2. The girls had _____ argument over _____ for-
    mer boyfriend.

3. You will come to _____ fork in the road after you pass over

    _____ covered bridge and _____ old farm-
    house.

Write sentences using *a* and *an*.

_____

_____

accept (ăk sĕpt′)   receive; agree to
except (ĕk sĕpt′)   exclude; but

"I would *accept* your loan," said Bill to the bartender, "*except* that I'm not
ready to pay 25 percent interest."

Fill in the blanks with the correct form of *accept* or *except*.

1. He was ready to _____ and forgive all the bad things she had

    done to him _____ one—her continuing to date other guys after
    they had become engaged.

2. _____ that she can't _____ any criticism, Lori
    is a good friend.

3. I would have felt very happy when _____ed the award,

_____ that my best friend Larry had been competing for the award, too.

Write sentences using *accept* and *except*.

_____

_____

advice (ăd vīs′)   a noun meaning "an opinion"
advise (ăd viz′)   a verb meaning "to counsel, to give advice"

I *advise* you to take the *advice* of your friends and stop working so hard.

Fill in the blanks with *advice* or *advise*.

1. Martha Grencher's doctor said, "I _____ you to follow my

diet, rather than take the _____ of the minister who promised you could lose weight through prayer."

2. Jake never listened to his parents' _____, and he ended up

listening to a cop _____ him of his rights.

3. I _____ you to listen carefully to any _____ you get from your boss.

Write sentences using *advice* and *advise*.

_____

_____

affect (uh fĕkt′)   a verb meaning "to influence"
effect (ĭ fĕkt′)   a verb meaning "to bring about something"; a noun meaning "result"

The full *effects* of marijuana and alcohol on the body are only partly known; however, both drugs clearly *affect* the brain in various ways.

Fill in the blanks with the correct form of *affect* or *effect*.

1. The special _____s in the monster movie always

_____ the audience; many people scream or faint at each performance.

2. The new tax laws go into _____ next month, and they are going
   to _____ the number of deductions I can claim.

3. My sister Sally cries for _____, but my parents caught on and
   her act no longer _____s_ them.

   Write sentences using *affect* and *effect*.

   _____

   _____

among   implies three or more
between   implies only two

   We selfishly divided the box of candy *between* the two of us rather than *among*
   all the members of the family.

   Fill in the blanks with *among* or *between*.

1. Of all the family squabbles, the one _____ my father and Uncle
   Ted lasted the longest.

2. A single Pepsi was shared _____ the five people in the car.

3. _____ the twenty-five girls on the camping trip, arguments
   developed only _____ the two counselors.

   Write sentences using *among* and *between*.

   _____

   _____

beside   at the side of
besides   in addition to

   Fred sat *beside* Martha. *Besides* them, there were ten other people at the
   Tupperware party.

   Fill in the blanks with *beside* or *besides*.

1. The panhandler sat down _____ me in the coffee shop and
   asked for money.

2. Clark stood _____ Vivian at the barbecue, whispering in her
   ear.

3. _____ studying for a math test, I also have to write a paper for English.

Write sentences using *beside* and *besides*.

_____

_____

can refers to the ability to do something
may refers to permission or possibility

If you *can* work overtime on Saturday, you *may* take Monday off.

Fill in the blanks with *can* or *may*.

1. _____ I try out your CB radio?

2. A mouse _____ get through the maze in less than five minutes.

3. You _____ come along if you're quiet.

Write sentences using *can* and *may*.

_____

_____

clothes articles of dress
cloths pieces of fabric

I tore up some old *clothes* to use as polishing *cloths*.

Fill in the blanks with *clothes* or *cloths*.

1. She cleverly made some doll _____ out of Handi-Wipe

_____ .

2. These dust _____ are so dirty they won't pick up dust anymore.

3. I never feel relaxed after work until I put on some old _____ .

Write sentences using *clothes* and *cloths*.

_____

_____

desert (dĕz'ərt) a stretch of dry land; (dĭ zûrt') to abandon one's post or duty
dessert (dĭ zûrt') last part of a meal

> Camels are animals on the *desert;* they are also cigarettes people smoke after dinner with their coffee and *dessert.*

Fill in the blanks with the correct form of *desert* or *dessert.*

1. After a hot day in the _____, the first things he wanted were a lot of iced tea and his favorite ice cream _____.

2. The cabin was _____ ed .

3. After their meal, they carried their _____ into the living room so that they would not miss the start of the old _____ movie.

Write sentences using *desert* and *dessert.*

_____

_____

does a form of the verb *do*
dose an amount of medicine

> Martha *does* not realize that a *dose* of brandy is not the best medicine for the flu.

Fill in the blanks with *does* or *dose.*

1. He _____ better on exams than I do because he drinks large _____ s of coffee to keep awake and study all night.

2. _____ anyone know where Mom hides the stamps?

3. _____ Sue really expect us to believe that she took that big a _____ of that medicine and never felt it?

Write sentences using *does* and *dose.*

_____

_____

_____

fewer used with things that can be counted
less refers to amount, value, or degree

I missed *fewer* classes than Tom; however, I wrote *less* effectively than he did.

Fill in the blanks with *fewer* or *less*.

1. I've had _____ attacks of nerves since I began drinking

   _____ coffee.

2. I've had _____ broken bones in my life than Al has had this
   year.

3. With _____ children to look after now, my parents can worry

   _____ .

Write sentences using *fewer* and *less*.

_____

_____

former refers to the first of two items named
latter refers to the second of two items named

I turned down both the service station job and the shipping clerk job: the
former involved irregular hours and the *latter* offered very low pay.

Fill in the blanks with *former* or *latter*.

1. I don't like figs or grapefruit: the _____ are too sweet and the

   _____ are too sour.

2. Howard doesn't like babies or dogs: the _____ cry when they

   see him and the _____ try to bite him.

3. I drink neither coffee nor milk; the _____ keeps me awake

   while the _____ puts me to sleep.

Write sentences using *former* and *latter*.

_____

_____

_____

Note: Be sure to distinguish *latter* from *later* (meaning *after some time*). Very
often people will use the word *latter* when in fact they mean *later*.

learn   to gain knowledge
teach   to give knowledge

   After Roz *learns* the new dance, she is going to *teach* it to me.

   Fill in the blanks with *learn* or *teach*.

1. Next year my mother is going to _____ me how to drive
   the car.

2. I wasn't able to _____ my dog how to roll over, but she did
   _____ how to play dead.

3. My brother thinks that what I _____ at school is completely
   useless.

   Write sentences using *learn* and *teach*.

   _____

   _____

loose (lo͞os)   not fastened; not tight-fitting
lose (lo͞oz)   misplace; fail to win

   Phil's belt is so *loose* that he always looks ready to *lose* his pants.

   Fill in the blanks with *loose* or *lose*.

1. Lola told Tony, "You look dumpy when you wear a _____
   fitting shirt. You _____ all the wonderful lines of your
   chest."

2. The shelf came _____ and fell with a terrible crash at
   4 A.M.

3. At least once a week our neighbors _____ their dog; it's because
   they let him run _____.

   Write sentences using *loose* and *lose*.

   _____

   _____

quiet (kwī′ĭt)   peaceful
quite (kwīt)   entirely; really; rather

> After a busy day, the children were now *quiet*, and their parents were *quite* tired.

> Fill in the blanks with *quiet* or *quite*.

1. She goes to the races _____ often, and he spends _____ afternoons in the garden.

2. My friends regarded Bob as _____ a catch, but he was just too _____ for me.

3. The _____ halls of the church become _____ lively during square dance evenings.

> Write sentences using *quiet* and *quite*.

_____

_____

though (thō)   despite the fact that
thought (thôt)   past form of *think*

> Even *though* she worked, she *thought* she would have time to go to school.

> Fill in the blanks with *though* or *thought*.

1. _____ I enjoyed the dance, I _____ the cover charge of $4 was too high.

2. Even _____ she looks well, she has been very sick.

3. I _____ I would like the job, but even _____ the pay was good, the traveling I had to do really bothered me.

> Write sentences using *though* and *thought*.

_____

_____

INCORRECT WORD FORMS

Starting on the next page is a list of incorrect word forms that people sometimes use in their writing. Complete the activities for each word, and check off and study the words that give you trouble.

being that—incorrect!   Use *because* or *since*.

because

I'm going to bed now ~~being that~~ I must get up early tomorrow.

Correct the following sentences.

1.   Being that she's a year older than I am, Mary thinks she can run my life.
2.   I think school will be canceled, being that the bus drivers are on strike.
3.   Being that I didn't finish the paper, I didn't go to class.

can't hardly, couldn't hardly—incorrect!   Use *can hardly* or *could hardly*.

can

Small store owners ~~can't~~ hardly afford to offer large discounts.

Correct the following sentences.

1.   I can't hardly understand why Nelson would cut class when he's madly in love with the teacher.
2.   You can't hardly imagine how I felt when I knocked over my aunt's favorite plant.
3.   You couldn't hardly see last night because of the heavy fog.

could of—incorrect!   Use *could have*.

have

I could ~~of~~ done better in that test.

Correct the following sentences.

1.   You could of made the basketball team if you had tried harder.
2.   I could of punched that salesman in the mouth.
3.   If Mary had wanted, she could of come with us.

irregardless—incorrect!   Use *regardless*.

Regardless

~~Irregardless~~ of what anyone says, he will not change his mind.

Correct the following sentences.

1.   They decided to buy the house irregardless of the price.
2.   That company insures people irregardless of their age or state of health.
3.   Irregardless of the risk, I started mountain climbing as a hobby.

must of, should of, would of—incorrect!   Use *must have, should have, would have*

I should ~~of~~ *have* applied for a loan when my credit was good.

Correct the following sentences.

1.   Anita must of gone home from work early.
2.   I should of started reading the textbook early in the semester.
3.   If the game had been canceled, they would of been very disappointed.

REVIEW TEST **1**

These sentences check your understanding of *its, it's; there, their, they're; to, too, two;* and *your, you're*. Underline the correct word in the parentheses. Rather than guessing, look back at the explanations of the words when necessary.

1.   Some stores will accept (your, you're) credit card but not (your, you're) money.
2.   I know (its, it's) late, but (its, it's) important to get this job done properly.
3.   (There, their, they're) is a good baseball game down at the playground, but (there, their, they're) (to, too, two) busy to walk down (there, their, they're).
4.   (Its, It's) an hour since I put the TV dinner in the oven, but (its, it's) still not ready.
5.   (There, Their, They're) going to be away for (to, too, two) weeks and want me to go over to (there, their, they're) yard to water (there, their, they're) rose bushes.
6.   (Your, You're) going to have to do a better job on (your, you're) final exam if you expect to pass the course.
7.   That issue is (to, too, two) hot for any politician (to, too, two) handle.
8.   If (your, you're) hoping to get good grades on (your, you're) essay tests, you need to improve (your, you're) handwriting.
9.   (There, Their, They're) planning to trade in (there, their, they're) old car for a new one before taking (there, their, they're) vacation.
10.   (Your, You're) going to have to put aside individual differences and play together for the benefit of (your, you're) team.

REVIEW TEST **2**

The sentences on the next page check your understanding of a variety of commonly confused words. Underline the correct word in the parentheses. Rather than guessing, look back at the explanations of the words when necessary.

1. I try to get (through, threw) each day without a cigarette. Once I (through, threw) away my latest magazines because their tempting cigarette ads were (affecting, effecting) my resolve.

2. We weren't sure (whether, weather) or not a storm was brewing until several hours had passed. (Then, Than) the air became (quiet, quite), clouds formed, and we (knew, new) enough to run indoors.

3. Even (though, thought) the (brakes, breaks) on my car were worn, I did not (quiet, quite) have enough money to get them replaced (right, write) away.

4. Take my (advice, advise) and hurry down (to, too, two) the radio station. They'll give you a (pair, pear) of free tickets to the rock concert.

5. For Sharon the (principal, principle) (course, coarse) of the meal—a (desert, dessert) of French vanilla ice cream and blueberry pie—was yet (to, too, two) come.

6. (Except, Accept) for the fact that my neighbor receives most of his mail in (plain, plane) brown wrappers, he is (know, no) stranger (than, then) anyone else in this (hole, whole) of a rooming house.

7. The first (course, coarse) of the meal was soup. Its (principal, principle) ingredient was cheese, to which I'm allergic. Trying to be polite, I ate one mouthful, but (than, then) I began to sneeze uncontrollably.

8. (Whose, Who's) the culprit who left the paint can on the table? The paint ruined a (knew, new) tablecloth. (Beside, Besides) that, it soaked (threw, through) the linen and (affected, effected) the varnish stain on the table.

9. The night after I watched the chiller movie, I dreamed that (a, an) gigantic (hole, whole) opened up in the earth, swallowed a whole city, and (than, then) tried to swallow me, (to, too, two).

10. "I'm going to let you be my (knew, new) woman," the man declared. (Your, You're) my (peace, piece) of property from now on."

   "(Whose, Who's) messed up (your, you're) head?" the woman replied. I can't believe I (hear, here) you (right, write). (Where, Wear) are you at? I think you have been (affected, effected) by the sun."

Slang

We often use slang expressions when we talk because they are so vivid and colorful. However, slang is usually out of place in formal writing. Here are some examples of slang expressions:

I've *gotten into* science fiction lately.
Tom spent Saturday afternoon *messing around with* his car.

I don't *hang around* with Jerry anymore.
They enjoyed the party because it was a *real blast*.
The tires on my Camaro make the car look like *something else*.

Slang expressions have a number of drawbacks: they go out of date quickly, they become tiresome if used excessively in writing, and they may communicate clearly to some readers but not to others. Also, the use of slang can be an evasion of the specific details that are often needed to make one's meaning clear in writing. For example, in "The tires on my Camaro make the car look like something else," the writer has not provided the specific details about the tires necessary for us to clearly understand his statement. In general, then, you should avoid the use of slang in your writing. If you are in doubt about whether an expression is slang, check a good dictionary.

PRACTICE

Rewrite the following sentences, replacing the slang words with more formal ones.

Example   My friend had wheels, so we decided to cut out of the crummy dance.
   We decided to use my friend's car to leave the
   boring dance.

1. If you don't get your act together in this course, you're going to be blown away by the midterm exam.

   _____

   _____

2. The car was a steal for the money until the owner got wise and jacked up the price.

   _____

   _____

3. The football game was a real wipeout; we got our butts kicked.

   _____

4. There are so many jerks and creeps at my school that it's a wonder I haven't flipped out.

   _____

   _____

5. I pushed the panic button when the teacher called on me. My brain was out to lunch.

   _____

   _____

Clichés

Clichés are expressions that have been worn out through constant use. Some typical clichés are

pain in the neck	sad but true
know the ropes	taking a big chance
drop in the bucket	wear yourself out
sight for sore eyes	end of the affair
a spoiled brat	cold, cruel world
had a hard time of it	at a loss for words

Clichés are common in speech but make your writing seem tired and stale. Also, they are often an evasion of the specific details that you must work to provide in your writing. You should, then, avoid clichés and try to express your meaning in fresh, original ways.

PRACTICE

Underline the cliché in each of the following sentences. Then substitute specific, fresh words for the trite expression.

Example   My father supported me through some <u>trying times</u>.

rough years

1. I am sick and tired of her dog's digging up my backyard.

2. Because I kept forgetting to clean my room, my mother decided to put her foot down.

3. Donna came out of her shell after she joined the theater group at school.

4. Helen could not have cared less whom Pete was dating.

5. Since my mother was feeling under the weather, she didn't go to work.

Wordiness

Wordiness—using more words than necessary to express a meaning—is often a sign of lazy or careless writing. Your readers may resent the extra time and energy they must spend when you have not done the work needed to make your writing direct and concise. Here are examples of wordy sentences:

> I would like to say that my subject in this paper will be the kind of person that my father was.

> The meaning of his statement is that he is of the opinion that the death penalty should be allowed.

Omitting needless words improves the sentences:

> My father was a generous person.
> He believes in the death penalty.

PRACTICE

Rewrite the following sentences, omitting needless words.

1. Due to the fact that since it was raining, I didn't go shopping.

    _____

2. As far as I am concerned, in my opinion I do not feel that prostitution should be legalized.

    _____

3. After a lot of careful thinking, I've arrived upon the conclusion that my golf clubs are my most valued material possession.

    _____

4. It is often hard and difficult for the inexperienced driver, who has had no previous experience, to drive in heavy traffic.

    _____

    _____

5. Way back in the past when my grandfather was a boy, gaslights lined the streets as a source of light at night.

    _____

    _____

6. With attractive brown-colored eyes and attractive chestnut-colored hair, Maria was a girl who made her father a proud man.

7. I have repeatedly asked you over and over again to turn off the lights when you get ready to retire and go to bed.

8. In order for you to write an effective paper, you must first of all before doing anything else decide what point it is that you want to make in the paper.

Answers to Practice Exercises

Note: Answers are not given for those practice exercises where more than one response is possible.

Subjects and Verbs (pp. 5–6)

PRACTICE 2	PRACTICE 4	PRACTICE 5
1. students	1. believes	1. Carol works
2. socks	2. like	2. watch loses
3. Melanie	3. sticks	3. car broke
4. windstorm	4. blinded	4. fog rolled
5. game	5. limits	5. Sparrows live
6. Pretzels and chips	6. was called	7. car needed
7. fan	7. fell	8. fly stung
8. wind	8. lit	9. Russ expected
9. children	9. tumbled	10. I ran
10. shrubs	10. starts	

More about Subjects and Verbs

PRACTICE (p. 7)

1. The attractive <u>woman</u> ~~over there in the corner~~ <u>is</u> my former wife.
2. The <u>dishes</u> ~~in the sink~~ <u>must be washed</u> before tomorrow.
3. <u>Both</u> ~~of my house keys~~ <u>are missing</u>.
4. The <u>hamburger</u> ~~on sale at 89¢ a pound~~ <u>looks</u> several days old.
5. ~~In the middle of the movie,~~ the <u>screen</u> suddenly <u>went</u> blank.
6. The water <u>stain</u> ~~on her suede shoes~~ <u>disappeared</u> ~~with brushing.~~
7. The last <u>rays</u> ~~of the sun~~ <u>faded</u> ~~into darkness.~~
8. ~~During the baseball game,~~ my twin <u>brother</u> <u>ate</u> five hot dogs.
9. ~~Without the help of a calculator,~~ <u>I</u> <u>could</u> not <u>balance</u> my checkbook.
10. ~~Over the river~~ and ~~through the woods to Grandmother's house~~ <u>we</u> <u>will go</u>.

PRACTICE (p. 8)

1. <u>He</u> <u>has been sleeping</u>
2. <u>foundations</u> <u>have been attacked</u>
3. <u>Sally</u> <u>should have gone</u>
4. <u>teacher</u> <u>had</u> not <u>warned</u>
5. <u>Carol</u> and <u>Arnie</u> <u>have received</u>
6. <u>You</u> <u>should pet</u>
7. <u>I</u> <u>have washed</u>
8. <u>He</u> <u>could make</u>
9. <u>bus</u> <u>must have been delayed</u>
10. <u>They</u> <u>have been married</u>

PRACTICE (p. 9)

1. <u>mother</u> and <u>daughter</u> <u>wore</u>
2. <u>people</u> <u>laughed</u> and <u>cried</u>
3. <u>Tuna</u> and <u>dolphins</u> <u>were trapped</u>
4. <u>hospital</u> <u>will serve</u>
5. <u>people</u> <u>will be admitted</u> and <u>be given</u>
6. <u>sister</u> and <u>I</u> <u>play</u>
7. <u>John</u> and <u>Marilyn</u> <u>looked</u>
8. <u>I</u> <u>sprayed</u> and <u>spread</u>
9. <u>Dodgers</u>, <u>Reds</u>, and <u>Giants</u> <u>occupied</u>
10. <u>student</u> <u>sat</u> and <u>volunteered</u>

Sentence Fragments

Dependent-word Fragments

PRACTICE 2 (pp. 14–15)

1. *Fragment:* After I slid my aching bones into the hot water of the tub.
   Correction: After I slid my aching bones into the hot water of the tub, I realized that there was no soap.
2. *Fragment:* Since they had come from a can.
   Correction: The peas and carrots had a flat taste since they had come from a can.

3. *Fragments:* Because he had eaten and drunk too much.
    That was ready to erupt.
    Corrections: Because he had eaten and drunk too much, he had to leave the party early. His stomach was like a volcano that was ready to erupt.

4. *Fragments:* Until you could go in swimming.
    If you tried to sneak in after only fifty-six minutes.
    Corrections: I used to believe that you had to wait exactly an hour after eating until you could go in swimming. If you tried to sneak in after only fifty-six minutes, your stomach would know and you would drown immediately.

5. *Fragments:* A boy that she had dated in high school.
    Although she had no intention of breaking off with her present boyfriend.
    Corrections: Today Pam got a call from James Wood, a boy that she had dated in high school. She agreed to have lunch with him although she had no intention of breaking off with her present boyfriend.

-ing and to Fragments

PRACTICE 1   (pp. 16–17)

1. *Fragment:* Then going to class for 2½ hours.
    Correction: Then he goes to class for 2½ hours.

2. *Fragment:* Wishing that he had a hundred thousand dollars.
    Correction: After the alarm rang, he lay in bed ten minutes longer, wishing that he had a hundred thousand dollars.

3. *Fragment:* His chief objection being that it lasted four hours.
    Correction: His chief objection was that it lasted four hours.

PRACTICE 2   (pp. 17–18)

1. *Fragment:* As a result, being late for class.
    Correction: As a result, I was late for class.

2. *Fragment:* Claiming that crumbs settle in the grass so you never see them.
    Correction: Martha Grencher is pleased with the carpet of Astro-Turf in her kitchen, claiming that crumbs settle in the grass so she never sees them.
    Or: Martha Grencher is pleased with the carpet of Astro-Turf in her kitchen. She claims that crumbs settle in the grass so she never sees them.

3. *Fragment:* Looking down at the grass, which had suddenly begun to seem very squishy.
    Correction: Looking down at the grass, which had suddenly begun to seem very squishy, I realized I had hiked into a marsh of some kind.
    Or: I looked down at the grass, which had suddenly begun to seem very squishy.

4. *Fragments:* Hiding in the back or in a corner or behind someone.
    But by sitting where you can have direct eye contact with teachers.

Corrections: Some students show through body language that they don't want to get involved in a class, hiding in the back or in a corner or behind someone. But by sitting where you can have direct eye contact with teachers, you can make a favorable impression on them.

5. *Fragments:* Knowing they would pity me if I forgot my lines.
   To make me laugh if possible.
   Corrections: I was afraid of the adults in the audience, knowing they would pity me if I forgot my lines.
   Or: I knew they would pity me if I forgot my lines.
   I was also worried that the kids would giggle at me, to make me laugh if possible.
   Or: They would make me laugh if possible.

Added-Detail Fragments

PRACTICE 1 (pp. 19–20)

1. *Fragment:* For example, managing to cut his hand while crumbling a bar of shredded wheat.
   Correction: He managed to cut his hand while crumbling a bar of shredded wheat.

2. *Fragment:* Such as bed sheets, pillowcases, towels, handkerchiefs, and underwear.
   Correction: The first load of wash should be white things such as bed sheets, pillowcases, towels, handkerchiefs, and underwear.

3. *Fragment:* For example, poker, blackjack, and pinochle.
   Correction: For example, I play poker, blackjack, and pinochle.

PRACTICE 2 (pp. 20–21)

1. *Fragment:* Like a land mine ready to explode.
   Correction: I could feel his anger building, like a land mine ready to explode.
   Or: It was like a land mine ready to explode.

2. *Fragment:* For example, the ability to lift weights for three hours and then play basketball all afternoon.
   Correction: For example, he has the ability to lift weights for three hours and then play basketball all afternoon.

3. *Fragment:* Such as cherry cheesecake or vanilla cream puffs.
   Correction: One of my greatest joys in life is eating desserts, such as cherry cheesecake or vanilla cream puffs.

4. *Fragment:* For instance, chewing with his mouth open.
   Correction: For instance, he chewed with his mouth open.

5. *Fragment:* With potatoes splattering all over the walls of the oven.
   Correction: A half hour later, there were several explosions, with potatoes splattering all over the walls of the oven.
   Or: Potatoes splattered all over the walls of the oven.

Missing-Subject Fragments

PRACTICE (p. 22)

1. *Fragment:* And discovered about one tablespoon of milk left in the carton.
   Correction: Tom went to the refrigerator to get milk for his breakfast cereal and discovered about one tablespoon of milk left in the carton.
   Or: He discovered about one tablespoon of milk left in the carton.

2. *Fragment:* But happily found it in the women's room after class.
   Correction: But happily, she found it in the women's room after class.

3. *Fragment:* Also, were asked to leave the parking lot as well.
   Correction: Also, they were asked to leave the parking lot as well.

4. *Fragment:* And even measured it with a ruler, so she'd have a figure to compare it with six months later.
   Correction: She started checking her nose in the mirror each day and even measured it with a ruler, so she'd have a figure to compare it with six months later.
   Or: She even measured it with a ruler, so she'd have a figure to compare it with six months later.

5. *Fragment:* Also, seated us in rows from the brightest students to the dumbest.
   Correction: Also, they seated us in rows from the brightest students to the dumbest.

Run-On Sentences

PRACTICE (p. 28)

1. summer. A
2. gunshot. Her
3. nut. She
4. jeans. They
5. apartment. The
6. bar. The
7. other. This
8. tinge. As
9. child. I
10. sink. The

PRACTICE 1   (pp. 30–31)

1. and
2. for
3. but
4. for
5. so

PRACTICE 3   (p. 32)

1. gas. Today
   or gas, but today
2. youth. I
   or youth, and
3. Sociology 201, for
   or Sociology 201. She
4. yogurt, for
   or yogurt. He
5. vacation, but
6. diapers, and
   or diapers. He
7. oily, so she
   or oily. She
8. himself. He
   or himself, for he
9. supper. Then
   or supper, and then
10. her, but

PRACTICE (p. 33)

1. living; at
2. anymore; he
3. apartment; I
4. week; parts
5. tree; a

PRACTICE (p. 34)

1. point; therefore, I
   (*or* as a result *or* consequently)
2. album; however, the
3. thinning; also, he
   (*or* in addition *or* moreover *or* furthermore)
4. movie; instead, they
5. lunch; otherwise, I

Verb Endings

Present Tense Endings

PRACTICE 1 (p. 39)

1. tows
2. sells
3. pleases
4. tastes
5. weakens
6. cries
7. Correct
8. drives
9. lives
10. feels

PRACTICE 2 (p. 39)

Charlotte reac*ts* badly when she ge*ts* caught in a traffic jam. She open*s* the dashboard compartment and pull*s* out an old pack of Marlboros that she keep*s* for such occasions. She light*s* up and drag*s* heavily, sucking the smoke deep into her lungs. She ge*ts* out of the car and look*s* down the highway, trying to see where the delay is. Back in the car, she drum*s* her fingers on the steering wheel. If the jam last*s* long enough, she start*s* talking to herself and angrily kick*s* off her shoes.

Past Tense Endings

PRACTICE 1 (p. 41)

1. enjoyed . . . started
2. warmed . . . gobbled
3. missed . . . resolved
4. started . . . turned
5. pinched . . . swelled
6. patched . . . collapsed
7. showed
8. walked . . . ordered
9. tried . . . ended
10. burned

PRACTICE 2 (p. 41)

Bill's boss shout*ed* at Bill. Feeling bad, Bill went home and curs*ed* his wife. Then his wife scream*ed* at their son. Angry himself, the son went out and cruelly teas*ed* a little girl who liv*ed* next door until she cr*ied*. Bad feelings were pass*ed* on as one person wound*ed* the next with ugly words. No one manag*ed* to break the vicious cycle.

Irregular Verbs

PRACTICE 1 (p. 46)

1. chosen
2. did (*or* had done)
3. worn
4. written
5. gave
6. was
7. broken
8. lent
9. saw
10. knew

3. (*a*) grows
   (*b*) grew
   (*c*) grown
4. (*a*) goes
   (*b*) went
   (*c*) gone
5. (*a*) throws
   (*b*) threw
   (*c*) thrown
6. (*a*) sees
   (*b*) saw
   (*c*) seen
7. (*a*) lies
   (*b*) lay
   (*c*) lain
8. (*a*) does
   (*b*) did
   (*c*) done
9. (*a*) begins
   (*b*) began
   (*c*) begun
10. (*a*) eats
    (*b*) ate
    (*c*) eaten

PRACTICE 2 (pp. 47–48)

1. (*a*) freezes
   (*b*) froze
   (*c*) frozen
2. (*a*) knows
   (*b*) knew
   (*c*) known

Troublesome Irregular Verbs

PRACTICE (p. 49)

1. lays
2. lay
3. Lying
4. laid
5. lay

PRACTICE (pp. 49–50)

1. sit
2. setting
3. set
4. sat
5. set

PRACTICE (p. 50)

1. rise
2. raise
3. risen
4. raised
5. rises

Subject-Verb Agreement

PRACTICE (p. 52)

1. needs	4. blares	7. looks
2. slither	5. loves	8. itches
3. drives	6. squeak	9. grow
		10. appears

Agreement Mistakes with Four Common Irregular Verbs

PRACTICE (pp. 53–54)

1. was	4. am	7. is
2. do . . . am	5. have . . . has	8. are . . . am
3. has . . . do	6. was . . . did	9. was . . . went
		10. has . . . has

Other Situations in Which Agreement Mistakes Are Made

PRACTICE (p. 56)

1. comes	4. were	7. do
2. sells	5. belong	8. need
3. are	6. seem	9. is . . . needs
		10. is

PRACTICE (pp. 56–57)	**PRACTICE (pp. 57–58)**	**PRACTICE (pp. 58–59)**
1. are	1. were	1. lacks
2. were	2. have	2. take
3. is	3. are	3. is
4. do	4. were	4. were
5. is	5. are	5. give
6. were	6. grow	6. blares
7. are	7. have	7. calls
8. are	8. are	8. brave
9. knows	9. visit	9. scare
10. was	10. are	10. stumble

PRACTICE (pp. 59–60)

1.	ignores	4.	were
2.	dances	5.	appears
3.	deserves	6.	volunteers

7. owns
8. has
9. thinks
10. has

Consistent Verb Tense

PRACTICE (pp. 61–62)

1.	decided	4.	hopes
2.	walked	5.	informs
3.	picked	6.	sprinkled

7. fail
8. asked
9. graduated
10. shrugged

Additional Information about Verbs

PRACTICE (p. 66)

1. Charlotte organized the surprise party.
2. The comedian offended many people.
3. The neighbors paid for the old woman's groceries.
4. The boys knocked the horse chestnuts off the trees.
5. The exorcist drove the devil out of Regan.

Misplaced Modifiers

PRACTICE (pp. 67–68)

1. with a newspaper
   He swatted with a newspaper the wasp that stung him.
   Or: With a newspaper, he swatted the wasp that stung him.

2. almost
   I had almost a dozen job interviews after I sent out my résumé.

3. to save money
   To save money, Joanne decided to live with her grandparents when she attended college.
   Or: Joanne decided to live with her grandparents to save money when she attended college.

4. which is very close to my heart
   I adopted from a junkyard a dog which is very close to my heart.

5. on the day she was born
   On the day their daughter was born, Tim and Rita decided to send her to college.

6. driving across the bridge
Driving across the bridge, we could see the football stadium.

7. angrily
I glared angrily at the man who slipped ahead of me in the ticket line.

8. going to work
Going to work, Clyde saw a three-car accident.

9. built by a gigantic spider
I noticed a gray, furry nest built by a gigantic spider in a corner of the apartment.

10. ranging from fried shrimp to chopped sirloin
The father ordered a meal ranging from fried shrimp to chopped sirloin for his family.
Or: For his family, the father ordered a meal ranging from fried shrimp to chopped sirloin.

Dangling Modifiers

PRACTICE 1 (pp. 71–72)

1. While I ate the hot dog, mustard dropped onto my blouse.
Or: Eating the hot dog, I dropped mustard onto my blouse.

2. After I put on a corduroy shirt, the room didn't seem as cold.
Or: After putting on a corduroy shirt, I didn't feel as cold in the room.

3. When I flunked out of school, my parents demanded that I get a job.
Or: My parents demanded that I get a job when I flunked out of school.

4. Confused about which road to take, I used my CB to get directions.
Or: Because I was confused about which road to take, I used my CB to get directions.

5. After Mike joined the Glee Club, his social life became more active.
Or: Joining the Glee Club, Mike found his social life becoming more active.

6. While they visited the Jungle Park Safari, a baboon scrambled onto the hood of their car.

7. Since her roses were under attack by beetles, Charlotte sprayed them with insecticide.
Or: Charlotte sprayed insecticide on her roses, which were under attack by beetles.

8. While I was standing at the ocean's edge, the wind coated my glasses with a salty film.

9. To pass Dr. Stein's course, students must attend class regularly.
Or: If you want to pass Dr. Stein's course, regular class attendance is necessary.

10. When I braked the car suddenly, my shopping bags tumbled off the seat.

Faulty Parallelism

PRACTICE 1 (p. 75)

1. to walk her fox terrier
2. ambition
3. nurse
4. embarrassed
5. long checkout lines
6. chasing squirrels
7. the potatoes were greasy
8. green eyes
9. riding around town with friends
10. difficult to handle

PRACTICE 2 (pp. 76–77)

1. Gail is a sweet, attractive, engaging woman.
2. My first grade teacher was an elderly, tall, friendly woman.
3. Instead of studying he listens to his stereo, flies paper airplanes, or shoots darts.
4. People in the lobby munched popcorn, sipped sodas, and shuffled their feet impatiently.
5. One by one the dry brown leaves fell from the plant and scattered on the floor.
6. I like Dan's easy manner, good humor, and sense of class.
7. Our city buses are frequently crowded, dirty, and late.
8. I headed for the pool, carrying with me a magazine, a Pepsi, and a lounge chair.
9. To deal with my cold, I purchased Kleenex, vitamin C, and several cans of fruit juice.
10. While watching television, Lana likes to paint, play solitaire, or prepare delicious desserts.

Pronoun Agreement, Reference, and Point of View

Pronoun Agreement

PRACTICE (p. 80)

1. their
2. it
3. their
4. they
5. it

PRACTICE (p. 81)

1. him
2. her
3. he
4. her
5. his
6. her
7. its
8. his
9. her
10. his

Pronoun Reference

PRACTICE (pp. 83–84)

Note: The practice sentences could be rewritten to have other meanings than the ones indicated below.

1. Because her aggressive children scratch and bite, Sarah never lets them play with the neighbor's cats.
2. Although Parmesan cheese does not always agree with me, I love to have it on veal.
3. An editorial in today's paper claims the chief of police is accepting bribes. *Or:* In today's paper the editors say they believe the chief of police is accepting bribes.
4. She wanted to go downstairs and say something to her arguing parents that would make things better.
5. When I asked why I had failed my driver's test, the officer said I had driven too slowly.
6. Angry at striking out, Tony broke the baseball bat by hurling it at the fence.
7. When the students at the high school are doing well, the teachers always tell them.
8. Because my brother didn't want to paint the garage doors, my Dad ordered him to do it.
9. Craig is quitting the basketball team because he feels the coaches emphasize winning too much.
10. He got a tutor to help him with psychology and began to enjoy the course. The tutoring led to a B on his next test.

Pronoun Point of View

PRACTICE (p. 85)

1.	we are hired	6.	you should take precautions
2.	I always have	7.	he (*or* she) should also have
3.	I do not get paid	8.	he (*or* she) got snapped at
4.	ruin my grade	9.	he (*or* she) used
5.	we had only a radio	10.	his (*or* her) place

Note: The last four sentences could also be recast in the plural:

7. People dieting should have the encouragement of friends; they should also have lots of will power.

8.   If people get near Rex, they get snapped at viciously.

9.   On the night the heat went off, people could not get warm, no matter how many blankets they used.

10.   Workers can take a break after relief persons come to take their place.

Pronoun Types

Subject and Object Pronouns

PRACTICE 1 (p. 89)

S   2.   I
S   3.   they (*did* is understood)
O   4.   her
S   5.   she
S   6.   he
S   7.   She
S   8.   We
S   9.   I (*am* is understood)
S   10.   She and I

PRACTICE 2 (pp. 89–90)

2.   me *or* him
3.   me *or* her *or* him *or* them
4.   me *or* her *or* him *or* them
5.   me *or* her *or* him
6.   I *or* he *or* she
7.   I *or* he *or* she
8.   them
9.   him *or* her *or* them
10.   us

Demonstrative Pronouns

PRACTICE 1 (p. 91)

1.   That dog
2.   This fingernail
3.   Those girls
4.   Those shopping bags
5.   that corner house

Possessive Pronouns

PRACTICE (p. 92)

1.   its
2.   his
3.   mine
4.   their
5.   ours

Reflexive Pronouns

PRACTICE (p. 93)

1.   himself
2.   themselves
3.   yourself
4.   themselves
5.   ourselves

Adjectives and Adverbs

PRACTICE (p. 96)

1.   violently
2.   quickly
3.   angrily
4.   considerable
5.   gently
6.   really
7.   regularly . . . regular
8.   quietly . . . angrily
9.   carefully . . . exact
10.   Slowly . . . surely

Well and Good

PRACTICE (pp. 96–97)

1.   well
2.   good
3.   well
4.   well
5.   well

Comparisons

PRACTICE (p. 98)		PRACTICE (pp. 99–100)
faster	fastest	1. most comfortable
more timid	most timid	2. most difficult
kinder	kindest	3. easiest
more ambitious	most ambitious	4. less
more generous	most generous	5. best
finer	finest	6. longest
more likable	most likable	7. most memorable
		8. more experienced . . . most experienced
		9. worse
		10. better

Paper Format

PRACTICE 1 (p. 102)

2. No quotation marks around the title.
3. Capitalize the major words in the title (''The Generation Gap in Our House'').
4. Skip a line between the title and the first line of the paper.
5. Indent the first line of the paper.
6. Keep margins on either side of the paper.

PRACTICE 2 (pp. 102–103)

1. ''Selfishness in Young Children''
2. ''The Health Benefits of Daily Exercise'' *or* ''The Values of Daily Exercise''
3. ''My Stubborn Son''
4. ''Essential College Study Skills''
5. ''Drawbacks and Values of Single Life''

PRACTICE 3 (pp. 103–104)

1. The worst day of my life began when my supervisor at work gave me a message to call home.
2. Catholic Church services have undergone many changes in the last few years.
3. An embarrassing moment happened to me when I was working as a waitress at the Stanton Hotel.
4. Correct
5. Many television commercials that I watch are degrading to human dignity.

Capital Letters

PRACTICE 1 (pp. 107–108)

1. Raid . . . Ratner Pest Control
2. January . . . August
3. Clark Kent . . . "You
4. Pepsis . . . Ritz . . . Oreo
5. Yamaha . . . Florida . . . Greyhound
6. "You're . . . "Watch . . . I'll
7. Friday . . . Morton's . . . Zenith
8. Empire . . . Square . . . Mets . . . Shea
9. Mary . . . *Sesame* . . . *Digest* . . . "Let's
10. Kellogg's . . . Dial . . . Pathmark . . . Safeway

PRACTICE 2 (p. 108)

1. summer . . . sun . . . magazines
2. week . . . tune . . . melody . . . gum . . . television
3. main . . . high school . . . states . . . country . . . goal . . . lawyer
4. title . . . paper . . . teacher . . . grade
5. friend . . . college . . . degree . . . job . . . life

Numbers

PRACTICE (p. 112)

1. Three boys
2. February 15, 1952.
3. $850
4. activity 4
5. four rabbits
6. 25 cases
7. two dollar bill . . . three
8. four courses
9. seven o'clock
10. 15 push-ups, 30 sit-ups

Abbreviations

PRACTICE (p. 113)

1. years . . . Avenue . . . Street
2. San Francisco, California . . . Hospital
3. December 5 . . . Saturday
4. minutes . . . television
5. biology and English . . . doctor . . . tranquilizer

End Marks

PRACTICE (p. 115)

1.	continue?	6.	cars.
2.	road!	7.	sunglasses!
3.	arthritis.	8.	*Rings*.
4.	visit?	9.	mess!''
5.	wallet.	10.	wig?''

Apostrophe

Apostrophe in Contractions

PRACTICE 1 (p. 116)

aren't	hasn't
you're	who's
they've	doesn't
wouldn't	there's
you've	

PRACTICE 2 (pp. 116–117)

1. I'll . . . you'll
2. It's . . . wouldn't
3. shouldn't . . . you're
4. isn't . . . weren't
5. I'd . . . who's . . . it's

Four Contractions

PRACTICE (p. 118)

1. They're . . . their
2. You're . . . your
3. Who's . . . whose
4. It's . . . it's
5. you're . . . their . . . it's

Apostrophe to Show Ownership or Possession

PRACTICE 1 (p. 119)

1. Lola's sneakers
2. Veronica's lipstick
3. His brother's house
4. The car's tires
5. Fran's bicycle
6. the blue jay's nest
7. my paper's title
8. My mother's arthritis
9. My sister's boyfriend
10. The little boy's energy level

PRACTICE 2 (p. 120)

1. (Done as example.)
2. Georgia's
3. friend's
4. teacher's
5. girl friend's
6. Albert's
7. daughter's
8. manager's
9. night's
10. son's

Apostrophe versus Simple Plurals

PRACTICE (pp. 121–122)

1. *Plurals:* strips . . . potatoes
   Possessive: Tony's favorite breakfast

2. *Plural:* brothers
   Possessive: father's influence

3. *Plurals:* persons . . . appointments
   Possessive: doctor's office

4. *Plural:* pigs
   Possessive: Bill's job

5. *Plural:* students
   Possessive: teacher's voice

6. *Plurals:* questions . . . grades
   Possessive: Rick's skill

7. *Plural:* noodles
   Possessive: friend's cooking

8. *Plural:* hangers
   Possessive: wife's habit

9. *Plural:* tapes
   Possessive: Carly Simon's
   latest album

10. *Plurals:* weeks . . . streams
    Possessive: lake's

Apostrophe with Words Ending in *-s*

PRACTICE (p. 122)

1. Jones' wife
2. workers' strike
3. students' gripes
4. Lois' dog
5. boys' father

Quotation Marks

PRACTICE 1 (p. 125)

1. "Don't shout at me," Lola said to her mother.
2. The teacher asked Sharon, "Why are your eyes closed?"
3. Christ said, "I come that you may have life, and have it more abundantly."
4. "I refuse to wear those itchy wool pants!" Ralph shouted at his parents.
5. His father replied, "We should give all the clothes you never wear to the Salvation Army."
6. The nervous boy whispered hoarsely over the telephone, "Is Linda home?"
7. "When I was ten," Lola said, "I spent my entire summer playing Monopoly."
8. Tony said, "When I was ten, I spent my whole summer playing basketball."
9. The critic wrote about the play, "It runs the gamut of emotions from A to B."
10. "The best way to tell if a mushroom is poisonous," the doctor solemnly explained, "is if you find it in the stomach of a dead person."

PRACTICE 2 **(p. 126)**

1. Fred said, "I'm going with you."
2. "Everyone passed the test," the teacher informed them.
3. My parents asked, "Where were you?"
4. "I hate that commercial," he muttered.
5. "If you don't leave soon," he warned, "you'll be late for work."

Indirect Quotations

PRACTICE 1 **(p. 127)**

2. Martha said, "You can listen to the game on the radio."
3. Fred said, "I'm tired of being told what to do."
4. Martha said, "As long as I'm bigger and stronger, I'll make the rules."
5. Fred said, "The day will come when the tables will be turned."

PRACTICE 2 **(p. 128)**

1. He said that as the plane went higher, his heart sank lower.
2. The designer said that shag rugs are back in style.
3. The foreman asked Jake if he had ever operated a lift truck.
4. My nosy neighbor asked if Ed and Ellen were fighting.
5. Martha complained that she married a man who eats Tweeties cereal for breakfast.

Quotes to Set Off Titles of Short Works

PRACTICE (p. 129)

1. Edgar Allan Poe's short story "The Murders in the Rue Morgue" and his poem "The Raven" are in a paperback titled Great Tales and Poems of Edgar Allan Poe.
2. My assignment is to research an article titled "A New Treatment for Hypertension" in the latest issue of Newsweek.
3. "States of Consciousness," the sixth chapter of Linda Davidoff's Introduction to Psychology, will be the basis for our next test.
4. Tony's favorite television show is Star Trek, and his favorite movie is Star Wars.
5. He bought the Ladies' Home Journal because he wanted to read the cover article titled "Secrets Men Never Tell You."

6. The assignment was to read the chapter titled "A Kite" in James Herndon's <u>How to Survive in Your Native Land</u>.

7. When she got her new <u>TV Guide</u>, she read an article titled "The New Comedians" and then thumbed through the listings to see who would be the guests that week on the <u>Tonight Show</u>.

8. The night before his exam, he discovered with horror that the chapter "Becoming Mature" was missing from <u>Childhood and Adolescence</u>, the psychology text that he had bought secondhand.

9. In Dr. Hickory's new book, <u>Black Walnuts and You</u>, there is a chapter titled "How to Make Walnut Peanut Butter."

10. Every holiday season our family watches the movie <u>A Christmas Carol</u> on television.

Comma

PRACTICE (p. 133)

1. Donald Duck, Archie, and Bugs Bunny
2. Cold eggs, burned bacon, and watery orange juice
3. rich, tangy, mellow beer
4. patties, special sauce, lettuce, cheese, pickles, and onions
5. laundry, helped clean the apartment, waxed the car, and watched

PRACTICE (pp. 133–134)

1. stomach, . . . In turn,
2. years,
3. money, . . . Also, . . . However,
4. accident, . . . Even so,
5. done, . . . there, . . . Also,

PRACTICE (p. 135)

1. deadline, the absolute final deadline,
2. cow, a weird creature, . . . dish, who must also have been strange,
3. husband, a mild man who works as a bookkeeper, . . . he, strange as it seems,
4. cheese, to be sure,
5. Tod, voted the most likely to succeed in our high school graduating class, . . . Kongs, a local motorcycle gang,

PRACTICE (p. 136)

1. car, but
2. Correct
3. shops, so
4. Correct
5. math, for
6. Novocain, and
7. Correct
8. dolls, and
9. drinking, but
10. speech, and

PRACTICE (p. 137)

1. fries," said
2. asked, "What
3. minute," said
4. beer," said
5. grief," said

PRACTICE (p. 138)

1. sorry, Sir,
2. you, Mike, and you, Susan,
3. September 12, 1978, and lived at 3865 Sunset Boulevard, Los Angeles, California, for one month.
4. 75,000 . . . $900,000
5. October 12, 1978, and

Unnecessary Use of Commas

PRACTICE (p. 139)

1. Frank said to me that the work was already done.
2. Eggs must be added to the recipe.
3. As the heavy Caterpillar tractor rumbled up the street, our house windows rattled.
4. I am allergic to wool rugs and cat fur.
5. The short, chubby blonde with the grin on her face is my sister.
6. The club members asked me whether I had ever taken karate lessons.
7. Las Vegas, Miami Beach, and Atlantic City are the three places where he has worked as a bartender.
8. The brown cotton shirt that Jay has worn for two years is threadbare and faded.
9. Thomas Farley, the handsome young man who just took off his trousers, is an escaped mental patient.
10. Because Mary is single, her married friends do not invite her to their parties.

Colon

PRACTICE (p. 143)

1. cars:
2. present:
3. class:
4. men:
5. situation:

Semicolon

PRACTICE (p. 144)

1. full; others
2. place; starting
3. me; yesterday
4. Abby''; the
5. cigarettes; he

Dash

PRACTICE (p. 144)

1. condition—
2. exercise—especially
3. you—in fact, I'm telling you—
4. arrived—badly
5. fishing—these

Hyphen

PRACTICE (p. 145)

1. High-flying jets and gear-grinding trucks
2. well-rounded
3. ten-legged . . . crumb-filled
4. seventy-two . . . twenty-two
5. ten-year-old . . . self-confident

Parentheses

PRACTICE (p. 146)

1. novel (especially Chapter Five) made
2. George (Amy's first husband) just
3. Freud (1856–1939) was
4. prepare (1) a daily list of things to do and (2) a weekly study schedule.
5. chapter (pages 72–96) of

Dictionary Use

Answers are in your dictionary. Check with your instructor if you are not able to locate certain answers.

Plurals

Irregular Plurals (p. 157)

1 sandwiches   crashes   foxes
       matches   dresses   passes

2 bodies   fallacies   donkeys
       countries   pennies   twenties

PRACTICE (pp. 158–159)

1. groceries   6. passes
2. towns   7. tragedies
3. supplies   8. watches
4. bodies   9. suits
5. lotteries   10. bosses

Omitted -S Ending

PRACTICE (pp. 159–160)

1. boyfriends . . . blows   6. days . . . times
2. curses   7. billboards
3. paragraphs . . . events   8. chairs . . . pillows
4. cars   9. watchtowers . . . states
5. houses . . . highways   10. Motorists . . . trucks

Omitted Words

PRACTICE (pp. 161–162)

1. When I began eating *the* box of chicken I bought at the fast-food restaurant, I found several pieces that consisted of *a* lot *of* crust covering nothing but chicken bones.

2. Sally had *a* teacher who tried *to* light a piece of chalk, thinking it was *a* cigarette.

3. In his dream, Harry committed *the* perfect crime: he killed his enemy with *an* icicle, so *the* murder weapon was never found.

4. Dr. Yutzer told me not *to* worry about *the* sore on my foot, but I decided to get *a* second opinion.

5. As *the* little girl ate *the* vanilla sugar cone, ice cream dripped out *of a* hole at the bottom onto her pants.

6. When thick black clouds began *to* form and we felt several drops *of* rain, we knew *the* picnic would be cancelled.

7. After spending most *of* her salary on new clothes, Susan looks like something out of *a* fashion magazine.

8. As wasps buzzed around *the* room, I ran for *a* can of Raid.

9. Sam put *the* pair of wet socks in the oven, for he wanted *to* dry them out quickly.

10. Because *the* weather got hot and stayed hot for weeks, my flower garden started *to* look like *a* dry flower arrangement.

Commonly Confused Words

Homonyms (pp. 162–173)

all ready/already

1. all ready . . . already
2. all ready
3. already . . . all ready

brake/break

1. brake . . . break
2. break . . . brake
3. breaking . . . brake

course/coarse

1. coarse . . . course
2. course
3. course . . . coarse

hear/here

1. hear . . . here
2. here . . . hear
3. Here . . . hear

hole/whole

1. whole . . . hole
2. whole . . . hole
3. whole . . . hole

its/it's

1. it's
2. It's
3. its . . . its

knew/new

1. knew . . . new
2. knew . . . new
3. knew . . . new

know/no

1. know . . . no
2. know . . . no
3. No . . . know

pair/pear

1. pair . . . pears
2. pear . . . pair
3. pairs

passed/past

1. past . . . passed
2. past . . . passed
3. past . . . passed

peace/piece

1. peace . . . piece
2. piece . . . peace
3. peace . . . piece

plain/plane

1. plain . . . plane
2. plain . . . plane
3. plain

principal/principle

1. principal . . . principles
2. principal . . . principle
3. principles . . . principal

right/write

1. write . . . right
2. write . . . right
3. write . . . right

than/then

1. then . . . than
2. than . . . then
3. than . . . then

their/there/they're

1. There . . . their
2. they're
3. there . . . there

threw/through

1. through . . . threw
2. through
3. through . . . threw

to/too/two

1. two
2. to . . . too
3. to . . . too

your/you're

1. You're . . . your . . . you're
2. your . . . your . . . you're
3. You're . . . you're

wear/where

1. wears
2. Where . . . wear
3. where

weather/whether

1. weather . . . whether
2. Whether
3. whether . . . weather

whose/who's

1. Who's . . . whose
2. Who's
3. Whose

Other Words Frequently Confused (pp. 174–181)

a/an

1. a . . . a . . . an
2. an . . . a
3. a . . . a . . . an

accept/except

1. accept . . . except
2. Except . . . accept
3. accepted . . . except

advice/advise

1. advise . . . advice
2. advice . . . advise
3. advise . . . advice

affect/effect

1. effects . . . affect
2. effect . . . affect
3. effect . . . affects

among/between

1. between
2. among
3. Among . . . between

beside/besides

1. beside
2. beside
3. Besides

can/may

1. May
2. can
3. may

clothes/cloth

1. clothes . . . cloths
2. cloths
3. clothes

desert/dessert

1. desert . . . dessert
2. deserted
3. dessert . . . desert

does/dose

1. does . . . doses
2. Does
3. Does . . . dose

fewer/less

1. fewer . . . less
2. fewer
3. fewer . . . less

former/latter

1. former . . . latter
2. former . . . latter
3. former . . . latter

learn/teach

1. teach
2. teach . . . learn
3. learn

loose/lose

1. loose . . . lose
2. loose
3. lose . . . loose

quiet/quite

1. quite . . . quiet
2. quite . . . quiet
3. quiet . . . quite

though/thought

1. Though . . . thought
2. though
3. thought . . . though

Incorrect Word Forms (pp. 182–183)

being that

1. Since (or Because) she's a year older
2. since (or because) the bus drivers
3. Since (or Because) I didn't

can't hardly/couldn't hardly

1. I can hardly
2. can hardly
3. could hardly

could of

1. You could have
2. I could have
3. she could have

irregardless

1. regardless of the price
2. regardless of their age
3. Regardless of the risk

must of/should of/would of

1. Anita must have
2. I should have
3. they would have

Slang

PRACTICE (p. 185)

1. If you don't start working regularly in this course, you're going to fail the midterm exam.
2. The car would have been a bargain, but the owner realized his asking price was too low and raised it.
3. We were badly beaten in the football game.
4. There are so many strange and unpleasant people at my school that it's surprising I've kept my sanity.
5. I got so anxious when the teacher called on me that my mind went blank.

Clichés

PRACTICE (p. 186)

1. Substitute *furious over* for *sick and tired*.
2. Substitute *discipline me* for *put her foot down*.
3. Substitute *opened up socially* for *came out of her shell*.
4. Substitute *did not care* for *could not have cared less*.
5. Substitute *not feeling well* for *feeling under the weather*.

Note: The above answers are examples of how the clichés could be corrected. Other answers are, of course, possible.

Wordiness

PRACTICE (pp. 187–188)

1. Because it was raining, I didn't go shopping.
2. I do not feel that prostitution should be legalized.
3. I've decided that my golf clubs are my most valued material possession.
4. It is hard for the inexperienced driver to drive in heavy traffic.
5. When my grandfather was a boy, gaslights lined the streets.
6. With her attractive brown eyes and chestnut hair, Maria made her father a proud man.
7. I have repeatedly asked you to turn off the lights when you go to bed.
8. To write an effective paper, you must first decide what point you want to make.

PART 2
Skills Reinforcement through Guided Composition

INTRODUCTION

This section of the book will help reinforce many of the grammar, punctuation, mechanics, and word use skills presented in Part 1. All too often, people can apply such skills when correcting individual sentences, but they can't apply those skills in their own compositions. The guided composition activities in Part 2 should increase your chances of transferring to actual writing situations the sentence skills you have learned.

Part 2 will also give you practice in proofreading. Frequently, persons understand a particular sentence skill but are not able to locate a mistake in that skill in their own writing. They must learn to proofread carefully for skills mistakes and to make such "proofing" a habit. To do successfully the activities in Part 2, you will have to practice the skill of careful proofreading.

Steps in Guided Composition

Each composition in this section contains a number of mistakes involving a single sentence skill. The first composition, for example, contains seven sentence fragments. Your assignment will be to rewrite each passage, correcting it for the skills mistake indicated. At the same time, you must copy perfectly the rest of the passage, without omitting a word, misplacing an apostrophe, dropping a verb ending, misspelling a word, or making any other change in the passage. If you miss even one skills error in a passage or make even one mistake in copying, you should rewrite a different passage that deals with the same skill.

Every skill presented in Part 2 is described as a separate step. Here is a list of the sentence skills you will practice:

Step 1 Correcting Fragments
Step 2 Correcting Run-on Sentences
Step 3 Adding Noun and Verb Endings
Step 4 Understanding Irregular Verbs
Step 5 Making Subjects, Verbs, and Pronouns Agree
Step 6 Maintaining Consistent Verb Tense and Pronoun Point of View
Step 7 Correcting Dangling Modifiers
Step 8 Correcting Faulty Parallelism
Step 9 Adding Capital Letters
Step 10 Adding Apostrophes
Step 11 Adding Quotation Marks
Step 12 Adding Commas
Step 13 Understanding Commonly Confused Words

There are three passages in each step. For example, under Step 1 there are three passages containing sentence fragments. After you rewrite and proofread carefully the first fragments passage, you will show it to your instructor. He or she will check it quickly to see that all the fragments have been corrected and that no copying mistakes have been made. If the passage is error-free, the instructor will mark and initial the appropriate box in the progress chart on pages 232–233 and you can move on to Step 2.

If even a single mistake is made, the instructor may question you briefly to see if you recognize and understand it. (Perhaps he or she will put a check beside the line in which the mistake appears, and then ask if you can correct it.) You will then be asked to write the second passage under Step 1. If necessary, you will remain on Step 1 and rewrite the third passage (and even perhaps go on to repeat the first and second passages) as well. You will complete the program in guided composition when you successfully work through all thirteen steps in Part 2. Completing the thirteen steps will strengthen your understanding of the skills, increase your chances of transferring the skills to actual writing situations, and improve your proofreading ability.

In doing the passages, note the following points:

1 For each step you will be told the number of mistakes that appear in the passages. Also, you will be given the page numbers for the section that explains the skill in question. Do not hesitate to turn back and review such pages when you are unsure about a skill.

2 Here is an effective way to go about correcting a passage. First, read it over quickly. Look for and mark off mistakes in the skill area involved. For example, in your first reading of a passage that has seven fragments, you may locate and mark only four fragments. Next, reread the passage carefully so you can find the remaining errors in the skill in question. Finally, make notes in the margin about how to correct each mistake. Only at this point should you begin to rewrite the passage.

3 Be sure to proofread with care after you finish a passage. Go over your writing word for word, looking for careless errors. Remember that you may be asked to do another passage on the same step if you make even one mistake.

STEP 1: CORRECTING FRAGMENTS

Mistakes in each passage: 7
Pages explaining fragments: 11 to 26

   a   A million cars were stolen in the United States last year. Millions more vandalized
and stripped. You should learn how to fight back. Before you become part of the statistics. Doors should always be locked. According to statistics, 80 percent of the cars stolen
last year were unlocked at the time. Forty percent had the keys in the car. Sitting right
there in the ignition. You should roll your windows up tightly. You should store spare keys 5
in your wallet, not in the car. Since a professional thief knows all the hiding places. Standard
door-lock buttons should be replaced with the slim, tapered kind. Because they are almost
impossible to pull up with a coat hanger. You should park your car in the driveway with the
nose toward the street. So anyone tampering with the engine can be seen more easily. In
summary, if you make it time-consuming to steal your car. The thief will probably try his 10
luck on someone else's.

   b   For her biology class, Ann lay stretched out on the grass in the park. Taking notes
on the insect life she observed around her. First off, a clear-winged bug set down from the
heat. And swayed on a blade of grass nearby. Next, landing suddenly on her hand, a
ladybug. Ann could count the number of dots on its tiny, speckled body. As it crawled
around and under her fingers. When the ladybug left, Ann picked up a low, flat rock. Three 5
black crickets slithered quickly away. Seeking shelter under other rocks or leaves. She
watched one camouflage itself under a leaf. Carefully, she removed the leaf. And watched
the cricket dig deeper into the underbrush. It kept crawling away from the light. Ann moved
her eyes away for a second as a car went by. When she looked back. The cricket had
disappeared.   10

   c   One factor that causes you to forget is lack of motivation. If you have no reason for
remembering certain information. You will probably forget it. Dr. Joyce Brothers, a
prominent psychologist, relates how she memorized facts on boxing. To win $64,000 on a
television quiz show. She and her husband were college students at the time. And, like
most students, could use some extra money. She was not as interested in boxing as she was 5
in winning the money. After she had won the money and used her memorized information
for its purpose. She promptly forgot the facts. Another factor in forgetting, interference.
Previous learning can interfere with new learning. Especially if there are similarities between
the two. If you have previously studied traditional math. You may experience difficulty
learning the new math.   10

STEP 2: CORRECTING RUN-ON SENTENCES

Mistakes in each passage: 6
Pages explaining run-on sentences: 27–37

a Monday morning was a miserable time for me, everything seemed to go wrong. The first mistake I made was to burn the breakfast, therefore, I had to resort to cold cereal. Then my younger son spilled a quart of milk on the dining room carpet as he poured milk into his bowl. I was cleaning the milk up when the telephone rang it was a bill collector reminding me of an overdue bill. As my two sons left for school, they were throwing a 5 rubber ball back and forth one of them missed the ball, and it cracked the living room window. My dog also added to my misery instead of staying home, he was across the street chasing my neighbor's cat. The neighbor came out and threatened to sue me if my dog ever came into her yard again, I had a splitting headache when I was through listening to her.

b What is plaque? Plaque is a sticky, almost invisible film that clings to tooth surfaces it is composed of saliva, cells from the tissues of the mouth, and living bacteria always present in the mouth. Even when you have just cleaned your teeth and have eaten no food, plaque continues to form, this is because saliva is continually bathing the teeth and gums. Your mouth produces approximately 1½ quarts of saliva a day, the saliva washes the plaque 5 and its bacteria into every tiny, minute crevice of teeth and gums these are exactly the spots where it can do most harm. When you eat food containing refined carbohydrates (such as sugar and starches), the bacteria in the plaque can produce acid while tooth enamel is the hardest substance in the body, this acid can actually dissolve the enamel and cause decay. Plaque must be removed daily, otherwise, it can harden between teeth and at the gum line 10 into a substance called tartar. The tartar can eventually contribute to gum disease—the main cause of tooth loss in adults.

c Americans use more energy per person than any other people in the world. We have only 6 percent of the world's population, however, we use about one-third of all the energy consumed on this globe. Our total national energy cost in 1975 amounted to about $170 billion, each year our energy needs are steadily rising. Most of the energy we use in the United States comes from crude oil, because domestic production falls short of our needs, 5 we have to import almost half of it. Expert estimates of our known and potential domestic reserves vary, we probably have somewhere between a 25- to 30-year supply of oil. We must, though, keep our energy-use growth rate at about 2 percent per year. If we continue using energy as we have become accustomed to, we could run out of domestic oil supplies in the year 2007, we may run out of natural gas even sooner. The overall energy situation 10 in the United States is not rosy. Energy demands and prices keep going up, therefore, the availability and future costs of supplies remain uncertain.

STEP 3: ADDING NOUN AND VERB ENDINGS

Mistakes in each passage: 5 missing -*s*, -*es*, or -*ies* endings on nouns
5 missing -*s*, -*d*, or -*ed* endings on verbs
Pages explaining noun and verb endings: 38–43; 159–160

a As cities get larger, the problems of keeping them clean and disposing of their wastes become more difficult. Some ancient cities solve these problem; for example, inhabitant of ancient Rome had water-borne sewage system and public baths. During the Middle Ages, these health-supporting systems disappear from the cities of Europe. Sewage and garbage were dump in yards and street, and bathing was consider to be bad for one's health. It was 5 not surprising that a great plague, the Black Death, rage through Europe during this period, killing about one-fourth of its inhabitants. Eventually people began to improve their sanitary facilities, and in modern cities, many social agency take care of removing sewage, disposing of garbage, and sweeping the streets.

b The river rambles for mile around trees and bushes. At one point, children throw small rock and laugh at the splashes they make. Further along, factories dump gallon of slime and pollutants into the water. Away from the factories, the river seem to smile as it ripples over stones. A waterfall appears near a clump of trees. Romantic couple sit there in the spring. Occasionally, a fisherman tries his luck at the river's edge. A mile or two past 5 the waterfall, the river roar angrily along. It rush noisily. Boys and girls pretend they are captains of many fleets. They sail paper ship and watch them sink. Where the river widen and grows calm once more, someone always seems to be paddling a canoe. Where a bridge stretch across the river, old men stand and look out over the water. The river never gets lonely, for someone is always there to use it.   10

c Sal should have stayed in bed yesterday. He knew it when he tried to shut off his alarm and accidentally pushed the clock on the floor. Sal decide to brave fate anyway. He dressed and headed for the breakfast table. After putting two slice of toast in the toaster, he went out to get the paper. Rain hurtled down from a dark sky. The paper was not under the shelter of the porch but was sitting, completely soak with water, on the walk. ''Thanks 5 a lot, paperboy,'' Sal said to himself as he left the paper where it was and return to the kitchen. After eating quickly, he gathered his books and ran down to the bus stop. No one was there, which meant he had miss the bus. As he stood for twenty minute waiting for the next bus, his pants were splashed by two car that went by. When the bus finally pulled up, Sal reached into his pocket for the fare. Two dime slipped out of his fingers and fell into the 10 water at the curb. After fishing out the coins and paying his fare, Sal discovered there were no empty seat on the bus. Standing there, he wonder what other kinds of bad luck awaited him at school.

STEP 4: UNDERSTANDING IRREGULAR VERBS

Mistakes in each passage: 10
Pages explaining irregular verbs: 44–51

a When the game show contestant learned she had chose the box with only a penny in it, she was badly shaken. She begun to cry and the game show host for a minute was froze with fear. Then he taked her hand and said, ''You have not gotten to the end of the line yet, Mrs. Waterby. Cheer up.'' When she learned she was going to be given one more chance, Mrs. Waterby stopped crying. At the host's signal, a tray was brang onto the stage and 5 placed in front of Mrs. Waterby. On the tray sat three shells. One shell, the host told her, covered the key to a new Lincoln Continental. Mrs. Waterby was to choose the shell she thoughted had the key under it. There was a long pause, and she gived her answer, ''Number three.'' The host lifted up the third shell; the key was underneath. Mrs. Waterby was ecstatic. She danced about the stage, just as she had been instructed to do if she winned. 10 Her husband run up on stage and embraced her. They had realized the great American dream: they had gotten something for nothing.

b Occasionally when I have drove to work, I have gotten behind a slow driver. This usually occurs when I have leaved the house late. I have tried to pass such drivers, but traffic always seems too heavy in the opposite direction. At this point, I have spoke to myself or sung to myself, trying to forget how slow I was traveling. I have never understanded the reason for going 25 miles per hour in a 50 mph zone. Once past the stage of trying to 5 keep calm, I have always expressed my anger to the fullest. I have shook the steering wheel and sayed the foulest words I know. I have imagined stealing a bazooka from an Army depot and blasting the slow driver with it. After I have wore myself out, I have gritted my teeth and waited for my sanity to return. Usually about a mile from my office, the driver in front of me has turned off the street and has rode out of my sight. Then I have forgetted 10 all about it and have went on with my day.

c Pete Jenkins had knew the meaning of fear before, like the time he got a cramp while swimming. Luckily, he had been saved from drowning then by a friend he always swum with. But Pete admits that his first job interview brang an even greater fear. On the morning of the interview, his stomach felt as if he had ate a block of cement the night before. In his throat, a lump had grew to the size of a football, and he wondered if he would be able 5 to speak at all. His mother realized Pete was nervous. She drove him to the interview office while the pressure builded within him. His mother looked over at him before he walked into the office and burst out laughing. ''Pete,'' she said, ''don't worry so much. This is only an interview for a job at McDonald's.'' Pete was angry at first with his mother for laughing, but when she apologized he forgived her. He also knowed his mother was right. He was 10 just going to be interviewed for a job making hamburgers. He kepted his composure during the interview and came through it with ease.

STEP 5: MAKING SUBJECTS, VERBS, AND PRONOUNS AGREE

Rewrite the passage, making the change indicated. Note that changing the subject will require you to make a number of verb and pronoun changes as well. Pages explaining subject-verb-pronoun agreement: 52–60; 79–81

a Change *a person* to *persons.*

A person suffering from hypochondria imagines she has ailments that in reality she does not have. As a result of watching a television medical program, for example, she may believe she has a certain disease. Or after reading about a certain disease, she suddenly realizes that she has some of the symptoms and becomes convinced she has the illness. Such a person is not deliberately pretending that she is ill, however, and doctors will have a difficult 5 time convincing her that she does not have, for instance, heart trouble or cancer.

Very often such a person is lonely. Typically an ill person gets more attention than one who is well. But a person who is continually describing her aches and pains and seeking sympathy turns other people away from her, leaving her even more lonely.

b Change *adolescents* to *adolescent.* Note that you have to add the article *an* before *adolescent* in some cases. Use either *he* or *she* consistently at places where a pronoun is needed.

Although adolescents don't realize it, they need their parents as much during their teenage years as at earlier points in their life. Adolescents have mixed feelings about growing up. They want the skills and freedom of adults but aren't quite ready to give up the sheltering of childhood. They are irritated about any resistance to their efforts to be grown-up, and they are also angered because they still need to depend on you. 5

Adolescents try on roles and behavior patterns—almost the way they try on new clothes—to find out which ones suit them best. They sense that they can no longer be an extension of you, so they are working to put together their own kind of person. They don't do this all at once; instead, their process of discovery can take years. All the bobbing around that adolescents do means they need a rock to rest upon when the process tires them. You 10 as parents must help provide this support.

c Change *boys* to *boy.*

My little boys are sick with the flu. They lie in bed perspiring, chilled, and scared. They want me to stay with them. As long as I'm with them, they will be all right. Sitting on the rocker next to their bed, I listen to their shallow, labored breathing. They cough and ask for water. Then they fall asleep.

After a long nap, they wake up and say they are hungry. They sip sweet tea and munch 5 toast spread with cherry jelly. They do some coloring in a little book and read some Donald Duck and Superman comic books. They watch some television and I take their temperatures, waiting for their fevers to subside. The thermometer reading is down; they still feel sick and scared, but they'll be better in the morning.

STEP 6: MAINTAINING CONSISTENT VERB TENSE AND PRONOUN POINT OF VIEW

Mistakes in each passage: 4 mistakes in verb tense

4 mistakes in pronoun point of view

Pages explaining consistent verb tense and pronoun point of view: 61–62; 84–85

a I lived in an old apartment house years ago where I got little peace and quiet. For one thing, you could hear the constant fights that went on in the adjoining apartment. The husband yelled about killing his wife, and she yells right back about leaving him or having him arrested. The people in the apartment above me had four kids. Sometimes one felt a football game was going on upstairs. The noise was especially bad when I got home from 5 work, which also happens to be the time the kids got home from school. If the kids and neighbors were not disturbing me, you had one other thing to depend on. The superintendent visits my apartment whenever he felt like it. He had various excuses, such as checking the water pipes or caulking the windows, but you felt he just wants to get away from his noisy family, which occupied the basement apartment. I moved out of the apartment as soon as 10 I could afford to.

b Riding with a teenager who is learning to drive is a disturbing experience. I have to ride with my brother Mickey, who just got his learner's permit. One does not look forward to going out in the car with Mickey. I think the instinct for survival has a lot to do with your attitude.

The lessons begin and end the same way each day. My brother and I climb into the 5 family Volvo. Mickey practically bounced in the seat with excitement. I feel like bouncing my head against the wall for volunteering my life. You try to remain calm. Mickey steps on the gas and the car responded by stalling. Mickey has not yet learned to coordinate the clutch with the gas pedal. Finally, the car moves forward, and we are quickly off. One wishes for a good luck charm to hold onto. As the car stutters along, my head gains an extra 10 pair of eyes. I watched for cars, telephone poles, stop signs, pedestrians, and anything else Mickey might possibly run into. Fortunately the ride always ended without harm to life, limb, or fender. I am safe for another day.

c Driving at night can be frightening for a variety of reasons. One danger is fog. Fog plays tricks on your eyes while a driver tries to concentrate on the road. Putting on high beams sometimes makes matters worse. Reflected light causes the driver to think he sees objects; he at times applied his brake suddenly. Even the low beams in a car may cause one's imagination to turn shadows into real things. Animals are another night problem. 5 They often crossed the highway at night and may damage your car and themselves. And a driver swerving to avoid animals often hits other cars or collided with a telephone pole or tree. At times the worst danger of all is rain. A pelting rain obscures a driver's already-limited vision, and if your windshield wipers are not working well, there is even less visibility. Rain also creates slick spots on the road, and a driver may skid on these when 10 he encountered curves that are sharper than expected. Everything considered, night driving is best avoided.

STEP 7: CORRECTING DANGLING MODIFIERS

Mistakes in each passage: 5
Pages explaining dangling modifiers: 70–73

a   My sister Kathy once drove an English car called a Morris Mini Minor. Smaller than a VW "Bug," other drivers chuckled and stared at it often. We kids called it the "Mouse." Called the "Rat" by my father, many hours were spent by him searching for cures for its many ailments. My father often spoke about pushing the car off a cliff or exploding it somewhere. He wasn't serious, of course, but one day the little car saved my 5 father the trouble. Driving one afternoon, smoke began pouring through the back seat of the Mini. My sister parked on the side of the road and was quickly pulled away from the car by another motorist. She watched the car smolder for a few minutes and then burst into flames. Arriving about ten minutes later, the fire was soon put out by firemen who towered over the car. Unfortunately, it was too late. Tires melted and body blackened, my sister 10 could hardly recognize the car. When she told the family what had happened, everyone was sympathetic. I suspect, however, that my father shed no tears that the "Rat" was gone from our lives.

b   Before heading to work in the morning, the streets are filled with joggers. They pound the sidewalks quietly in their brightly colored sweatsuits and sneakers. Groups of early feeding birds and squirrels scatter as the joggers move easily down the streets. Wondering where they get their energy, the joggers are gazed at by milkmen and people at bus stops. Kneeling on the cement, a shoelace is sometimes tied during a quick stop. The 5 joggers pass supermarkets and the fresh produce trucks parked at loading ramps. Breathing rhythmically, they soon pass the post office, firehouse, and city hall. On rainy days, the runners watch for slick spots on the sidewalk, but they don't worry about the rain or cold. Pushing on at a steady pace, the number of miles traveled is counted. Finally, the joggers are back at their homes. Taking quick showers, their thoughts are now on the 10 workday ahead. They will return to their special world of running the next morning.

c   When my brother Rick gets hold of a best seller, he forgets the rest of the world exists. Absorbed in his book, dinner is forgotten. He must be reminded to eat even when we have meat loaf, his favorite meal. Rick not only ignores the other people in the family, but he also forgets his chores. Reading after breakfast, lunch, and dinner, a lot of dishes pile up and wastebaskets are not emptied. We try to understand; in fact, we think he's lucky. 5 Sitting in the middle of a room, his book seems to drown out the television, radio, and screaming children. Never wanting any sleep, his book still has his attention at 1 A.M. We bought a new rocking chair once when Rick was in the middle of a best seller. Rocking away, his eyes never left the pages long enough to notice the chair. Days later, when he finished the book, he asked, "When did we get the new chair?"   10

STEP 8: CORRECTING FAULTY PARALLELISM

Mistakes in each passage: 5
Pages explaining faulty parallelism: 74–78

a Human beings attempt to protect themselves psychologically as well as in physical ways. If someone harms you physically, you may want to fight back. To guard yourself psychologically, you may use defense mechanisms. You may be unaware of the real cause of your behavior in adjusting to a situation that is undesirable or a threat.

Three common defense mechanisms are regression, rationalization, and trying to com- 5 pensate. Regression means returning to an earlier form of behavior. A person who regresses temporarily rejects the "hard cruel world" and is seeking the greater sensitivity of childhood. Rationalization is excuse making. A student not wanting to study for a test decides that she doesn't know what to study. Compensation is a form of substitution. If a person wants a better education but cannot attend school, she may try studying on her own or to 10 learn more through experience.

b In shopping for a good used car, be cautious and have suspicion. Remember that the previous owner had some reason for getting rid of the car. The reason may have been that he wanted to buy a new car or the avoidance of costly repairs. A car that appears to have a "dirt-cheap" price may turn out to have "sky-high" costs. Remember, too, that the older a car is, the chances are better that it will soon require major repairs. If you buy an 5 older car, be sure that repair parts and service facilities are available in your area. Try to pick a used car with the lowest mileage on the odometer, the best overall condition, and that the dealer guarantees for the longest time. There are several ways to protect yourself from a falsified odometer. You should ask for a mileage disclosure statement, examine closely the condition of the vehicle, and to contact the prior owner. 10

c Almost everyone suffers from headaches occasionally. Some people say they have a headache if they feel tense, lightheaded, or have dizziness. Most often, however, people associate headache with pain. The pain may last for minutes, hours, or days.

Doctors believe that a headache is a sympton. It tells you that something is wrong in your body. You feel the pain, but others see the signs. People suffering from migraine, for 5 example, may look pale, greenish-colored, or there may be puffy eyes.

Headaches interfere with an employee's job, cause bad feelings between friends, and family life is hurt. The employee with a headache is less productive. His quick temper may upset fellow workers or annoy customers. The man or woman with migraines may irritate a spouse, frighten the children, or the disturbance of neighbors. 10

Repeated headaches are not something to hide with aspirin. If they continue, check them out. On the other hand, simple daily headaches may be relieved by lying down for a while, breathing fresh air, or the massage of neck muscles.

STEP 9: ADDING CAPITAL LETTERS

Mistakes in each passage: 10
Pages explaining capital letters: 105–111

a   Last friday while at work I began to feel sick. I asked my boss, Mr. Johnson, if he could have someone drive me to my doctor's office in danville. He responded, "here are the keys to my car." I said that I could not drive and had felt this way ever since I had been in a car accident two months before. He said, "you can drive or you can die for all I care." As a result, I had no choice but to try to drive. I got into his gremlin and began to shake and   5 cry. I finally got enough courage to start the car. I drove a block, stopped and inhaled some smelling salts, and then started again. I finally did get to dr. cooper's office, and he told me there was nothing wrong with me but a bad case of nerves from the car accident. He gave me a prescription for a tranquilizer named valium and, after getting it filled at the white cross drug store, I returned to the shop. I gave the keys back to my boss and he asked, "Are you   10 feeling better now?" I said that I was and he then said, "I'm sorry I spoke to you so hard before, but if you didn't get in a car then, you might never have driven a car again." I guess I have my boss to thank for my driving today.

b   Credit cards have been abused by both the people that own them and the companies that issue them. Some people fall into the habit of using their visa charge card for hotels and meals, their texaco card for gasoline, and other cards for department store purchases. The danger in this, as was pointed out recently on the television program *sixty minutes*, is that people can quickly reach a point where they cannot meet the monthly payments on their   5 charge cards. Such people can appreciate the warning in a texas newspaper, "it isn't buying on time that's difficult, it's paying on time." Magazines such as *time* and *newsweek* have also pointed out how quickly people lose a sense of their financial resources with charge cards. perhaps charge cards should carry a message that reads, "warning—excessive use of credit cards may be hazardous to your economic health."   10

c   I would like to introduce all of you to Dan Rossi, one of the members of our writing class. Dan has been at buckley Community College since last fall. He is majoring in math and minoring in English. Dan's hobby is space and the planets. he speaks about jupiter and Mars as though they are family. Dan subscribes to the magazine *telescope* so that he'll know the positions of the planets each month. He recently joined a group called the star   5 gazers. The members meet once a month on tuesday night at the keystone lodge on Second Street. Dan impressed the group with the pictures he took through his telescope with his nikon camera. If Dan could be anything he wanted in life, he'd like to become a professor of astronomy at a large university somewhere.

STEP 10: ADDING APOSTROPHES

Mistakes in each passage: 9
Pages explaining apostrophes: 115–123

a Working as a house packer for Jerrys moving service was an enjoyable job for me. First of all, almost no other job allows you to go into peoples houses and see at close range how they live. I encountered a lot of interesting surprises. For example, one womans house was as neat as a display room in a museum, but her basement was as littered as our towns dump. Another person had converted a bedroom into a small library. In the room 5 there were about seven rows of storage shelves, all filled with issues of magazines like *Reader's Digest* and *Redbook*. Another positive feature of the job was the sharing of some close moments. Memories often awakened as people helped pack up items from their past. Many couldnt stop talking once they started. I also liked the job because people would give me things they didnt want anymore. For instance, I received a lot of childrens 10 toys and a complete set of tools. In fact, my mothers cellar started filling with items I received from customers cellars. Final benefits of the job included plenty of snacks and sodas and handsome tips when the job was over. In summary, as a temporary job, house packing was one of my favorites.

b Mrs. Bartlett is our towns strangest person. She has lived in the big house on Pine Street, without once setting foot outside, for more years than most people remember. In her yard she keeps several cocker spaniels thatll rip your pants in a second. While the regular mailmans face is familiar to the dogs, they treat a substitute mailman like a juicy bone. In addition to the dogs, there are dozens of tame blackbirds perched in the trees. 5 Hitchcocks movie *The Birds* could have been made using her yard and house as a setting. If you are on her good side, Mrs. B. (everyones name for her) will invite you in for tea. Her gardener, Willy, watches the dogs while you hurry to the porch. Willys job, by the way, is also to serve as night watchman. Since he's almost seven feet tall, its not surprising that no prowlers have troubled the property. Inside the house, a maid named Tina will take your 10 coat. Tina is completely close-mouthed about what Mrs. B. is like. A curiosity-seekers question will get only a scowl from her and a short, ''Thats not your business.'' People in general seem to respect this answer, and no one has really challenged the right of Mrs. B. to live life her own way.

c In a small park near the center of Millville, a group of bronze statues stand in a circle. Most of them are models of the individual rich men who provided money for the towns beginning. The center of the circle is occupied by a nameless man. Citizens call him Joe because hes a symbol of the common man. Joes clothes appear tattered, but his body seems strong. His face looks tired, but his eyes look proud. Many people who have stopped 5 in the small park talk about that face when they leave. Each person Joe represents couldnt give money to the town but gave strength and sweat instead. A farmers back worked to keep the town in food. A womans hands wove, knitted, and sewed clothes. A blacksmiths arms struggled to provide horseshoes and tools. Joe's eyes must talk to passers-by. People seem to realize that without the ordinary mans help, that circle of rich men wouldnt exist. 10

STEP 11: ADDING QUOTATION MARKS

Sets of quotation marks needed in each passage: 9
Pages explaining quotation marks: 124–131

a Once when I was walking down a lonely street, three boys came up to me. Will you give us a nickel, Mister? one of them said.

Sorry, fellows, I replied, but I don't have any change to spare.

All we want are three nickels, Mister, they said over and over, and suddenly they were surrounding me.   5

Get out of my way, will you? I asked, trying to be polite. I'm in a hurry.

At this point the boy in front of me said, Stop trying to walk over me, Mister.

As I raised my arm to move him aside, I felt a hand going into my back pocket. I spun around and yelled, Give me that wallet! to the boy who had taken it. I grabbed the wallet and the coin purse snapped open, with change spilling out over the sidewalk. The boys 10 began scooping up the coins, all the time chanting, Thanks for the change, Mister. I wanted to belt one of them, but thought better of it. Instead, I put my wallet back in my pocket and walked quickly away.

b Tony and Lola were standing in the express line at the Safeway supermarket. Tony noticed that a sign above the checkout counter read, Express line—10 items or less. He then said to Lola, Look at that guy in front of us. He has at least seventeen items in his cart. He shouldn't be in the express lane.

Be quiet, said Lola, or he'll hear you.   5

I don't mind if he does hear me, Tony replied. People like that think the world owes them a favor. I hope the cashier makes him go to another lane.

The man in front of them suddenly turned around and said, Buddy, stop acting as if I've committed a federal crime. If you look more closely, you'll see I don't have more than ten separate items. See those five cans of Alpo—that counts as one item. See those four packs 10 of Twinkies—that counts as one item.

Let's just say this, Mister, Tony answered. You certainly have an interesting way of counting.

c Irene Bates, a lawyer, scowled as she gazed down at the meal that Al Bates, a house husband, had prepared. TV dinners again, Al? she asked.

Listen, Irene, I have other things to do than to plan elaborate dinners every night, Al replied.

Irene sat at her place and glared across the table. I know you have things to do, Irene 5 growled. For instance, you must rack your brain each morning to decide whether to pop frozen pancakes or frozen waffles into the toaster.

Al gritted his teeth between mouthfuls of instant potatoes. Then he asked, What's the matter, Irene? Did you have a tough day at the office?

Irene could feel her temper rumbling as she snarled, Al, I buy you nice things and take 10 you out every weekend. Why should I have to eat frozen, instant ingredients filled with artificial everything?

Al sighed. You have a point, Irene. The truth is that I'm tired of spending all my time at home. Maybe I should start looking for a job.

Let's talk about it after dinner, Irene said. I'm not sure I want any husband of mine to 5 go out and work.

STEP 12: ADDING COMMAS

Mistakes in each passage: 9
Pages explaining commas: 132–141

a Studies have found that people have a psychological need for plants. People who grew up in urban areas one survey revealed often mentioned the presence or absence of lawns in their neighborhood. One person observed "I realized how much I missed lawns and trees after living in a city where concrete covered everything."
The city is a difficult environment for plants. The soil of the city is covered mostly with   5
buildings and pavements so there is little space for plants to grow. Plants that are present are often hurt by haze smog and air pollution. Some plants are more sensitive to pollution than others; snapdragons for example do poorly in polluted air. When planners choose the kind of plants to place in urban areas they must consider the plants' chances for survival under the difficult growing conditions of city streets.   10

b As businesses look for new ways to attract customers retailing has become more specialized. In West Germany where the automobile is a central part of everyday life a new chain of gas stations is now the last word in one-stop drive-ins. Each of the gas pumps is equipped with a pushbutton grid. A customer pushes one button for a pound of butter another button for a favorite cereal and a third button for a head of fresh lettuce. Groceries   5
are loaded into the car while the gas tank is filling up and a customer pays a pretotaled bill at a drive-up window. Such specialization is also seen in the growing services provided by U.S. supermarkets. Markets now provide prescription drugs banking services and clothing for all members of the family. Because of such expanding services Americans are often able to do one-stop shopping.   10

c If you want to become a better note-taker you should keep in mind the following hints. You should attend class on a regular basis. The instructor will probably develop in class all the main ideas of the course and you want to be there to write the ideas down. Students often ask "How much should I write down?" By paying close attention in class you will probably develop an instinct for the material that you must write down. You should   5
record your notes in outline form. Start main points at the margin indent major supporting details and further indent more subordinate material. When the speaker moves from one aspect of a topic to another show this shift on your paper by skipping a line or two. A final hint but by no means the least is to write down any points your teacher repeats or takes the time to put on the board.   10

STEP 13: UNDERSTANDING COMMONLY CONFUSED WORDS

Mistakes in each passage: 12
Pages explaining commonly confused words: 162–184

a   Anyone whose stayed up all night studying for a test knows the dizzy, foggy feeling you're head gets. Although I have had this terrible experience more then once, I can't seem to discipline myself enough to avoid it. As a result, I always have to cram at exam time, and I am up righting notes and studying all threw the night.

Hear are some of the techniques I use to stay awake. I drink large doses of coffee. I   5
take No-Doz, to, if I feel that the coffee begins to lose its affect on me. And I eat candy bars, though the fewer the better, for they can upset my stomach. There are also two study methods that really help me. I take regular little brakes—about ten minutes an hour, I lie down for a few minutes' peace. Secondly, I pace back and forth when I'm studying. The principle value of this study method is that I don't get sleepy if I am physically moving 10 about. Its probably a strange sight to see me walking up and down the hallway reciting notes to myself, but the plane fact is that the technique works.

b   If your ever in a city park, take time to study the people and the life their. Accept for the sad alcoholics who pester you for money, there is a hole cast of characters to enjoy. The life of the park reaches a peak at lunchtime when the benches are usually packed. By than elderly couples have gotten out for some air. They sit closely beside each other and watch the young people walk by, alone or in pears. Its sad that the generations seldom talk 5 to each other. Lunchtime also brings the city vendors. You can hear the hot dog man announcing his presence. Pigeons and squirrels join the bustle that continues threw the noon hour. Since some people consider pigeons dirty birds, it's against their principles to feed them. But others love to watch the birds edging about, and the birds flock to these people.   10

By the time two o'clock has past, the activity has died down. The fields wear the city workers threw Frisbees have emptied. And perhaps because the whether has become too hot, the elderly people accept one another's advise and head home for the day.

c   When the weather is still cold enough, the new ice skating rink is open for business. Hal, an old man whose in his early seventies, entertains those lucky enough to catch his act. Each day around lunchtime, he starts his performance. A retired showman, Hal is quite good at recapturing his passed. Whereing a blue sweatshirt and blue pants, Hal first balances a broom on his head. Next, he goes through a hat routine. After letting his hat 5 fall too the ice, he kicks it into the air and catches it on his head. His act than begins to get more fancy. Hal must no his audience is growing. Music plays from somewhere as Hal twists and turns around the whole rink twice. He skillfully avoids a patch of lose ice in one corner. People smile at one another and Hal. Half the time there prompted to applaud, though for Hal their smiles are enough. He skates only for peace of mind and youthfulness. 10

Its getting past lunchtime now. Hal does a final lap and goes to the edge of the rink to take off his skates and put on warmer cloths. Since he is a quite man, he will not speak to anyone. But people know he will return hear to the rink the following day.

PROGRESS CHART FOR GUIDED COMPOSITIONS

Date	Step	Comments	To Do Next	Instructor's Initials
9/27		Missed -ing frag; 3 copying mistakes	1b	JL
9/27	1b	No mistakes—Good job!	2a	JL

Date	Step	Comments	To Do Next	Instructor's Initials

PART 3
Skills Reinforcement through Mastery and Editing Tests

INTRODUCTION

Part 3 consists of a series of mastery and editing tests. The mastery tests include most of the individual sentence skills covered in the book. Such tests may be used as homework assignments, supplementary activities, in-class quizzes at the end of a section, or review tests at any point during the semester. The series of editing tests measure your understanding of a variety of sentence skills. Along with the controlled composition activities in Part 2, the editing tests will reinforce many of the skills treated in Part 1 and give you practice in the essential skill of careful proofreading. A progress chart on page 281 makes it easy for you to score your answers to the mastery tests in Part 3.

Note: The mastery tests are perforated and so can be easily removed for "hand-in" assignments.

Mastery Tests

SUBJECTS AND VERBS

 MASTERY TEST 1

Draw one line under the subjects and two lines under the verbs. Cross out prepositional phrases where needed to help find subjects. (Be sure to underline all the parts of a verb. Also, remember that you may find more than one subject and one verb in a sentence.)

1. She walked barefoot down to the store.
2. That man on the corner may ask you for a quarter.
3. My son pours chocolate milk on his cereal.
4. The salad and the potatoes fed only half the guests.
5. The family played badminton and volleyball at the picnic.
6. Sara hates pickles but loves olives.
7. The nail under your rug barely missed my toe.
8. Behind all that mud you will see my son's face.
9. A solution to the problem suddenly popped into my head.
10. Will and Angie just bought matching sweatshirts.
11. I often play the stereo but almost never watch television.
12. The fallen power line jumped and sparked on the street.
13. The game has been postponed because of bad weather.
14. Betty and Robert sang together and banged on the piano.
15. We sat by a large rock, munched peanuts, and talked for hours.

SUBJECTS AND VERBS

 MASTERY TEST **2**

Draw one line under the subjects and two lines under the verbs. Cross out prepositional phrases where needed to help find subjects. (Be sure to underline all the parts of a verb. Also, remember that you may find more than one subject and verb in a sentence.)

1. I have not been eating in the cafeteria this year.
2. Those tulips make my eyes itch.
3. I may hitchhike to the Mardi Gras this year.
4. He does not often drive his car at night.
5. Carol will be studying all day for the test.
6. Strange behavior in our house is the norm rather than the exception.
7. I walked out to the garage last night and ran into a rug on the clothesline.
8. The rising tide will wash away that sand castle soon.
9. Harriet buys clothing impulsively, sends off for lots of mail-order items, and in general quickly spends her money.
10. The girls paddled their canoe across the lake and visited some boys at the camp on the other side.
11. At the top of the canyon, you can speak softly and still hear an echo.
12. The newspaper boy shouted out the headlines and soon sold all his papers.
13. The shattered glass, cracked foundations, and fallen signs throughout the city resulted from earthquake tremors.
14. They won a lifetime supply of dishwashing liquid on the game show but do not have any room for it in their house.

SENTENCE FRAGMENTS

 MASTERY TEST **1**

In the space provided, write *C* if a word group is a complete sentence; write *frag* if it is a fragment.

_____ 1. I awoke with a start last night.

_____ 2. With the loud buzzing of a mosquito in my ear.

_____ 3. Also a swelling on my arm that was just starting to itch.

_____ 4. I knew I wouldn't get back to sleep again until I had killed the mosquito.

_____ 5. I got up and turned on all the lights in the room and closed the windows.

_____ 6. To keep any more mosquitoes from coming in while the lights were on.

_____ 7. I then rooted around among the fishing rods, kite sticks, and other items in my closet.

_____ 8. Looking for the flyswatter that I knew was there.

_____ 9. The night was warm, but I felt a slight chill.

_____ 10. Also a sense of excitement and anticipation.

_____ 11. At four o'clock in the morning while the rest of the world slept.

_____ 12. A little war went on between the mosquito and me.

_____ 13. I suddenly saw it cruise by my bare leg, and I moved quickly.

_____ 14. Stepping back and swatting at it in midair.

_____ 15. I didn't know whether or not I connected.

_____ 16. So went back to my bed and waited under the light, swatter in hand.

_____ 17. I kept moving my left hand over my head and behind my neck.

_____ 18. To keep the mosquito from getting at me from behind.

_____ 19. Fifteen minutes went by, and suddenly there it was on my arm.

_____ 20. I smashed at the mosquito with my bare palm.

_____ 21. Killing it and smearing my arm with blood.

SENTENCE FRAGMENTS

MASTERY TEST 2

In the space provided, write *C* if a word group is a complete sentence; write *frag* if it is a fragment.

_____ 1.   I was seventeen on the night I died.

_____ 2.   In the spring of 1977.

_____ 3.   I had a severe case of the flu.

_____ 4.   And had spent the first three days of my illness in bed.

_____ 5.   Running a temperature between 102° and 107°.

_____ 6.   Only getting up to take care of the necessities of life.

_____ 7.   On Friday, the sixth day of my illness, rain from early morning on.

_____ 8.   The wind howled outside, the house was damp and chilly, and my fever seemed higher than ever.

_____ 9.   In late afternoon, I took my pillow and blanket into the living room.

_____ 10. Because I was sick of bed and decided I'd lie on the sofa and watch television.

_____ 11. I watched Mike Douglas and read a magazine for a while.

_____ 12. Then I must have fallen asleep.

_____ 13. When I was suddenly conscious again.

_____ 14. I was in the middle of total darkness.

_____ 15. And total silence.

_____ 16. I was absolutely terrified.

_____ 17. Because I was sure that I had died.

_____ 18. Then, somewhere in the blackness ahead of me, I saw and recognized a small, dissolving spot of light.

_____ 19. I slowly realized it was coming from the television set.

_____ 20. And that there had been a power failure.

SENTENCE FRAGMENTS

 MASTERY TEST **3**

Underline the fragment in each selection. Then make whatever change is needed to turn the fragment into a sentence.

Example   In grade school, I didn't want to wear glasses. <u>*a*nd avoided having to get them by memorizing the Snellen eye chart.</u>

1. The people at the diner save money. By watering down the coffee. Also, they use the cheapest grade of hamburger.

2. After a day at the beach. There were several itchy red spots on my arm. I must have been bitten by sandflies.

3. I enjoy routine things. Such as eating, sleeping, and watching television. Sometimes I go to the movies.

4. My brother has a large dream. To become an astronaut someday. Space fascinates him.

5. Fred recently bought a hair unit. To cover the bald spot on the back of his head.

6. Martha doesn't enjoy a steam bath. Feeling like a steamed clam. She'd rather soak in a hot tub.

7. June yelled out, "Is anyone home?" She had exciting news to tell. To anyone who was there to listen.

8. We threw out the feather-stuffed cushions. Since they were beyond mending. They had belonged to my grandmother.

9. I hated my new shoes. Because of the way they squeaked on our kitchen floor.

10. Gathering speed with enormous force. The plane was suddenly in the air. Then it began to climb sharply.

SENTENCE FRAGMENTS

 MASTERY TEST 4

Underline the fragments in each selection. Then correct the fragments using the space provided.

1. Clyde loved fire drills in school. Since they were usually the most exciting moment in the day. Everyone worked together for a change. Moving briskly and obediently. So that the building was cleared in a hurry.

   _____

   _____

   _____

   _____

2. Because the miracle soles on my shoes have never worn down. I have used the same pair for two years. Also in good condition is the shoes' fabric. Which looks like a tan suede.

   _____

   _____

   _____

   _____

3. She buys only name brands at the store. Because she feels safer with them. For example, she will buy Green Giant peas rather than A & P peas. Which are lower in price and therefore, she suspects, in quality.

   _____

   _____

   _____

   _____

4. Chatting with the meter man who had ticketed my car. I hoped to persuade him to tear up my ticket. However, when I asked him how much the fine was. His answer was, "I'm not authorized to tell you that." I gave up then. Knowing I would not have any luck with him.

   _____

   _____

   _____

   _____

RUN-ON SENTENCES

 MASTERY TEST **1**

Correct each run-on sentence with (1) a period and a capital letter or (2) a comma and a joining word. Do not use the same method of correction for each sentence.

1. Bill can crush walnuts with his teeth he is also good at biting the caps off beer bottles.

2. At one time Bill used to bend nails with his teeth this feat ended when a wise guy slipped him a tempered nail.

3. After wearing shorts all summer, Lola found it hard to return to slacks in the fall, she did not like the confining feel of the clothes against her bare skin.

4. They always had either chicken or hamburger for dinner there were no other meats they could afford any more.

5. I wondered why the time was passing so slowly then I realized my watch had stopped.

6. The long ash fell off Fred Grencher's cigar and into the cuff of his baggy pants, two minutes later his pantleg was on fire.

7. Fred's wife put out the fire quickly, she dumped a pitcher of iced tea on it.

8. The Economics I class is a bore if there were a clock in the room, I would spend all my time looking at it.

9. Everything on the menu of the Pancake House sounded delicious they wanted to order the entire menu.

10. She took a year of accounting courses in school then she decided that she wanted to go into journalism.

11. He pressed a cold washcloth against his eyes, it was the only thing that would relieve his headache.

12. Darlene washes her hair before she goes to the hairdresser she cleans her house before the cleaning woman comes.

13. The course on the history of UFOs sounded interesting, it turned out to be very dull.

14. That clothing store is a strange place to visit you keep walking up to dummies that look like real people.

15. As a little girl she pretended she was a hairdresser her closet was full of bald dolls.

RUN-ON SENTENCES

 MASTERY TEST 2

Correct each run-on sentence with (1) a period and a capital letter, (2) a comma and a joining word, or (3) a semicolon. Do not use the same method of correction for each sentence.

1. Fast cars and fast people can be lots of fun, they can also be very dangerous.
2. He enjoys watching a talk show she prefers watching a late movie.
3. No one bought the bananas tarantulas huddled in every bunch.
4. Lola does yoga exercises every morning she strongly believes in a healthy body.
5. He had forgotten to get his gas tank filled he only realized this about midnight when most stations were closed.
6. I ate too quickly at the fast-food restaurant, as a result, I now have a bad case of indigestion.
7. Silence roared in her ears she sat waiting for her date to arrive.
8. I forced myself to eat the yogurt my doctor said it would help my digestion.
9. Fred had a bad headache yesterday, moreover, his arthritis was bothering him as well.
10. Our teacher has gained a lot of weight this semester every two weeks he has opened his belt another notch.
11. I could not get a definite commitment from Beth I decided not to count on her.
12. Clyde pulled the cellophane off the cake the icing came along with it.
13. The wind tore at me as I crossed the open parking lot I thought I would be swept into the adjoining lake like a scrap of paper.
14. The plumber said he would come in the early morning he didn't arrive until midafternoon.
15. Thunder doesn't scare my cat, he always clings to my head this way.

RUN-ON SENTENCES

 MASTERY TEST 3

Correct each run-on sentence with (1) a period and a capital letter, (2) a comma and a joining word, or (3) a semicolon. Do not use the same method of correction for each sentence.

1. The storm blew up quickly it pelted the thick dust of the road with large raindrops.

2. His nose had become very cold he pressed the warm underside of his forearm against it.

3. Plants take up every available shelf space in his apartment he loves growing things.

4. She saw a young woman putting flowers on a grave in the cemetery with a stab of sorrow, she thought of her brother's recent death.

5. I have no illusions about the papers that I write for my English composition course I know they will not be put in a time capsule for future generations to read.

6. My toes are predictable as soon as I get into bed, they turn ice cold.

7. The man reached for the bottle of rye in his desk he kept the bottle there for nonmedicinal purposes.

8. Everyone in class had to read two paragraphs from the story, he sweated as his turn to read approached.

9. Martha chewed on a juicy lemon, meanwhile, mouths puckered around the room.

10. On sweltering summer afternoons, fire hydrants explode with water, dozens of young children shriek with delight.

11. The rain fell softly outside it was a relaxing day to stay indoors.

12. Saturday is the worst time to shop people mob the stores.

13. I spoke to the growling dog in a friendly way I hoped his owner would quickly appear and call him away.

14. The soup was too hot to eat I dropped in two ice cubes and cooled it off quickly.

15. Bill does not appear to be a good dart player, however, his aim becomes deadly when money is involved.

RUN-ON SENTENCES

MASTERY TEST **4**

Correct the run-on selections with (1) a period and a capital letter, (2) a comma and a joining word, or (3) a semicolon. Do not use the same method of correction for each sentence.

1. Every night Bob reads the help-wanted ads he has also signed with a local employment agency. He is determined to find a new job, his old job has given him an ulcer.

2. Confined to bed with hepatitis, I faced all the disadvantages of being ill. I had to use a bedpan, which was very unpleasant, also, I couldn't have visitors the first few days of my illness.

3. Theresa can be blunt, she does not hesitate to point out things that I don't like to hear. For example, she calls my stomach a spare tire, she says there are handlebars on my hips.

4. In paging through my high school yearbook, I saw many people I fondly remember on one page was Sue, who kept a list of all the guys she dated. On another page was Jerry he was the biggest con man in the class now he is a political candidate.

5. By halftime of the television football game, our refreshments were gone, the six-packs of beer and soda I had bought the day before were now empty cans. A half-pound wedge of sharp cheese was reduced to a few crumbs, the salty pretzels which I had bought that morning had disappeared.

6. As I neared the end of my day-long drive, I began to get sleepy, I opened all the windows to let in gusts of fresh air. Then I turned the radio on loud, I began singing along with the music.

7. The automobile is a mixed blessing, it has, for instance, made commuting long distances possible. However, parents often leave for work so early and return home so late that they see their children only on weekends, they also miss the opportunity to enjoy the space and greenery that was their reason for moving to the suburbs.

8. There is little quality in much of the merchandise that I buy, for example, yesterday I went to a well-known department store and bought a portable air conditioner. When I got it home, I opened the carton it was in, then I pulled on the long plastic carrying handle to lift the air conditioner out of the carton, almost immediately the handle snapped. I swore angrily as I realized I had purchased another inferior product.

VERB ENDINGS

 ## MASTERY TEST **1**

Add -s, -es, -d, or -ed endings where needed. Cross out the incorrect form of the verb and write the correct form above it. The context will often show you whether present or past time is involved. In a few cases, you can use either the present or past tense.

Example The job offer I just got ~~seem~~ *seems* too good to be true.

1. Joan pretend that she did not understand the teacher's question while she attempt to think of the answer.

2. After he shaves, shower, and splash on Aqua-Velva in the morning, he feel like a different person.

3. Electric lines were knock down between 2 and 3 A.M. last night; as a result, I punch in late for work.

4. I remember how my wet mittens use to steam when I place them on the living room radiator.

5. The rocking chair squeak when I use it; the noise bother me so much I can't relax.

6. When I was learning how to drive, I strip the gears on my father's car.

7. Last week I move into a five-room apartment. Yesterday, a fire destroy the contents of four of the rooms.

8. She change into comfortable clothes when she get home from a day at work.

9. The little girl in the car in front of us wave, and we wave back.

10. When he discover he lock his keys in the car, he went to a phone and call a gas station.

11. They suspect that their neighbors stole their lawn furniture until the police caught someone else.

12. He think of her when he take his work breaks during the day.

13. Tea contain so much caffeine that it stimulate some people more than coffee.

14. Bill prefer riding his motorcycle to just about any other activity.

15. The young man stand at the intersection every afternoon, selling soft pretzels to anyone who stop at the light.

VERB ENDINGS

MASTERY TEST **2**

a Rewrite the short selection below, adding present tense *-s* or *-es* verb endings wherever needed.

The man lounge on his bed and watch a spider as it crawl across the ceiling. It come closer and closer to a point directly above his head. It reach the point and stop. If it drop now, it will fall right into his mouth. For a while he try to ignore the spider. Then he move nervously off the bed.

_____

_____

_____

_____

_____

_____

b Rewrite the short selection below, adding past tense *-d* or *-ed* verb endings wherever needed.

I smoke for two years and during that time suffer no real side effects. Then my body rebel on me. I start to have trouble falling asleep, and I awaken early every morning. My stomach digest food very slowly, so that at lunchtime I seem to be still full with breakfast. My lips and mouth dry up and I sip water constantly. Also, mucus fill my lungs and I cough a lot. I decide to stop smoking when my wife insist I take out more life insurance for our family.

_____

_____

_____

_____

_____

_____

IRREGULAR VERBS

MASTERY TEST 1

Cross out incorrect forms of irregular verbs and write the correct forms directly above them.

Example   He ~~breaked~~ *broke* the video game I ~~lended~~ *lent* him.

1. The body that the men drug out of the water was a terrible thing to see.

2. A sudden banging on my door shaked me out of sleep quickly.

3. I blowed up the balloon until I was afraid it would explode in my face.

4. Life has dealed Mary a number of hard moments.

5. When the boys throwed stones at us, we decided to throw some back.

6. He begun to yell at me as soon as I walked in the door.

7. The mop that I left by the back door has froze stiff.

8. My car was stole and I had no way of getting to school.

9. The teacher did not remember that I had spoke to her about my absence.

10. Someone leaved their books in the classroom.

11. Our gym teacher speaked on physical fitness, but we slept through the lecture.

12. If the phone had rang once more, my mother would have throwed a pot at it.

13. I choosed the blueberry pie for dessert because the pudding looked watery.

14. The fishing rod slipped out of his hand and sunk to the bottom of the pond.

15. That sweater was tore yesterday.

IRREGULAR VERBS

MASTERY TEST 2

Write in the space provided the correct form of the verb shown in the margin.

write   1. Morris had _____ me five times before the letters stopped.

do   2. Did you see the damage that maniac _____ to the laundromat?

see   3. The fever made me hallucinate, and I _____ monkeys at the foot of my bed.

freeze   4. After dicing the vegetables, Sara _____ them to use later.

drink   5. I _____ at least six cups of coffee while working on the paper.

come   6. That last commercial _____ close to making me scream.

go   7. The foreman asked why I had _____ home early from work the day before.

wear   8. I should have _____ heavier clothes to the picnic.

throw   9. If I hadn't _____ away the receipt, I could have gotten my money back.

bring   10. Willy _____ his volleyball to the picnic.

become   11. I would have _____ very angry if you had not intervened.

swim   12. I was exhausted before I had _____ two lengths of the pool.

eat   13. Albert _____ four slices of almond fudge cake before he got sick.

break   14. How long has your watch been _____?

know   15. If we had _____ how the weather would be, we would not have gone on the trip.

SUBJECT-VERB AGREEMENT

 MASTERY TEST 1

Underline the correct verb in the parentheses.

Note: You will first have to determine the subject in each sentence. To help find subjects in certain sentences, you may find it helpful to cross out prepositional phrases.

1. The sweater and the books on the table (belongs, belong) to Sidney.
2. I envy people who (plays, play) a musical instrument well.
3. The plywood under your carpets (is, are) rotting.
4. Inside the bakery shop carton (is, are) your favorite pastries.
5. The shirts that you thought (was, were) too expensive are now on sale.
6. Hurrying down the street after their father (was, were) two small children.
7. Bob and Ellen (enjoys, enjoy) watching old movies but hate almost everything else on television.
8. Someone on the team (has, have) forgotten her warm-up jacket.
9. Here (is, are) the screwdriver you were looking for all weekend.
10. At the end of the long movie line (is, are) about twenty people who will not get into the next show.
11. A little time for rest and relaxation (is, are) what I need right now.
12. Neither of the coats (looks, look) good on you.
13. Janet and her mother (shops, shop) together on Thursday nights.
14. My brother and I (has, have) season tickets to the games.
15. There (is, are) about ten things I must get done today.

SUBJECT-VERB AGREEMENT

MASTERY TEST **2**

Cross out the incorrect form of the verb. Then write the correct form of the verb in the space provided. Mark the one sentence that is correct with a *C*.

1. The price of those stereo speakers have been reduced. _____

2. The marigolds that was planted yesterday were accidentally mowed over today. _____

3. Many tables at the auction was covered with very old books. _____

4. The old woman rooting through those trash baskets have refused to enter a nursing home. _____

5. Why do Jim always look so depressed on Mondays? _____

6. Bob checked with the employment agencies that was helping him look for a job. _____

7. Trucks and cars uses our street heavily since the road construction began. _____

8. The vicious gossip about our new neighbor have begun to anger me. _____

9. The plastic slipcovers on their furniture has started to turn yellow. _____

10. John and his brother play duets on the piano. _____

11. Why has Cindy and Mary quit their jobs as telephone repair persons? _____

12. One actress at the rehearsals have become ill from the heat. _____

13. The buildings across the street is all going to be demolished. _____

14. Those old coats in your closet has a dust line on their shoulders. _____

15. Archery and soccer is the new sports in our school. _____

CONSISTENT VERB TENSE

 MASTERY TEST 1

In each selection, make all verbs consistent with the first verb used. Cross out the incorrect verbs and write the correct form above.

1. As we walked through the forest, we check the trail markers that are posted periodically.

2. I wiped my hands on my trousers before I walk in for the job interview. I did not want the personnel officer to know my palms were sweating. I was very nervous, for I need the job badly.

3. They used to live in an old farmhouse but moves to an apartment to be closer to town.

4. He graduated from Maple Shade High School, attends Illinois State University, works as a carpenter for two years, and then returned to school.

5. Fred reached way down into the bread bag. He skips the first couple of pieces and grabbed one of the fresher, bigger pieces from the middle. He wants the best bread the bag had to offer.

6. The lightning struck and we watch a tree split and then burn.

7. Walter believes he is smarter than us, but we realized he just has an ego problem.

8. When we asked for the menu, the waitress looks as though we were speaking Russian.

9. Most of them enjoyed the movie, even though it turns violent in parts.

10. When I noticed the way Bill cocked his head, I realize he had an earache.

11. My eyes always close when I listened to an afternoon lecture in that class.

12. Our son and daughter clean the house and feed the dog before we arrived home.

CONSISTENT VERB TENSE

 MASTERY TEST **2**

   In each selection *one* verb must be changed so that it agrees in tense with the other verbs. Cross out the inconsistent verb and write the correct form in the space at the right.

1.   After he bought a stereo and collects a lot of records, my brother wound up listening mostly to his FM radio.   _____

2.   The little boy raced his Lionel train too fast, so that it topples off the track when rounding a curve.   _____

3.   She let her mother cut her hair until her friends began saying that her hairstyle looks very strange.   _____

4.   The air pollution is so bad that the weather bureau urges people not to exercise outside until it cleared.   _____

5.   Sandy greeted the mailman and flips quickly through the letters he handed her to see if there was a letter from her boyfriend.   _____

6.   After the truck overturned, passing motorists parked their cars on the side of the road and walk back to look at the damage.   _____

7.   The lights went out and we all jump because we were watching a horror movie at the time.   _____

8.   The wind came up quickly, knocks down a lot of dead tree branches, and blew in the front window of the bank across the street.   _____

9.   After the wolf unsuccessfully huffed and puffed at the little pig's brick house, he realizes he would have to hire a demolition contractor.   _____

10.   While in the hospital, she read lots of magazines, watched daytime television, shuffles up and down the corridor, and generally felt very bored.   _____

11.   Roger is so unaggressive that when a clerk overcharged him for an item, he pays the money and makes no complaint.   _____

12.   At our holiday dinners, people continue to stuff themselves even when it seemed obvious that they are already full.   _____

MISPLACED AND DANGLING MODIFIERS

MASTERY TEST 1

a Place an *MM* for *Misplaced Modifier* or a *C* for *Correct* in front of each sentence.

———————— 1. Bill received a bad shock fiddling with his radio.

———————— 2. Bill, while fiddling with his radio, received a bad shock.

———————— 3. While fiddling with his radio, Bill received a bad shock.

———————— 4. The suburbs nearly had five inches of rain.

———————— 5. The suburbs had nearly five inches of rain.

———————— 6. Ben ran over a dog's tail roller-skating.

———————— 7. While roller-skating, Ben ran over a dog's tail.

———————— 8. Roger visited the old house, still weak with the flu.

———————— 9. Roger, still weak with the flu, visited the old house.

———————— 10. While still weak with the flu, Roger visited the old house.

b Place a *DM* for *Dangling Modifier* or a *C* for *Correct* in front of each sentence. Remember that opening words are dangling when there is no logical subject nearby for them to modify.

———————— 1. Waiting in the icy rain for twenty minutes, the bus finally arrived.

———————— 2. Waiting in the icy rain for twenty minutes, I was relieved when the bus finally arrived.

———————— 3. Feeling like a good Samaritan, the injured bird touched him.

———————— 4. Feeling like a good Samaritan, Tom was touched by the injured bird.

———————— 5. When overweight, desserts are especially tempting.

———————— 6. When overweight, I find desserts especially tempting.

———————— 7. After a nap in my room, my mother always gave me a snack.

———————— 8. After I napped in my room, my mother always gave me a snack.

———————— 9. While depositing a check, an alarm suddenly rang in the bank.

———————— 10. While I was depositing a check, an alarm suddenly rang in the bank.

MISPLACED AND DANGLING MODIFIERS

 MASTERY TEST 2

Make the changes needed to correct the misplaced or dangling modifier in each sentence.

Examples   I asked him if he wanted to see a movie, *N* (nervously).

Because she had been
O
Out late the night before, her eyes were red and strained.

1. Hot and sizzling, we bit into the apple tarts.

2. Feeling extra lucky, the black cat didn't scare Sue.

3. While on the phone, my hot tea turned to cold tea.

4. I decided to send fewer Christmas cards out this year in October.

5. I was attacked by a stray dog working in the yard.

6. At the age of five, my mother bought me a chemistry set.

7. Piled high with dirty dishes, I hated to look at the kitchen sink.

8. I planned to start a garden while preparing dinner.

9. Marty is the guy carrying packages with curly brown hair.

10. While focusing the camera, several people wandered out of view.

11. I watched the traffic pile up bumper-to-bumper from my window.

12. Cut and infected, I took my dog to the vet.

13. Mary Ann dozed on the sand growing redder by the minute.

14. To drive the school bus, a special license is needed.

15. Christmas shoppers roam the stores trying to find just the right color sweater with aching legs.

FAULTY PARALLELISM

MASTERY TEST 1

Make the changes needed to correct the nonparallel part of each sentence.

Example   Kathy doesn't like her job or ~~the school she goes to~~. *her school*

1. My little brother asked for a bowl of cereal, a glass of orange juice, and to have a comic book to read.

2. My sister's peculiar habits include yelling in her sleep and to do her homework in the bathtub.

3. Filling out an income tax form is worse than wrestling a bear or to walk on hot coals.

4. Sally enjoys reading mystery novels and tennis.

5. I had to correct my paper for fragments, misplaced modifiers, and there were apostrophe mistakes.

6. That new blond-haired boy is both handsome and he is personable.

7. Shoppers stop in pet stores to buy a pet, to pick up pet supplies, or just looking at the animals.

8. Our children can watch television, talk on the phone, and their homework all at the same time.

9. Frustrated, annoyed, and feeling depression, Steve returned to work after the strike.

10. Jane's favorite people include those who have thoughtfulness and are unselfish.

11. His headache was so bad Mel was ready to give all his money or the confessing of all his secrets to anyone who would stop the pain.

12. I awoke from the nightmare with sweaty palms and a head that was dizzy.

FAULTY PARALLELISM

 MASTERY TEST 2

Make the changes needed to correct the nonparallel part of each sentence.

1. Victor wants to find a job with short hours and having good pay.

2. Science fiction, popular music, and to watch television sports—these are the things my father enjoys most.

3. In the evening, our family likes struggling with a giant jigsaw puzzle or to play Scrabble.

4. Pesky mosquitoes, humidity that is high, and sweltering heat make summer an unpleasant time for me.

5. Our professor warned us that he would give surprise tests, the assignment of ten papers, and allow no make-up exams.

6. My job with a travel agency paid well and excitement was provided.

7. The obnoxious hotel clerk asked me how big a room I wanted and my age.

8. Walking in the moonlight and to play the piano relax me.

9. With rings on her fingers and having bells on her toes, she can make music wherever she goes.

10. Reading comic books, finger painting, or just to stare out his bedroom window kept the boy happy while he recovered from the flu.

11. Visiting the house I grew up in and to wander through the old schoolyard brought back happy memories.

12. The course taught me how to take more effective notes, how to study a textbook chapter, and preparing for exams.

PRONOUN AGREEMENT, REFERENCE, AND POINT OF VIEW

 MASTERY TEST **1**

Underline the correct word in the parentheses.

1. I realized that each of the coaches had done (her, their) best to motivate me.
2. Either of the television sets has (its, their) good and bad features.
3. I hated my job as an office mailboy because (I, you) got taken advantage of by everyone.
4. Somebody has not been doing (his, their) share of the house cleaning.
5. I stopped my pottery classes because (it, the ceramic dust) made me sneeze.
6. If a person goes barefoot through the store, (she, they) can expect to meet a security guard.
7. We went to Disney World on a Sunday, and (you, we) had to wait an hour for every ride.
8. My cat got hold of a lollipop, and (it, the cat) got very sticky.
9. When Jack argues with Ted, (he, Ted) always gets in the last word.
10. One of my sisters has decided to separate from (her, their) husband.
11. I've been taking cold medicine and now (it, the cold) is better.
12. The ten girls in our cabin developed a closeness that (you, we) could feel grow as the summer at camp progressed.
13. Sarah was nervous about her speech, but (it, the nervousness) didn't show.
14. Everybody I spoke to is signing (his, their) name on the petition.
15. When we reached the station, (you, we) realized that the train had left.

PRONOUN AGREEMENT, REFERENCE, AND POINT OF VIEW

 MASTERY TEST **2**

Cross out the pronoun error in each sentence and write the correction above it.

Examples   Each of the boys explained ~~their~~ *his* project.

"*You are too considerate.*"
Mark told Jed, ~~he was too considerate~~.

As we watched the lightning storm, ~~you~~ *we* were in awe.

1. People will enjoy the movie if you don't mind a sentimental ending.

2. When the picture tube on the television burned out, I had to replace it.

3. Everyone who donates their time for the project will receive a free admission to the union picnic.

4. People should never go for a job interview if you don't prepare in advance.

5. If one intends to pass that chemistry course, you have to be good at math.

6. Millie told her mother she needed a new pair of shoes.

7. We wanted to see the exhibit, but you couldn't push through the crowds.

8. Everybody in the class should be ready to deliver their report by next Monday.

9. I enjoyed the volleyball match even though I'm not very good at it.

10. I wanted a free pencil sharpener, but you first had to buy $5 worth of pencils.

11. Has everybody finished their work for the committee?

12. I went fishing yesterday and caught three of them.

13. The article was about the movie, which pleased me.

14. No one whom I spoke to felt they had taken very good notes at the lecture.

15. I arrived late for the surprise quiz in English, which is why I failed it.

PRONOUN TYPES

 MASTERY TEST 1

Underline the correct word in the parentheses.

1. Harold pretended to be at ease, but he didn't fool Susan or (me, I).
2. (This, This here) tree is full of sparrows at night.
3. I believe that coat is (hers', hers).
4. Talking intimately, Ellen and (I, me) didn't see Fred walking up to our front porch.
5. The two of you must give (yourself, yourselves) another chance.
6. Al and (I, me) are equally poor in math.
7. (That there, That) car has given me nothing but frustration.
8. (Those, Them) newspapers have to be carried down to the incinerator.
9. That last hamburger on the grill is (yourn, yours) if you want it.
10. Though the furry black tarantula was in a cage, it still scared Bill and (I, me).
11. Whenever our neighbor sees me on the porch, he invites (hisself, himself) over.
12. You are getting more of your work done than (I, me).
13. Ted (hisself, himself) takes full responsibility for the accident.
14. The teacher glared at Sarah and (I, me) and then dismissed the class.
15. Though younger than (I, me), Andrea acts like my superior.
16. If it were up to (they, them), that old building would be torn down.
17. Of all the children in the class, Dora and (he, him) are the least reliable.
18. The teacher asked Chico and (I, me) to volunteer.
19. I recently met a friend of (her, hers).
20. (Those, Them) boots weren't made for walking.

PRONOUN TYPES

 MASTERY TEST 2

Cross out the incorrect pronoun in each sentence and write the correct form in the space at the right.

1. The coach's decision didn't suit Charlie or I. _____

2. Our teacher gave us homework in all of those there books. _____

3. That rabbit of yourn just became a mother again. _____

4. Joel won because he has played chess much longer than her. _____

5. Our brothers were very proud of themself when they caught the vandal at Walburn Creek. _____

6. Peter and her will be married in January. _____

7. The mailman says that Paul and me get more mail than all the other people on the block combined. _____

8. Lee never gets tired of talking about hisself. _____

9. Even the U.S. mail gets things done faster than her. _____

10. This here toothbrush looks like someone used it to scrub potatoes. _____

11. Angela and me go hiking together each fall. _____

12. The firemen theirselfs were puzzled by the source of the smoke in my basement. _____

13. Our garden is more cared for than theirs'. _____

14. The stone barely missed the children and we. _____

15. Them mosquitoes will bite you faster than you can blink your eyes. _____

16. If you want that old garden shovel, it's yours'. _____

17. I heard that her and her sister were expelled from school. _____

18. Me mother had a bad accident last month. _____

19. Juan jogs on a more regular basis than me. _____

20. The pages are torn in many of them books. _____

ADJECTIVES AND ADVERBS

 MASTERY TEST 1

Underline the correct adjective or adverb form in the parentheses.

1. For a week after his accident, Tom could not walk (steady, steadily) or think very (clear, clearly).

2. To sit (silent, silently) in a group of people will not help you make friends very (easy, easily).

3. I did so (good, well) in my first visit to the race track that I (unwise, unwisely) decided to try my luck a second time.

4. My brother was (furious, furiously) with his sister, who had teased him (cruel, cruelly).

5. Sammy spoke (truthful, truthfully) about what he'd seen, but his story sounded (odd, oddly).

6. The parents wondered (sad, sadly) why all their boys had turned out so (bad, badly).

7. If you would smile more (pleasant, pleasantly), people would treat you more (kind, kindly).

8. Waitressing was (easy, easily) for Marge, but since my coordination was not as (good, well) as hers, I was fired.

9. (Deep, Deeply) involved with the motorcycle gang, Tommy was (close, closely) to landing in jail.

10. The dark clouds formed (sudden, suddenly) and everyone made a (frantic, frantically) dash for shelter.

11. The major spoke neither (truthful, truthfully) nor (agreeable, agreeably) to the assembled members of the press.

12. (Patient, Patiently), the teacher instructed Carl, who was (painful, painfully) slow at learning.

ADJECTIVES AND ADVERBS

 MASTERY TEST **2**

Underline the correct adjective or adverb form in the parentheses.

1. The doctor said I was not (good, well) enough to travel, but I (stubborn, stubbornly) refused to listen to him.

2. The parakeet squawked (furious, furiously) until I was (wise, wisely) enough to refill his seed cup.

3. My mother spoke (blunt, bluntly) to the salesperson, and he responded (aggressive, aggressively).

4. If you'd be more (forceful, forcefully) with him, Jimmy might listen to you more (respectful, respectfully).

5. Since half a dozen doctors assured Jay he's not (insane, insanely), he's been acting far more (intelligent, intelligently).

6. If you think your decision was (right, rightly), you are likely to sleep (peaceful, peacefully) tonight.

7. Your cupcakes are so (good, well) that they are (rapid, rapidly) disappearing.

8. I feel (envious, enviously) of Marion, who has been sticking (faithful, faithfully) to her exercises.

9. Because the children sat (quiet, quietly) during the movie, their parents were (happy, happily) to buy them some ice cream.

10. Lola reacts (quick, quickly) with angry words if anyone speaks (unkind, unkindly) about Tony.

11. The spade cut (deep, deeply) and (quick, quickly) severed the tree root in half.

12. Tim is a (good, well) team player, but (unfortunate, unfortunately) he is not very talented.

ARISONS

MASTERY TEST 2

Correct the errors in comparison. Put *C* beside the one sentence that is correct.

Example   Andy considers himself $\overset{more}{\wedge}$ important~~x~~ than other people.

1.   Lenny is the most worst basketball player I have ever met.

2.   Her hair is the most shortest that she has ever worn it.

3.   That orange moth may be the beautifulest one I'll get for my collection.

4.   My boyfriend Freddy has a more handsomer smile than Robert Redford.

5.   That scruffy dog is the most meanest in our alley.

6.   Mrs. Partridge owns several banks, but she's the most stingiest person in town.

7.   Sally Ann Brant is the attractivest and most egotistical girl that Tom has ever dated.

8.   The water in Mudville is more dirtier than the name of the town.

9.   Lisa's boss assured her that she's got a more better chance of getting the promotion than anyone else.

10.   Despite the reviews, I think *The Killer Frogs* was the most entertaining movie released this year.

11.   After five hours of sunbathing, Andrea had a more severer burn than Ellen.

12.   It is importanter that you pass chemistry than that you be the highest scorer on the basketball team.

13.   His chain of doughnut stores was the successfulest business in our state last year.

14.   Earthworms are less likelier to make Willy squeamish than are spiders.

15.   The most good book I read recently was *Watership Down* by Richard Adams.

COMPARISONS

MASTERY TEST 2

Correct the errors in comparison. Put *C* beside the one sentence that is correct.

Example   Andy considers himself ^more^ important~~er~~ than other people.

1. Lenny is the most worst basketball player I have ever met.

2. Her hair is the most shortest that she has ever worn it.

3. That orange moth may be the beautifulest one I'll get for my collection.

4. My boyfriend Freddy has a more handsomer smile than Robert Redford.

5. That scruffy dog is the most meanest in our alley.

6. Mrs. Partridge owns several banks, but she's the most stingiest person in town.

7. Sally Ann Brant is the attractivest and most egotistical girl that Tom has ever dated.

8. The water in Mudville is more dirtier than the name of the town.

9. Lisa's boss assured her that she's got a more better chance of getting the promotion than anyone else.

10. Despite the reviews, I think *The Killer Frogs* was the most entertaining movie released this year.

11. After five hours of sunbathing, Andrea had a more severer burn than Ellen.

12. It is importanter that you pass chemistry than that you be the highest scorer on the basketball team.

13. His chain of doughnut stores was the successfulest business in our state last year.

14. Earthworms are less likelier to make Willy squeamish than are spiders.

15. The most good book I read recently was *Watership Down* by Richard Adams.

COMPARISONS

 MASTERY TEST 1

Add to each sentence the correct form of the word in the margin.

hard 1. My science exam was the _____ of my two tests.

old 2. Mr. McMurry was the _____ of all the used car dealers at the convention.

dark 3. Your yellow bedroom walls are _____ than a New York City cab.

little 4. That is the _____ of my many worries.

young 5. Mrs. Martin's husband was the _____ man at the company Christmas party.

pleasant 6. Barbara is the _____ of the two Grencher sisters.

good 7. Some people believe that everything happens for the _____ in life.

strong 8. Jerry is probably the _____ player on the crew team.

uncomfortable 9. Her sofa is one of the _____ pieces of furniture that I have ever sat on.

bad 10. That barley and hot dog concoction is by far her _____ creation yet.

good 11. Joe always does a _____ job on his compositions than Jerry does.

rude 12. Anne is the _____ of the three Clemens children.

bitter 13. The coffee always tastes _____ when I, rather than Brian, make it.

wonderful 14. Even though the painting was hideous, I told Bobby it was his _____ work yet.

boring 15. Of all the new television shows I have watched this year, that comedy is the _____.

CAPITAL LETTERS

 ## MASTERY TEST **1**

Correct the capital letter mistakes in the following sentences. Add or omit capital letters, as needed.

Example We don't like ~~T~~*t*raveling during ~~n~~*N*ew ~~y~~*Y*ear's weekend.

1. I asked the Clerk, ''do you have any italian olives?''

2. When the company transferred his mother to the west coast, he wound up as a Student at beverly hills high school.

3. I drove ed to the auto shop to get the Estimate on repairs to his 1970 thunderbird.

4. ''because of the bad weather conditions,'' said the manager, ''our Store will be closing at four o'clock.''

5. I can't decide whether to buy the boots I saw at butler's or to see if I can find a better pair at Roger's on third street.

6. I am so Brainwashed by Advertising that I always want to buy both skippy and peter pan peanut butter.

7. Cindy works at the farmers' national bank in williamstown on mondays, wednesdays, and fridays.

8. He got low grades in his Math Courses but straight A's in English and spanish.

9. The third-grade Children sang ''jingle bells'' during the school christmas ceremony.

10. The epitaph on W. C. Fields' Tombstone reads, ''on the whole, I'd rather be in Philadelphia.''

11. Because we were out of listerine mouthwash, i gargled using ordinary Salt Water instead.

12. That woman reminds me of the person who played the mean witch in *the wizard of Oz*.

CAPITAL LETTERS

 MASTERY TEST 2

Correct the capital letter mistakes in the following sentences. Add or omit capital letters, as needed.

1. Our neighbor, mr. Charles Reynolds, accidentally backed into our Maple tree today.

2. The restaurant refuses to serve people dressed in Jeans.

3. "Last week I bought Adidas sneakers and a jogging sweatshirt," Janie said. "But my Asthma is so bad that my doctor won't let me start running."

4. Joe and Leslie love Kentucky, but we prefer north or south Carolina.

5. The statue in boyle's square is supposed to represent all the soldiers killed in the civil war.

6. I hired a Lawyer after my VW Rabbit was scraped by a united parcel delivery truck.

7. If you've ever worked in a Nursing Home, you know the drawbacks of working there on saturdays or sundays.

8. Lisa complained, "this pearl bracelet I bought at woolworth's has started to turn green."

9. Although howard no longer lives on third street, he likes to return there on Weekends to visit old friends.

10. I don't like Instant Coffee, but that's all they serve at the pta meetings on wednesday nights.

11. After I flunked math 101, I decided not to become an Engineer.

12. The united mine workers rejected the contract offer because they felt the Health benefits were inadequate.

APOSTROPHE

MASTERY TEST 1

Underline the word in each sentence that needs an ' or an '*s*. Then write the word correctly in the space at the right.

1. I walked casually around the parking lot, trying to conceal the fact that Id no idea where I left my car. _____

2. My brother CB was stolen by vandals who broke his car window. _____

3. I think that Marie diet has only helped her gain weight. _____

4. When the students complained about the teacher assignment, he said they would never make it through college. _____

5. Martha ignored the police officer siren and ended up in jail last night. _____

6. No one in our family looks forward to my sister tuna salad. _____

7. Sally typing might improve if she would cut an inch off her nails. _____

8. The man said his name was Elmer Fudd, but I didnt believe him. _____

9. I am amazed by my sister perfect recall of how much she has weighed for any important social event of her life. _____

10. Our tough sheriffs campaign promise is that he will replace the electric chair with electric bleachers. _____

11. Dick habit of sucking in spaghetti noodles makes him unpleasant to eat with. _____

12. My friend warned me about Robert false charm. _____

13. He entered the clubs running marathon. _____

14. A ride in my parents old station wagon is like a ride on a roller coaster. _____

15. Vinnie has been on Hal blacklist since she revealed he sleeps with his socks on. _____

APOSTROPHE

 MASTERY TEST 2

Add an ' or an 's where needed.

1. Freds day started going sour when he noticed that everyone in the doughnut shop had gotten fatter doughnuts than he did.

2. The animals footsteps were all around our tent.

3. While the team was in the showers, someone tied all the players sneakers together.

4. If youll check the noise in the attic, Ill stand by the phone in case you scream.

5. Tony would rather visit the dentist than eat one of his brothers meals.

6. Alans hamster has gotten fat from eating lettuce.

7. Despite the driver warning that smoking was not allowed, several people lit up in the back of the bus.

8. When I sat on the fender of Ted car, he stared at me until I slid off.

9. Isnt it your turn to give the Saint Bernard his bath?

10. After a hard day work, I get into the shower to wash off the grime.

11. Joan hair began to fall out two days after she dyed it.

12. Her husband beauty, more than his brains, is what first attracted her to him.

13. Well meet your hockey team at the pond.

14. If youre thinking of entering the contest, youll need to pay a $10 admission fee.

15. The womens room in that service station is always clean.

QUOTATION MARKS

 MASTERY TEST 1

Place quotation marks where needed.

1. Abraham Lincoln once wrote, My father taught me to work. He did not teach me to love it.

2. A friend of mine used to say, There's nothing wrong with you that a few birthdays won't cure.

3. After I've run in the morning, said Lola, there's a smoky fragrance to my skin.

4. Fire torpedoes! the captain shouted. Then abandon ship!

5. The food critic wrote, The best test of a fast-food hamburger is to eat it after all the trimmings have been taken off.

6. Well, this is just fine, she mumbled. The recipe calls for four eggs and I have only two.

7. Murphy's law states, Whatever can go wrong, will.

8. After Bill pulled the flip-top cap off the can, he noticed that the label said, Shake well before drinking.

9. Eating Ann's chili, he whispered, is a breathtaking experience.

10. How would you feel, the teacher asked the class, if I gave you a surprise quiz today?

11. Judy Collins' song, Clouds, is one of my all-time favorites.

12. The school I went to was very tough, the comedian said. If you got into the lunchroom and out alive, you were given a diploma.

13. A recent cover story in *Newsweek* was titled Cubans in Africa.

14. The tag on the pillow read, Do not remove under penalty of law.

15. After I finished James Thurber's story, The Secret Life of Walter Mitty, I started to write a paper on it.

QUOTATION MARKS

MASTERY TEST **2**

Place quotation marks or underlines where needed.

1. You know, Bill said to the bartender, there are times in my life when I kind of panic. I want to go to bed and never get out again.

2. When I know I have a long day ahead, Judy said, I always have trouble sleeping well the night before.

3. I told the dentist that I wanted Novocain. He said, Don't be a sissy. A little pain won't hurt you. I told him that a little pain might not bother him, but it would bother me.

4. Immanuel Kant once wrote: Two things fill me with constantly increasing admiration and awe the longer and more earnestly I reflect on them—the starry heavens without and the moral law within.

5. The slogan we learned in school was, Do unto others as you would have them do unto you. The slogan that I now have on the wall of my study reads, Remember the golden rule: he who has the gold makes the rules.

6. When Clyde got home from work, he said, At times I feel I'm in a rat race and the rats are winning. Charlotte consoled him by saying that everyone feels like that from time to time.

7. One of the questions in Sharon's American literature test was to identify the book in which the following line appears: You don't know about me without you have read a book by the name of The Adventures of Tom Sawyer; but that ain't no matter.

8. In a Consumer Reports article titled What's Inside Frozen Pot Pies? the editors write, The filth we discovered is not a health hazard. But it's unpleasant to discover that these pies contain big and little parts of aphids, flies, moths, weevils, cereal beetles, and rodent hairs.

9. Sharon based her English paper on two lines from George Eliot's novel, Middlemarch: If we had a keen vision and feeling of all ordinary human life, it would be like hearing the grass grow and the squirrel's heart beat, and we should die of that roar which lies on the other side of silence. As it is, the quickest of us walk about well wadded with stupidity.

10. In her book Adolescent Development, Elizabeth B. Hurlock suggests why activities such as drinking and smoking marijuana attract adolescents. She writes, The status value of some forbidden pleasures is so great that adolescents who feel socially insecure and anxious to improve their status in the peer group may engage in them to excess. Another reason Hurlock gives for the appeal of forbidden activities is that the very fact they are forbidden makes them desirable.

COMMA

 MASTERY TEST **1**

Add commas where needed. Place a *C* beside the one sentence that needs no comma.

1. The hot dogs that we bought tasted delicious but they reacted later like delayed time bombs.

2. The loan shark may send a message to you a message you won't like unless you pay your money soon.

3. The old graveyard was filled with vampires werewolves crooked politicians and other monsters.

4. When she got back from the supermarket she realized she had forgotten to get cereal grape jelly and Drano.

5. Because it was the thing to do Tony pretended he had dated a lot of women when he talked with the guys.

6. Clyde had no idea what his weight was but Charlotte always knew exactly how much she weighed.

7. Navel oranges which Cheryl as a little girl called belly-button oranges are her favorite fruit.

8. The bedspread handwoven and handsewn was her favorite possession.

9. "I wish there was some pill" Chuck said "that would give you the equivalent of eight hours' sleep in four hours."

10. She loves to spend her afternoons paging through a mail-order catalog and watching soap operas on television.

11. Guys looking for pick-ups went to Rexy's Tavern and they found some women also looking for pick-ups.

12. Fred chose what he thought was the shortest waiting line at the post office but suddenly the man in front of him began pulling a number of tiny packages out of his pocket.

13. If you don't stay away from that raspberry patch you'll probably be stung by yellow jackets.

14. The child's eyes glowed at the sight of the glittering tree colorful packages and stuffed stockings.

15. "Before you crack open another walnut" Tony's father warned him "remember that we're going to be eating shortly."

COMMA

MASTERY TEST 2

Add commas where needed. Also, cross out any unnecessary commas.

1. I remember how with the terrible cruelty of children we used to make fun of the retarded girl who lived down the street.

2. After drinking five glasses of orange juice, and eating some bacon and eggs I began to recover from my hangover.

3. On Friday my day off I went to get a haircut.

4. Even though King Kong was holding her at the very top of the Empire State Building Fay Wray kept yelling at him "Let me go!"

5. Cindy attended class for four hours worked at the hospital for three hours and studied at home for two hours.

6. She was not happy about having to drop the math course but there were too many other demands, being made on her time.

7. If you have a bad cold Bob you shouldn't play in the game tonight.

8. The aliens in the science fiction film visited our planet in peace but we greeted them with violence.

9. George and Ida sat down to watch the Rams game with crackers sharp cheese salty beer pretzels and two frosty bottles of beer.

10. A jar of chicken noodle soup which was all he had in the refrigerator did not make for a very satisfying meal.

11. Frank does not like, cooked carrots and he cares even less for lima beans.

12. A neat appearance, warm smile, and positive attitude, will make an employer respond to you.

13. Although he is normally a careful, and defensive driver he drives recklessly if he is in a bad mood.

14. According to rumors, our school janitor, has made himself a millionaire through real estate investments.

15. Tinkerbell Peter Pan's little friend was acted in the school play by a little girl carrying a flashlight.

COMMA

 MASTERY TEST 3

Add commas where needed.

1. Clyde and Charlotte took Paul their son to see Walt Disney's *Bambi*.

2. The film covers the birth of Bambi the loss of his mother his escape from a forest fire and his growth to young fatherhood.

3. Featured characters include Thumper the rabbit; Flower the skunk; and Feline Bambi's loved one.

4. Just before the film started Clyde decided to get a giant box of Jujyfruits.

5. He loved the varied flavors of the sticky gooey candy but he didn't like the way the candy stuck to his teeth.

6. "Charlotte" he asked "do you want anything?"

7. "Get me a box of popcorn Clyde" she replied.

8. At the lobby's busy refreshment counter Clyde waited to buy popcorn Jujyfruits and a box of chocolate-covered raisins.

9. While he was standing there the house lights dimmed the stage curtains opened and the movie started.

10. When he reentered the theater Clyde paused briefly for his eyes had trouble adjusting to the dark.

11. He then moved uncertainly down the aisle almost stumbling and slipped into the empty aisle seat that he thought was his.

12. He rested his left hand which held the popcorn in the lap of the woman he assumed was Charlotte.

13. With his right hand Clyde pried open the box of Jujyfruits and popped three of the chewy goodies into his mouth.

14. They were lemon cherry and licorice in flavor.

15. He bit down hungrily on all three of them and they all stuck like glue to his teeth.

16. Meanwhile the woman next to Clyde pleased by the touch of his left hand leaned closer and nestled her head on his shoulder.

17. As Clyde's eyes grew accustomed to the dark he became aware suddenly of an elderly man standing near him in the aisle.

18. "Excuse me sir" the man said. "You're in my seat aren't you?"

19. Hearing the man's voice the woman's head lifted from Clyde's shoulder.

20. When the woman saw Clyde's face rather than her husband's she screamed.

21. ''I'm really sorry madam'' Clyde said.

22. He jumped up and ran down the aisle and then he saw Charlotte's hand waving at him.

23. When he sat down and told her what had happened they both squirmed in their seats to keep from laughing out loud.

24. Paul who was only four years old didn't know why they were laughing.

25. However the little boy soon picked up their mood.

26. He began to squeal gurgle and laugh with pleasure.

27. After quieting Paul down Clyde and Charlotte settled back happily to watch the movie.

28. When *Bambi* was over Charlotte asked Clyde to point out the elderly couple to her.

29. However the couple was nowhere to be seen and Clyde guessed they must have left quickly to avoid embarrassment.

30. ''Clyde you dope I don't know how I put up with you'' Charlotte laughed.

COMMONLY CONFUSED WORDS

 MASTERY TEST 1

These sentences check your understanding of a variety of commonly confused words. Underline the correct word in the parentheses.

1. As he (passed, past) by the church, he (though, thought) of the Sunday mornings he had spent (there, their, they're) in the (passed, past).

2. (Being that, Since) "Stormy (Weather, Whether)" is her favorite song, I (should of, should have) gotten her an album with that song on it.

3. My dog lost (its, it's) tail when run over by a truck that had lost (its, it's) (brakes, breaks).

4. (Irregardless, Regardless) of what her coworkers think, Susan always (wears, wheres) (plain, plane) (clothes, cloths) to work.

5. (Its, It's) obvious why (know, no) one is eating the cheese; (there, their, they're) frightened by (its, it's) unusual smell.

6. Pete (could of, could have) used the money, but he refused to (accept, except) the check his parents offered him.

7. Morris can't stand to (hear, here) (advice, advise). He lives by the (principal, principle), "If I make my own decisions, I have only myself to praise or blame."

8. Kevin and Judy have to make (there, their, they're) handwriting neater and more legible if (there, their, they're) after good grades.

9. Just (among, between) us, I'd (advice, advise) you not to take Dear Abby's (advice, advise) as gospel.

10. That lion over (there, their, they're) clawed at the attendant cleaning (its, it's) cage.

11. I (would of, would have) tried out for that role, but the director told me that she had (all ready, already) filled the part.

12. (Being that, Because) (there, their, they're) are only (to, too, two) days left to take advantage of (there, their, they're) special offer, you (can hardly, can't hardly) afford to wait any longer.

13. (Its, It's) hard to deny the fact that (there, their, they're) are many fools in the world.

14. Lori was (among, between) the ten best salespeople in the company last year, right (among, between) Terry and Dick in volume of sales.

15. The (affect, effect) of the medication is that many of my symptoms have disappeared.

COMMONLY CONFUSED WORDS

 MASTERY TEST 2

Cross out the mistakes in usage in each sentence. Write the correct words in the spaces provided. The number of spaces tells you how many corrections to make in each sentence.

1. Beside the twins, the Forsters have three other children—more then anyone else on the block.

   _____   _____

2. Larry should of realized by now that the less he worries, the less headaches he'll have.

   _____   _____

3. Its to bad that the pair of you didn't apply for an job their.

   _____   _____   _____   _____

4. Nothing was further from his mind then the possibility of excepting the advise I had given him.

   _____   _____   _____

5. Irregardless of what you say, I believe we could of learned our collie how to be a good watchdog.

   _____   _____   _____

6. I pursue both rug making and gardening: the latter allows me to be creative and the former allows me to enjoy the piece of nature.

   _____   _____   _____

7. I'll be quiet surprised if the promise of a delicious desert doesn't make my little sister agree to be quiet.

   _____   _____

8. Being that its sinking into the water, their must be to many people in the boat.

   _____   _____   _____   _____

9. The car past me at 90 miles a hour, but I new it wouldn't get past the speed trap that is write down the road.

   _____   _____   _____   _____

10. Weather or not I take that coarse depends on whose teaching it and how much righting is required.

   _____   _____   _____   _____

WORDINESS

MASTERY TEST **1**

Rewrite the following sentences, omitting needless words.

1. The main point that I will try to make in this paper is that our state should legalize and permit gambling.

   _____

2. Owing to the fact that I was half an hour late, I did not do well on the test and failed it.

   _____

3. In my opinion, our neighbor has more types of flowers for you to look at than you would see in the county park.

   _____

   _____

4. Jay always keeps his hand covered over his eyes, so that his teacher in school can't tell he's dozing when she looks at him.

   _____

   _____

5. Those two spiders, to be exact, have lived in that corner over there since we moved ourselves into the apartment.

   _____

   _____

6. Playing around with and having fun with his basketball in the living room, Jerry knocked over a bowl of nuts so that they scattered all over the floor.

   _____

   _____

7. After a great deal of much driving practice with the family car, my sister said she felt she was ready and prepared to take her driver's test.

   _____

   _____

8. The fact of the matter why I don't watch television is there are too many television commercials to look at.

   _____

WORDINESS

 MASTERY TEST 2

Rewrite the following sentences in the space provided, omitting needless words.

1. You can tell by looking at her that she's been outside in the fresh air because her cheeks are a red color in tone.

_____

2. One reason, of course, for visiting the library is the borrowing of books that you want to use.

_____

3. If you are out on the job market looking for a job, you should have professional help to assist you in your search to find employment.

_____

4. The newsstand has available a wide selection of printed matter—books, magazines, and newspapers—that people who are interested in them can buy.

_____

5. After the storm ended, children listened eagerly to the radio in order to see if they could hear any news about school closings.

_____

6. When the motorcycle roared by the house with a loud noise, I was so angry I wanted to get on the phone and call the police to complain.

_____

7. At this point in time I have not yet reached a decision about whether I will return to school next year.

_____

8. Due to the fact that Midge's car refused to start up, she had to take public transportation by bus to her place of work.

_____

PROGRESS CHART FOR MASTERY TESTS

This chart lets you keep a numerical record of your performance on the mastery tests. To determine your score for a given test, first count the number of your mistakes. (Each incorrect answer is a mistake; in a sentence where two answers are required, you may have two mistakes.) Multiply the number of your mistakes by the number shown in the chart. Then subtract the resulting figure from 100.

Test	Number of Mistakes		Score
Subjects and Verbs 1	_____ × 3 =	_____ 100 − _____ =	_____ %
Subjects and Verbs 2	_____ × 3 =	_____ 100 − _____ =	_____ %
Sentence Fragments 1	_____ × 5 =	_____ 100 − _____ =	_____ %
Sentence Fragments 2	_____ × 5 =	_____ 100 − _____ =	_____ %
Sentence Fragments 3	_____ × 5 =	_____ 100 − _____ =	_____ %
Sentence Fragments 4	_____ × 5 =	_____ 100 − _____ =	_____ %
Run-on Sentences 1	_____ × 6 =	_____ 100 − _____ =	_____ %
Run-on Sentences 2	_____ × 6 =	_____ 100 − _____ =	_____ %
Run-on Sentences 3	_____ × 6 =	_____ 100 − _____ =	_____ %
Run-on Sentences 4	_____ × 6 =	_____ 100 − _____ =	_____ %
Verb Endings 1	_____ × 3 =	_____ 100 − _____ =	_____ %
Verb Endings 2	_____ × 5 =	_____ 100 − _____ =	_____ %
Irregular Verbs 1	_____ × 6 =	_____ 100 − _____ =	_____ %
Irregular Verbs 2	_____ × 6 =	_____ 100 − _____ =	_____ %
Subject-Verb Agreement 1	_____ × 6 =	_____ 100 − _____ =	_____ %
Subject-Verb Agreement 2	_____ × 6 =	_____ 100 − _____ =	_____ %
Consistent Verb Tense 1	_____ × 6 =	_____ 100 − _____ =	_____ %
Consistent Verb Tense 2	_____ × 8 =	_____ 100 − _____ =	_____ %
Misplaced and Dangling Modifiers 1	_____ × 5 =	_____ 100 − _____ =	_____ %
Misplaced and Dangling Modifiers 2	_____ × 6 =	_____ 100 − _____ =	_____ %
Faulty Parallelism 1	_____ × 8 =	_____ 100 − _____ =	_____ %

Test	Number of Mistakes		Score
Faulty Parallelism 2	_____ × 8 =	_____ 100 − _____	= _____ %
Pronoun Agreement, Reference, and Point of View 1	_____ × 8 =	_____ 100 − _____	= _____ %
Pronoun Agreement, Reference, and Point of View 2	_____ × 6 =	_____ 100 − _____	= _____ %
Pronoun Types 1	_____ × 5 =	_____ 100 − _____	= _____ %
Pronoun Types 2	_____ × 5 =	_____ 100 − _____	= _____ %
Adjectives-Adverbs 1	_____ × 4 =	_____ 100 − _____	= _____ %
Adjectives-Adverbs 2	_____ × 4 =	_____ 100 − _____	= _____ %
Comparisons 1	_____ × 6 =	_____ 100 − _____	= _____ %
Comparisons 2	_____ × 6 =	_____ 100 − _____	= _____ %
Capital Letters 1	_____ × 2 =	_____ 100 − _____	= _____ %
Capital Letters 2	_____ × 3 =	_____ 100 − _____	= _____ %
Apostrophe 1	_____ × 6 =	_____ 100 − _____	= _____ %
Apostrophe 2	_____ × 6 =	_____ 100 − _____	= _____ %
Quotation Marks 1	_____ × 3 =	_____ 100 − _____	= _____ %
Quotation Marks 2	_____ × 3 =	_____ 100 − _____	= _____ %
Comma 1	_____ × 4 =	_____ 100 − _____	= _____ %
Comma 2	_____ × 2 =	_____ 100 − _____	= _____ %
Comma 3	_____ × 4 =	_____ 100 − _____	= _____ %
Commonly Confused Words 1	_____ × 2 =	_____ 100 − _____	= _____ %
Commonly Confused Words 2	_____ × 3 =	_____ 100 − _____	= _____ %
Wordiness 1	_____ × 3 =	_____ 100 − _____	= _____ %
Wordiness 2	_____ × 3 =	_____ 100 − _____	= _____ %

Note: In calculating figures, decimals have been rounded off to the next *lowest* whole number. The number given for "Quotation Marks" assumes two mistakes are possible for each complete set of quotation marks. The number given for "Wordiness" assumes there are roughly three areas of wordiness in each sentence.

Editing Tests

Find and correct the sentence-skills mistakes in the following selections. The kind and number of errors have been indicated in each case.

A good way to proceed in correcting each selection is first to read through it quickly. Place a light check mark at those spots where mistakes seem to occur. Then read the selection more carefully, looking for the skill mistakes listed above the selection. After correcting the mistakes for a particular skill, cross the skill off the opening list.

1 1 fragment   1 run-on sentence

One game we played as little boys was to go down to the railroad tracks. And see who could walk farthest on the rail without falling off. Once we walked over a railroad trestle a train came five minutes after we got across.

2 1 fragment   1 run-on sentence

Helen couldn't decide whether to stay home that evening. Or to go out and try to meet a guy. Going out required too much preparation, she would have to iron a blouse and wash her hair.

3 1 fragment   1 missing capital letter
1 run-on sentence   1 missing apostrophe

Right before easter, Clyde bought his mother some roses. And planted them in her back yard. Each year he got a different color, the garden was now filled with roses of many colors. Clyde father had begun this special tradition before he died.

4 1 fragment   1 missing -s ending on a noun
1 run-on sentence   1 missing -ed ending

Often when I was called on in school. My brain just stopped working. I got decent grades on written test. But my marks for oral work were very low, my teacher seem angry that I never had anything to say.

5 2 fragments
   1 subject pronoun mistake
3 missing capital letters
2 missing quotation marks

My brother and me were always different. When we were little boys. Once my parents took us to see Santa Claus. Who was at the local department store instead of the north pole. My brother asked Santa for a red wagon and world peace. I asked Santa, how much money do you make?

6 1 fragment
   1 inconsistent verb tense
2 missing quotation marks
1 missing comma to set off a quotation

In the first class meeting, the instructor said It is your decision to come to class or not to come. As a result, low class attendance. After the midsemester exam, which half the class fails, the instructor announced that class attendance would be required from that point on.

7 1 fragment
   1 run-on sentence
1 missing capital letter
1 missing apostrophe

Fred poured a little water in the heinz catsup bottle. Then shook it to loosen the last bit of catsup at the bottom. He couldnt stand veal cutlet without catsup, it was like eating a baked potato without butter and salt.

8 1 missing apostrophe
   1 missing -*ed* ending
1 mistake in agreement between a pronoun
   and the word it refers to
2 missing commas between items in a series

The cigarette ashtray in Bills car was overflowing with ashes matchsticks and wooden Popsicle sticks. One day Bill left a lighted cigarette in the tray and all the debris, especially the Popsicle sticks, start on fire. Air from the window vent fanned the blaze. Bill had to pour half a Coke on them to put out the fire.

9 2 misplaced modifiers
   3 irregular verb mistakes
2 misspelled words

One of the strangest experiences of my life was the time I on the top of my arm fell asleep. I must have cut off all the blood cirkulation to the arm. When I hours later woke up, my arm was completely numb. In fact, when I sat up in bed, the arm seemed detached from my body. I begun to rub it, and soon I feeled a ''pins and needles'' sensation. After another couple of minutes of rubbing, the arm had became again a normel part of my body.

10 1 dangling modifier
2 fragments
1 unclear pronoun reference

1 dropped *-ly* ending (adverb mistake)
1 subject pronoun mistake
2 missing capital letters

Cindy had a weird but fascinating dream last night. Simply by turning the dial on her magical television set. She could see what anyone in the world was doing at the time. On one channel she could see her English teacher. He was sitting quiet by himself in a small room. Watching a late movie. On another channel, she could see the President of the United States fast asleep with his wife in a white 5 house bedroom. Turning to another channel, the first boyfriend Cindy ever had was on screen. A young woman and him were having a conversation at a singles bar, which seemed very intimate.

11 3 fragments
2 run-on sentences

2 missing commas between items in a series
1 nonparallel structure

When I was a child, my brother took advantage of my fear of ghosts. I would be taking a shower and my brother would open the door turn out the lights and start ''wooing'' until I began to cry. Then he would almost suffocate from laughing. Other times, he would make moaning sounds through the keyhole of my bedroom door. Rattling the doorknob as well. One night he did the worst thing of all he took 5 out the main fuse in the fuse box and all the lights in the house went out. No one was home at the time, I was so petrified that at first I couldn't move. But I sure did move when he came running down the hall with a white sheet over his head. Screaming at the top of his lungs. He must have chased me around the house for almost a half hour until I finally stopped, grabbed an apple out of the fruit basket, 10 and was throwing it at him as hard as I could. I missed him but not the kitchen window. When my parents got home, I told them what had happened, and my brother got spanked. But thanks to him, even today I can't walk down a dark street. Without thinking there is someone behind me.

12 1 fragment
2 run-on sentences
1 missing apostrophe
4 missing capital letters

2 missing quotation marks
1 missing comma to set off a quotation
2 missing commas to set off an interruptor
in a sentence

I remember a recent event that made me angry. It happened last saturday afternoon. When my wife, my little girl, and I went out to lunch. We were driving down madison avenue when, all of a sudden, a tan Labrador retriever darted out in front of the car, I tried to stop but there wasn't enough time. The dog though

hit by the car got up and ran down the street. Looking back, I could see some 5
people standing in front of a house on the corner. I turned my car around, went
back, and asked the people if the dog belonged to them. All at once, one man went
into a rage. He shouted You maniac. You almost killed my dog. Then he started
coming toward me. With this, I pulled away. The reason his action made me angry
was that I had tried to stop my car in time. I had applied my brakes I had attempted 10
to find the dogs owner. Finally, to make matters worse, and me even more frustrated
and angry, I found after I got home that the bumper on my 1974 buick was dented.

13 2 fragments
   3 run-on sentences
   2 missing apostrophes
   2 missing quotation marks

2 missing commas after introductory
   words
2 missing commas between items in a
   series
1 nonparallel structure

While shopping one morning, I passed a weird-acting character on the street.
He was sitting on a car fender rocking violently up and down. I was puzzled and,
along with several other people, stopped and turned after I passed him. In order
to stare. The man suddenly reached into his back pocket. And took out a small
packet containing miniature tools. With a screwdriver in his right hand he leaned 5
over while still sitting on the fender and began to unscrew the license plate on the
rear of the car, soon the license plate fell clattering to the ground. The man then
put his screwdriver away and just sat on the bumper for a minute, perhaps thinking
of what to do next. Then, without using his hands but getting enormous thrust
from his legs, he leaped to the sidewalk. He ran over to the open-air fruit stand 10
nearby grabbed a banana and to start eating it with the skin still on. A woman
working at the stand shouted, Get out of here, you wild man. However, she didnt
try to take the banana away from him. The man suddenly seemed to become aware
of the crowd watching him he heard someone laughing, and he began to laugh just
like them, but louder. At the same time, his eyes filled with tears, I suddenly felt 15
ashamed and guilty about watching him. As I turned and walked away I heard the
mans terrible laughing and sobbing sounds echo behind me.

14 4 fragments
   2 missing apostrophes
   5 missing capital letters
   6 missing quotation marks

1 missing *-s* ending on a verb
4 missing *-d* or *-ed* endings
2 mistakes in verb tense
1 subject pronoun mistake

Steve Miller is a stingy friend of mine. When he comes to work, he never
bring any money. But always asks me if I have a nickel or a dime to lend him so

he can buy a mounds bar or a small bag of potato chips. One time he asked me to lend him a dollar, so he could buy a chance from another employee for a thanksgiving turkey. I refuse at first, but he practically begged me. Resulting in my 5 giving him the money. As I expected, he never offer to return my dollar, and when Id remind him, he'd say, Oh yeah, I'll get it to you soon, but he never did. Another example of Steves stinginess was the time he and me and two of our friends decided to go out and eat during our lunch hour at the red rooster, a new restaurant. Steve suggest that we take his car, and as we were driving to the res- 10 taurant, he said his gas tank was empty. I couldn't believe that he would have the nerve to ask us for gas money. With only a total of eight miles to the restaurant and back. However, he pulls into an exxon gas station, and cheerfully says that a dollar for gas from each of us would be fine. I was really fuming. Because I could see that his gas tank was at least a quarter full. After we pulled into the 15 restaurant parking lot, Steve inform us that he would wait in the car while the rest of us ate. I asked him with a hard voice, Don't you have any money? Steve's reply was, Yeah, but I'm not going to spend it eating out when I can go home and eat for nothing.

Note: The kind and number of sentence skills mistakes are not identified in the remaining passages. Find and correct the mistakes. Your instructor may ask you to rewrite the selections that require extensive editing.

15 The worst thing that happen to me recently was when I decide to play a quick game of touch football with some friends. I felt good physically when the game was over. The next morning however I learned that I was not in the shape I thought I was. When I tried to get out of bed and couldnt. After my wife help me out of bed. I felt a little better. But all during the day I had to struggle whenever 5 I got in or out of my car. I thought the "monday soreness" was the end of it. Until tuesday morning when my wife had to help me put my shoes on. I could barely walk all day. And needed help getting out of my car. My body has delivered a loud and clear message to me. That has made me reconsider my imagined physical prowess.

10

16 Kathryn, my sister, is a self-centered person for example, she spends hours getting ready to go out. Putting on makeup, combing her hair, and getting dressed.

After she finish, she walk into the living room carrying herself in a way that you know is self-conscious, she thinks everyone is looking at her. If I try not to 5 look at her, she draw my attention by asking, "does this outfit look all right, Pat? or Do you like my hair this way?

My sister is always asking what other people say about her. I tell her, They're not saying anything about you, Kathy. She can't believe there not thinking about her. Just because shes always thinking about herself.   10

Kathryn is always putting down people who have accomplish something. If somebody wins an award at school. She calls them a show-off. If somebody get a job as a salesperson in a department store. She say their not good enough to do anything else. My sister has few friends. According to her, because everyone is jealous of her. The truth is that no one can stand her.   15

17 When I met a girl name Barbara, my life started to change. Our relationship begin one lonely night this past winter. I was sitting in the dewdrop inn with a friend. We were having a couple of beers and shooting a game of dart's. The place was almost empty, I guess there were about four people at the bar. Then Barbara and her friend walk in. Passing in front of us. At the jukebox they played some 5 records. On there way to the bar, I ask Barbara if she and her friend would like to play some darts. To my surprise, she said, yes, we would. I still can't believe what happened then, they beat us.

The night went on then Barbara and her friend said they had to go home. I felt sort of sad. I walked with her to her car we kissed good-night and made a date to 10 go bowling on saturday afternoon. However, I didnt show up for our date. Because I was afraid that she wouldnt be there. I went to the auto races with a buddy instead. A couple of days went by before I saw her again. I didnt think that she would talk to me. But she fool me we made another date, and this time I kept it.

We started to see each other several nights a week. Becoming closer and 15 closer to one another. Its hard to explain what I felt about her. When she met me. I was often drinking from early in the morning to late at night. I did not have a job, I felt as though I had nothing to work for. She changed me, I went out and got a job and did well at it.

Then I applied to college here I am now in school trying to learn and do well 20 in life. Barbara is helping me out as I try to achieve these goals'. We are married now we are both happy. In this strange world of ours, if a man has something to work for. He will do his best in order to achieve. I can honestly say that I now have a meaning in my life.

18 The main problem in my work as a substitute mail carrier is contending with dogs. Who are used to the regular carrier but not to me. Regarding me as a foreign presence worthy of attack. The route I was assigned to last week featured a German shepherd, the dog had been hit once while chasing a car and had lost a leg. Even though he had only three legs. He still chased cars. As I walked up the 5 lawn of the house where the German shepherd stood guard I felt very uneasy. Sitting in the side yard, I could see the dog out of the corner of my eye. Giving me a hateful stare. As I opened the screen door of the house, he let out several vicious snarls and barks, I could see his teeth showing. His owner appeared to get the mail, she yelled over to him, You stay right where you are, Rex. You just stay put, 10 now. I felt like asking the woman to stand there and watch Rex until I was back on the sidewalk, however, I didn't want to seem afraid. I head back away from the house. Walking slowly but eagerly. I hear the door click behind me and you knew the owner had gone back into the house. I wished that I felt as confident as she did that her dog would behave. When I was almost at the sidewalk. Rex began 15 to bark again, then his barking became louder and closer, I turned around and saw Rex coming at me in full, three-legged stride. With only three legs, I was sure that I could outrun him at least up to my truck. I felt foolish but that didn't stop me from running. Just as fast as I could. Rex were tearing at my pants' cuff as I reached the truck. Grateful that I had left the door open. At the same instant that 20 I leaped inside, I was sliding shut the door. Using it as a wedge to detach Rex from my trousers. Rex hurled himself at the door several times, then he backed off when his owner began to call. After catching my breath, I resolve not to return to Rex place again. At least not without a can of mace in my hand.

PART 4
Sentence Variety through Combining Activities

INTRODUCTION
Part 1 of this book gives you practice in skills needed to write clear sentences. Parts 2 and 3 help you work on reinforcing those skills. The purpose of this part of the book is to provide you with methods for writing varied and interesting sentences. Through the technique of sentence combining, you will learn about the many different options open to you for expressing a given idea. At the same time, you will develop a natural instinct and "ear" for choosing the option that sounds best in a particular situation. By the end of Part 4, you will be able to compose sentences that bring to your writing style a greater variety and ease. You will also be able to write sentences that express more complex thoughts.

How sentence combining works: The combining technique used to help you practice various sentence patterns is a simple one. Two or more short sentences are given and then combined in a particular way. You are then asked to combine other short sentences in the same way. Here is an example:

- The diesel truck chugged up the hill.
- It spewed out black smoke.

Spewing out black smoke, the diesel truck chugged up the hill.

- The crowd of dancers moved as one.
- They swayed to the music.

_____

_____

(The correct combination for the second example above would be, "Swaying to the music, the crowd of dancers moved as one.") The content of most sentences is given to you, so that instead of focusing on *what* you will say, you can concentrate on *how* to say it.

The sentence-combining activities are presented in a three-section sequence. The first section describes the four traditional sentence patterns in English and explains the important techniques of coordination and subordination central to these patterns. The second section presents other patterns that can be used to add variety to writing. And the last section provides a number of practice units in which you can apply the combining patterns you have learned as well as compose patterns of your own.

Four Traditional Sentence Patterns

Sentences have been traditionally described in English as being simple, compound, complex, or compound-complex. This section explains and offers practice in all four sentence types. The section also describes coordination and subordination—the two central techniques you can use to achieve different kinds of emphasis in your writing.

THE SIMPLE SENTENCE

A simple sentence has a single subject-verb combination.

Children play.
The game ended early.
My car stalled three times last week.
The lake has been polluted by several neighboring streams.

A simple sentence may have more than one subject:

Lola and Tony drove home.
The wind and water dried my hair.

or more than one verb:

The children smiled and waved at us.
The lawn mower smoked and sputtered.

or several subjects and verbs:

Manny, Moe, and Jack lubricated my car, replaced the oil filter, and cleaned the spark plugs.

ACTIVITY

On separate paper, write:

Three sentences with a single subject and verb
Three sentences with a single subject and a double verb
Three sentences with a double subject and a single verb

In each case, underline the subject once and the verb twice. (See page 3 if necessary for more information on subjects and verbs.)

THE COMPOUND SENTENCE

A compound or "double" sentence is made up of two (or more) simple sentences. The two complete statements in a compound sentence are usually connected by a comma plus a joining or coordinating word (*and, but, for, or, nor, so, yet*).

A compound sentence is used when you want to give equal weight to two closely related ideas. The technique of showing that ideas have equal importance is called *coordination*. Following are some compound sentences. In each case, they contain two ideas that are about equal in importance.

The rain increased, so the officials canceled the game.

Martha wanted to go shopping, but Fred refused to drive her.

Tom was watching television in the family room, and Marie was upstairs on the phone.

I had to give up woodcarving, for my arthritis had become very painful.

ACTIVITY 1

Combine the following pairs of simple sentences into compound sentences. Use a comma and a logical joining word (*and, but, for, so*) to connect each pair of statements.

Note: If you are not sure what *and, but, for,* and *so* mean, review page 30 before starting.

Example   • We hung up the print.
              • The wall still looked bare.

We hung up the print, but the wall still looked bare.

1. • My cold grew worse.
   • I decided to see a doctor.

   _____

2. • My uncle always ignores me.
   • My aunt gives me kisses and presents.

   _____

   _____

3. • We played softball in the afternoon.
   • We went to a movie in the evening.

   _____

   _____

4. • I invited Richard to sleep overnight.
    • He wanted to go home.

    _____

5. • Police raided the club.
    • They had gotten a tip about illegal drugs for sale.

    _____

ACTIVITY 2

On separate paper, write five compound sentences of your own. Use a different joining word (*and, but, for, or, nor, so, yet*) to connect the two complete ideas in each sentence.

THE COMPLEX SENTENCE

A complex sentence is made up of a simple sentence (a complete statement) and a statement that begins with a subordinating word.* Here is a list of common subordinating words:

after	if	when, whenever
although, though	since	where, wherever
as, as if	so that	which, whichever
because	that	who, whoever
before	unless	while
even, even though	until	

A complex sentence is used when you want to show that one idea is more important than another. The technique of emphasizing one idea over another is called *subordination*. Look at the following complex sentence:

Because I forgot the time, I missed the final exam.

The idea considered more important here—*I missed the final exam*—is emphasized by making it a complete thought. The idea considered less important—*Because I forgot the time*—is subordinated to the complete thought. A subordinating word, *Because*, is used to show that forgetting the time is the less important idea.

On the following page are other examples of complex sentences. In each case, the part starting with the subordinating word is the less-emphasized part of the sentence.

_____

* The two parts of a complex sentence are sometimes called an independent clause and a dependent clause. A *clause* is simply a word group that contains a subject and a verb. An *independent clause* expresses a complete thought and can stand alone. A *dependent clause* does not express a complete thought in itself and "depends on" the independent clause to complete its meaning. Dependent clauses always begin with a dependent or subordinating word.

While Sue was eating breakfast, she began to feel sick.
I checked my money *before* I invited Tom for lunch.
When Jerry lost his temper, he also lost his job.
Although I practiced for three months, I failed my driving test.

ACTIVITY 1

Use logical subordinating words to combine the following pairs of simple sentences into complex sentences. Place a comma after a subordinate statement when it starts the sentence.

Examples
- I obtained a credit card.
- I began spending money recklessly.

When I obtained a credit card, I began spending money recklessly.

- Alan dressed the turkey.
- His brother greased the roasting pot.

Alan dressed the turkey while his brother greased the roasting pot.

1. • The teacher announced the quiz.
   • The class groaned.

   _____

2. • Gene could not fit any more groceries into his cart.
   • He decided to go to the checkout counter.

   _____

   _____

3. • Your car is out of commission.
   • You should take it to Otto's Transmission.

   _____

   _____

4. • I finished typing the paper.
   • I proofread it carefully.

   _____

5. • We owned four cats and a dog.
   • No one would rent us an apartment.

   _____

   _____

ACTIVITY 2

Rewrite the following sentences, using subordination rather than coordination. Include a comma when a subordinate word group starts a sentence.

Example The hair dryer was not working right, so I returned it to the store.

Because the hair dryer was not working right, I returned it to the store.

1. Ruth turned on the large window fan, but the room remained hot.

   _____

2. The plumber repaired the hot water heater, so we can take showers again.

   _____

   _____

3. I washed the sheets and towels, and I scrubbed the bathroom floor.

   _____

4. You should go to a doctor, for your chest cold may get worse.

   _____

5. The fish tank broke, and guppies were flopping all over the floor.

   _____

ACTIVITY 3

Combine the following simple sentences into complex sentences. Omit repeated words. Use the subordinating words *who, which,* or *that.*

> *Note: who* refers to persons
> *which* refers to things
> *that* refers to persons or things

Use commas around the subordinate word group only if it seems to interrupt the flow of thought in the sentence. (See also page 134.)

Examples • Clyde picked up a hitchhiker.
           • The hitchhiker was traveling around the world.

Clyde picked up a hitchhiker who was traveling around the world.

           • Larry is a sleepwalker.
           • Larry is my brother.

Larry, who is my brother, is a sleepwalker.

1. • The magazine article was about abortion.
    • The article made me very angry.

    _____

2. • The woodshed has collapsed.
    • I built the woodshed myself.

    _____

3. • The power drill is missing.
    • I bought the power drill at half price.

    _____

4. • Alan Thorn was indicted for bribery.
    • Alan Thorn is our mayor.

    _____

5. • The chicken pies contain dangerous preservatives.
    • We ate the chicken pies.

    _____

ACTIVITY 4

On separate paper, write eight complex sentences using, in turn, the subordinating words *unless, if, after, because, when, who, which,* and *that*.

THE COMPOUND-COMPLEX SENTENCE

The compound-complex sentence is made up of two (or more) simple sentences and one (or more) subordinate statements. In the following examples, a solid line is under the simple sentences and a dotted line is under the subordinate word group.

> When the power line snapped, Jack was listening to the stereo, and Linda was reading in bed.
>
> After I returned to school following a long illness, the math teacher gave me make-up work, but the history teacher made me drop her course.

ACTIVITY 1

Read through each sentence to get a sense of its overall meaning. Then insert a logical coordinating word (*and, but, for,* or *so*) and a logical subordinating word (*because, since, when,* or *although*).

1. Fred had a closet full of leisure suits, _____ Martha would not let him wear them _____ they were no longer in style.

2. _____ I put on my new flannel shirt, I discovered a button was missing, _____ I angrily went looking for a replacement button in the sewing basket.

3. _____ the typewriter was just repaired, the carriage return still sticks, _____ certain keys keep jamming.

4. _____ I have lived for all my life on the East Coast, I felt uncomfortable during a West Coast vacation, _____ I kept thinking that the ocean was on the wrong side.

5. _____ water condensation continues in your basement, either you should buy a dehumidifier _____ you should cover the masonry walls with waterproof paint.

ACTIVITY 2

On separate paper, write five compound-complex sentences.

REVIEW OF COORDINATION AND SUBORDINATION

Remember that coordination and subordination are ways of showing the exact relationship of ideas within a sentence. Through coordination we show that ideas are of equal importance. When we coordinate, we use the words *and, but, for, or, nor, so, yet*. Through subordination we show that one idea is more important than another. When we subordinate, we use words like *when, although, since, while, because,* and *after*. A list of common subordinating words is given on page 295.

ACTIVITY

Use coordination or subordination to combine the groups of simple sentences on the next page into one or more longer sentences. Omit repeated words. Since a variety of combinations are possible, you might want to jot several combinations on separate paper. Then read them aloud to find the combination that sounds best.

Keep in mind that, very often, the relationship among ideas in a sentence will be clearer when subordinating rather than coordinating words are used.

Example   • My car is not starting on cold mornings.
             • I think the battery needs to be replaced.
             • I already had it recharged once.
             • I don't think it would help to charge it again.

Because my car is not starting on cold mornings, I think the battery needs to be replaced. I already had it recharged once, so I don't think it would help to charge it again.

Comma hints:
   • Use a comma at the end of a word group that starts with a subordinating word (as in "Because my car is not starting on cold mornings, . . .")
   • Use a comma between independent word groups connected by *and, but, for, so,* and other joining or coordinating words (as in "I already had it recharged once, so . . .")

1. • Louise used a dandruff shampoo.
    • She still had dandruff.
    • She decided to see a dermatologist.

    _____

    _____

    _____

2. • Al's parents want him to be a doctor.
    • Al wants to be a salesman.
    • He impresses people with his charm.

    _____

    _____

    _____

3. • The teacher conducted a discussion period.
    • Jack sat at the desk with his head down.
    • He did not want the teacher to call on him.
    • He had not read the assignment.

    _____

    _____

    _____

    _____

4. • Lola wanted to get a quick lunch at the cafeteria.
   • All the sandwiches were gone.
   • She had to settle for a cup of yogurt.

   _____

   _____

   _____

5. • I was leaving to do some shopping in town.
   • I asked my son to water the back lawn.
   • He seemed agreeable.
   • I returned three hours later.
   • The lawn had not been watered.

   _____

   _____

   _____

   _____

6. • I ate too quickly.
   • My stomach became upset.
   • It felt like a war combat zone.
   • I took two Alka-Seltzer tablets.

   _____

   _____

   _____

   _____

7. • Midge is always buying plants and flower seeds.
   • She enjoys growing things.
   • Not many things grow well for her.
   • She doesn't know why.

   _____

   _____

   _____

   _____

8. • My car was struck from behind yesterday.
   • I slowed suddenly for a red light.
   • The driver of the truck behind me slammed on his brakes.
   • He didn't quite stop in time.

   _____

   _____

   _____

   _____

9. • Ed skimmed through the help-wanted ads.
   • Nothing was there for him.
   • He desperately needed a job.
   • He would have to sell his car.
   • He could no longer keep up the payments.

   _____

   _____

   _____

   _____

10. • The meat loaf didn't taste right.
    • The mashed potatoes had too much salt in them.
    • We sent out for a pizza.
    • It was delivered late.
    • It was cold.

    _____

    _____

    _____

    _____

Other Patterns That Add Variety to Writing

This section gives you practice in other patterns or methods that can add variety and interest to your sentences. The patterns can be used with any of the four sentence types already explained. Note that you will not have to remember the grammar terms that are often used to describe the patterns. What is important is that you practice the various patterns extensively, so that you increase your sense of the many ways available to you for expressing your ideas.

-ING WORD GROUPS

Use an *-ing* word group at some point in a sentence. Here are examples:

The doctor, *hoping* for the best, examined the x-rays.
Jogging every day, I soon increased my energy level.
The rabbit perched on the edge of the patio, *chewing* a dandelion.

More information about *-ing* words, also known as *present participles,* appears on page 65.

ACTIVITY 1

Combine the sentences on the next page into one sentence by using an *-ing* word and omitting repeated words. Use a comma or commas to set off the *-ing* word group from the rest of the sentence.

Example
- The diesel truck chugged up the hill.
- It spewed out black smoke.

Spewing out black smoke, the diesel truck chugged up the hill

or *The diesel truck, spewing out black smoke, chugged up the hill.*

or *The diesel truck chugged up the hill, spewing out black smoke.*

1. • Ginger refused to get out of bed.
   • She pulled the blue blanket over her head.

   _____

   _____

2. • Dad is able to forget the troubles of the day.
   • He putters around in his basement workshop.

   _____

   _____

3. • The crowd of dancers moved as one.
   • They swayed to the music.

   _____

   _____

4. • George tried to protect himself from the dampness of the room.
   • He wrapped a scarf around his neck.

   _____

   _____

5. • The woman listened intently to the earnest young man.
   • She caressed her hair softly.

   _____

   _____

ACTIVITY 2

On separate paper, write five sentences of your own that contain *-ing* word groups.

-ED WORD GROUPS

Use an *-ed* word group at some point in a sentence. Here are examples:

Tired of studying, I took a short break.
Mary, *amused* by the joke, told it to a friend.
My eyes opened wide, *shocked* by the red "F" on my paper.

More information about *-ed* word groups, also known as *past participles,* appears on page 65.

ACTIVITY

Combine the following sentences into one sentence by using an *-ed* word and omitting repeated words. Use a comma or commas to set off the *-ed* word group from the rest of the sentence.

Example • Tim woke up with a start.
         • He was troubled by a dream.

Troubled by a dream, Tim woke up with a start.
or Tim, troubled by a dream, woke up with a start.
or Tim woke up with a start, troubled by a dream.

1. • I called an exterminator.
    • I was bothered by roaches.

    _____

2. • Sam grew silent.
    • He was baffled by what had happened.

    _____

3. • The crowd began to file slowly out of the stadium.
    • They were stunned by the last-minute touchdown.

    _____

    _____

4. • I tried to stifle my grin.
    • I was amused but reluctant to show it.

    _____

    _____

5. • Cindy lay on the couch.
    • She was exhausted from working all day.

    _____

    _____

APPOSITIVES

Use appositives. An *appositive* is a word group that renames a noun (any person, place, or thing). Here is an example:

Rita, a good friend of mine, works as a police officer.

The word group *a good friend of mine* is an appositive that renames the word *Rita*.

ACTIVITY 1

Combine the following sentences into one sentence by using an appositive and omitting repeated words. Most appositives are set off by commas.

Example • Alan Thorn got lost during the hiking trip.
• He is a former Eagle Scout.

Alan Thorn, a former Eagle Scout, got lost during the hiking trip.

1. • Houston is a rapidly growing city.
   • Houston is my hometown.

   _____

   _____

2. • Roger refused to get involved in the argument.
   • Roger is a gentle man.

   _____

   _____

3. • *Cutter and Bone* is a fascinating book.
   • *Cutter and Bone* is a novel by Newton Thornburg.

   _____

   _____

4. • The city park is where I go to think.
   • The city park is a shady retreat.

   _____

   _____

5. • The bungalow did not look safe enough to enter.
   • The bungalow is a tilted structure with a sagging roof.

   _____

   _____

ACTIVITY 2

On separate paper, write five sentences of your own that contain appositives.

-LY OPENERS

Use an *-ly* word to open a sentence. Here are examples:

Gently, he mixed the chemicals together.
Anxiously, the contestant looked at the game clock.
Skillfully, the quarterback rifled a pass to his receiver.

More information about *-ly* words, also known as *adverbs,* appears on page 95.

ACTIVITY 1

Combine the following sentences into one sentence by starting with an *-ly* word and omitting repeated words. Place a comma after the opening *-ly* word.

Example
- I gave several yanks to the starting cord of the lawn mower.
- I was angry.

Angrily, I gave several yanks to the starting cord of the lawnmower.

1.
- The burglars carried the television out of the house.
- They were quiet.

_____

2.
- Mary squirmed in her seat as she waited for her turn to speak.
- She was nervous.

_____

3.
- I reinforced all the coat buttons with a strong thread.
- I was patient.

_____

4.
- He finished answering the last question on the test.
- He was quick.

_____

5.
- I tore the wrapping off the present.
- I was excited.

_____

ACTIVITY 2

On separate paper, write five sentences of your own that begin with *-ly* words.

TO OPENERS

Use a *to* word group to open a sentence. Here are examples:

To succeed in that course, you must attend every class.
To help me sleep better, I learned to quiet my mind through meditation.
To get good seats, we went to the game early.

The *to* in such a group is also known as an *infinitive*, as explained on page 65.

ACTIVITY **1**

Combine the following sentences into one sentence by starting with a *to* word group and omitting repeated words. Use a comma after the opening *to* word group.

Example • I fertilize the grass every spring.
           • I want to make it greener.

To make the grass greener, I fertilize it every spring.

1. • Doug ran five miles a day all summer.
    • He wanted to prepare for the track season.

    _____

    _____

2. • You should meet Al's parents.
    • This will help you to understand him better.

    _____

    _____

3. • She wants to get the stain off her hand.
    • She will have to use an abrasive soap.

    _____

    _____

4. • I left the house early.
    • I had to get to the church on time.

    _____

    _____

5. • I punched in my code number.
   • I did this to make the automatic banking machine work.

_____

_____

ACTIVITY 2

On separate paper, write five sentences of your own that begin with _to_ word groups.

PREPOSITIONAL PHRASE OPENERS

Use prepositional phrase openers. Here are examples:

From the beginning, I disliked my boss.
In spite of her work, she failed the course.
After the game, we went to a movie.

Prepositional phrases include words like _in, from, of, at, by,_ and _with._ A full list is on page 7.

ACTIVITY 1

Combine the following sentences into one sentence by omitting repeated words. Start each sentence with a suitable prepositional phrase and place the other prepositional phrases in places that sound right. Generally you should use a comma after the opening prepositional phrase.

Example • A fire started.
   • It did this at 5 A.M.
   • It did this inside the garage.

At 5 A.M., a fire started inside the garage.

1. • I sat napping.
   • I did this during my work break.
   • I did this in the lunchroom corner.
   • I did this with my head in my arm.

_____

_____

2.
- We played basketball.
- We did this in the church gym.
- We did this during the winter.
- We did this on many evenings.

_____

_____

3.
- Fred Grencher studies his balding spot.
- He does this with grave concern.
- He does this in the bathroom mirror.
- He does this before going to bed.

_____

_____

4.
- The car skidded.
- It did this on an oil slick.
- It did this on a sharp curve.
- It did this during the race.

_____

_____

5.
- The teenage driver raced his car to the busy intersection.
- He did this without slowing down.
- The intersection is in the heart of town.

_____

_____

ACTIVITY 2

On separate paper, write five sentences of your own that begin with prepositional phrases and that contain at least one other prepositional phrase.

SERIES OF ITEMS

Use a series of items. Following are two of the many items that can be used in a series: adjectives and verbs.

Adjectives in Series

Adjectives are descriptive words. Here are examples:

The *husky young* man sanded the *chipped, weather-worn* paint off the fence.

Husky and *young* are adjectives that describe *man; chipped* and *weather-worn* are adjectives that describe *paint.* More information about adjectives appears on page 95.

ACTIVITY 1

Combine the following sentences into one sentence by using adjectives in a series and omitting repeated words. Use commas between adjectives only when *and* inserted between them sounds natural.

Example • I sewed a set of buttons onto my coat.
• The buttons were shiny.
• The buttons were black.
• The coat was old.
• The coat was green.

I sewed a set of shiny black buttons onto my old green coat.

1. • The boy stomped on the bug.
 • The boy was little.
 • The boy was angry.
 • The bug was tiny.
 • The bug was red.

2. • The man slowly wiped his forehead with a bandanna.
 • The man was tall.
 • The man was thin.
 • His forehead was sweaty.
 • His bandanna was dirty.
 • His bandanna was blue.

3. • My sister is intelligent.
 • My sister is good-natured.
 • My sister is humorous.

4. • The boy looked at the girl.
   • The boy was shy.
   • The boy was timid.
   • The girl was grinning.
   • The girl was curly-haired.

   _____

   _____

5. • The man wearing work clothes strode into the tavern.
   • The man was short.
   • The man was muscular.
   • The man was bald.
   • The work clothes were wrinkled.
   • The work clothes were green.
   • The tavern was noisy.
   • The tavern was smoke-filled.

   _____

   _____

   _____

ACTIVITY 2

On separate paper, write five sentences of your own that contain a series of adjectives.

Verbs in Series

Verbs are words that express action. Here are examples:

In my job as a cook's helper, I *prepared* salads, *sliced* meat and cheese, and *made* all kinds of sandwiches.

Basic information about verbs appears on pages 3 to 10.

ACTIVITY 1

Combine the sentences on the next page into one sentence by using verbs in a series and omitting repeated words. Use a comma between verbs in a series.

Example • In the dingy bar Sam shelled peanuts.
         • He sipped a beer.
         • He talked up a storm with friends.

In the dingy bar Sam shelled peanuts, sipped a beer, and talked up a storm with friends.

1.
   - When the popular comedian walked from behind the curtain, the crowd applauded.
   - The crowd stomped their feet.
   - The crowd shouted, "Hi . . . oh!"

   _____

   _____

2.
   - Everywhere in the cafeteria students were putting on their coats.
   - They were scooping up their books.
   - They were hurrying off to class.

   _____

   _____

3.
   - By 6 A.M. in the morning, I had read the textbook chapter.
   - I had taken notes on it.
   - I had studied the notes.
   - I had drunk eight cups of coffee.

   _____

   _____

4.
   - I pressed the Rice Krispies into the bowl.
   - I poured milk on them.
   - I waited for the milk to soak the cereal.

   _____

   _____

5.
   - I am afraid the dentist's drill will slip off my tooth.
   - I am afraid it will bite into my gum.
   - I am afraid it will make me jump with pain.

   _____

   _____

ACTIVITY 2

On separate paper, write five sentences of your own that use verbs in a series.

Note: The section on parallelism (pages 74 to 78) gives you practice in some of the other kinds of items that can be used in a series.

Sentence-combining Exercises

This section provides a series of combining exercises. The exercises are made up of a number of short sentence units, each of which can be combined into one sentence. (Occasionally, you may decide that certain sentences are more effective if they are not combined.) The patterns you have already practiced will suggest combining ideas for the units that you work on. However, do not feel limited to previous patterns. Use your own natural instinct to explore and compose a variety of sentence combinations. It will help if you write out possible combinations and then read them aloud. Choose the one that sounds best. You will gradually develop an ear for hearing the option that reads most smoothly and clearly and that sounds most appropriate in the context of surrounding sentences. As you continue to practice, you will increase your ability to write more varied, interesting, and sophisticated sentences.

Here is an example of a short sentence unit and some possible combinations:

- Martha moved in the desk chair.
- Her moving was uneasy.
- The chair was hard.
- She worked at her assignment.
- The assignment was for her English class.

Martha moved uneasily in the hard desk chair, working at the assignment for her English class.

Moving uneasily in the hard desk chair, Martha worked at the assignment for her English class.

Martha moved uneasily in the hard desk chair as she worked at the assignment for her English class.

Working at the assignment for her English class, Martha moved uneasily in the hard desk chair.

While she worked at the assignment for her English class, Martha moved uneasily in the hard desk chair.

Note: In combining short sentence clusters into one sentence, omit repeated words where necessary. Use separate paper.

1 DEPARTMENT STORE SALE

- There's a sale at the large chain store.
- The sale is in all departments.

- Shoppers flood the store.
- They hurry down the aisles.

- Teenage girls grab up the bikinis.
- The bikinis disappear quickly.

- Men and women buy many items for the house.
- They act as though they never saw household goods before.

- The goods include bath accessories.
- The goods include air conditioners and table fans.
- The goods include rugs and draperies.
- The goods include furniture.
- The goods include televisions and stereo equipment.

- Some people buy things they don't need.
- Other people buy things they don't want.

- Nobody brings cash.
- They do something else instead.
- They bring their charge plates.

- Everyone will be sorry.
- They will be sorry when the bills come.
- They will be sorry they didn't keep control of themselves.

- The manager smiles at the success of the sale.
- His employees don't smile.

- The shoppers mistreat the salespeople.
- The shoppers act like animals.
- The salespeople hate sales.

- The shoppers throw clothes on the floor.
- The shoppers throw dirty looks at each other.

- At the end of the day the store has made money.
- At the end of the day the manager is happy.
- At the end of the day the salespeople feel like quitting.

2 KIDS AND MUD

- Two toddlers sit on the ground.
- They play in the mud.
- The mud is wet and gooey.

- The children bury their hands in the mud.
- The children bury their toys in the mud.
- The children bury their feet in the mud.

- Mud is the pal of kids.
- Mud makes great pies and cakes.

- Kids don't need expensive toys.
- Kids don't need a television set.
- Kids don't need their parents' help.

- They do need some wet dirt.
- They do need nice parents.
- Nice parents won't yell about their clothes.

- Kids have imaginations.
- Their imaginations are marvelous.
- Their imaginations turn mud into cakes.
- Their imaginations turn dust into icing.
- Their imaginations turn twigs into candles.

- Kids are lucky.
- Mud can't be taken away by adults.
- Mud can't be improved upon.

- No one will package mud in a can.
- No one will sell it on television.

- Mud will always be clean fun.

3   TELEVISION

- Many people depend on the television set.
- The television set is nicknamed TV.
- It is nicknamed "the tube."

- People use the tube as a baby-sitter.
- People use the tube as a sports arena.
- People use the tube as a movie theater.

- You can tell some people are TV addicts.
- The TV runs day and night.

- They turn the TV on to keep them company.
- They leave it on throughout the day.

- The tube delivers messages.
- The messages are irritating.
- It does this frequently.
- The messages are called commercials.

- Commercials persuade people.
- Commercials mislead people.
- Commercials leave an aching in people's ears.

- The commercials are predictable.
- Certain kinds of programming are predictable.
- The programming includes soap operas.
- The programming includes talk shows.

- Soap operas sink their claws into viewers.
- Soap operas keep the viewers questioning.
- The viewers want to know, "What's next?"

- On talk shows people laugh.
- But often there is no humor.
- On talk shows people talk.
- But often nothing is said.

- Television can be like a drug.
- It is like this sometimes.
- It is a drug that people use too often.

4   STRAY DOG

- A dog trots down the street.
- The dog is a stray.
- The dog is hungry.

- He has a lovable face.
- He has a healthy coat.
- But someone has abandoned him.

- A house is nearby.
- The dog's nose works.
- It draws him to the trash can.

- The can is filled with garbage.
- The garbage is luscious to the dog.

- The dog knocks the can over.
- Garbage spills to the ground.

- Inside the house, the owner is alerted.
- He is alerted by the sound of the fallen can.

- The dog digs into his find.
- He doesn't hear the owner coming.

- The owner opens his back door.
- He yells at the dog.
- The dog is quickly scared off.

- The owner cleans up the mess.
- The dog appears out of the shadows.
- The dog is still hungry.

- The owner feels sorry for the dog.
- He returns to his house.
- He gets the dog some real food.

5 JACK ALONE

- Jack entered his apartment.
- He locked the door.
- The muscles in his face began to relax.
- The muscles in his body began to relax.

- He felt happy to be at home.
- He felt happy after an exhausting day at work.
- The work was as a delivery man for United Parcel.

- He was carrying a newspaper.
- He was carrying his mail.
- He dropped both of them on the sofa.

- He walked into the kitchen.
- He opened the freezer door.
- He took out a TV dinner.
- The TV dinner was a Swanson's Hungry Man Salisbury Steak dinner.

- He placed the dinner in his toaster oven.
- He set the oven at 450°.

- Then he went into the bedroom.
- He undressed.
- He hung on a chair his heavy brown shirt.
- He hung on a chair his heavy brown pants.
- The hanging was neat.

- In the bathroom he washed his face.
- He washed his arms and hands.
- He brushed the tangles out of his hair.
- His hair was curly.
- His hair was black.

- He put on a corduroy shirt.
- The shirt was soft.
- He pulled on a pair of trousers.
- The trousers were old.
- The trousers were baggy.
- The trousers hung loosely around his waist.

- Then he put on a pair of slippers.
- The bootees were blue.
- The bootees were fleece-lined.

- Jack shuffled back to the kitchen.
- He boiled water.
- He made a large cup of tea.

- To the tea Jack added a tablespoon of honey.
- To the tea Jack added a tablespoon of bourbon.

- Jack carried the tea to the living room.
- He sat down beside his newspaper and mail.
- He flicked on the television.

- Later Jack might feel lonely.
- Now he was relaxed.
- Now he was comfortable.
- Now he was happy to be by himself.

6 COCOA AND DOUGHNUT

- A cup of cocoa sat on the high-chair tray.
- Half a doughnut sat on the high-chair tray.
- The cocoa was dark brown.
- The doughnut was a white sugar doughnut.

- A little boy was in the high chair.
- He stuck his finger in the cocoa.
- The sticking of his finger was careful.

- Then he picked up the doughnut half.
- He pushed the doughnut into the cup.
- His pushing was deep.

- Cocoa flowed over the top of the cup.
- It ran onto the tray.
- It dropped off the tray onto a tablecloth.
- The tablecloth was white linen.

- The little boy grabbed at the doughnut.
- The doughnut was spongy.
- The doughnut would not come out of the cup.

- The boy pushed at the cup.
- The cup rolled onto its side.
- It rocked back and forth on the metal tray.
- The rocking was gentle.

- The boy dug his hand into the cup.
- He pulled out a piece of doughnut.

- He pressed the doughnut against the metal tray.
- He pressed it with his fist.
- The doughnut flattened.
- The flattening was like a pancake.

- The boy shoved the pressed doughnut.
- He shoved most of it off the tray.
- It splattered onto the floor.
- It splattered onto the tablecloth.

- The boy picked up a fistful of doughnut.
- He jammed it into his mouth.

- He sat chewing the doughnut.
- His chewing was contented.

- The boy's father walked into the room.
- The boy looked at his father.
- The boy was happy.

7 WRITING A PAPER

- Martha has writer's block.
- She can think of nothing to write.

- She scribbles words on the page.
- The words do not develop the subject.
- She crosses out the words.

- Martha is sweating.
- Martha is frustrated.
- She feels bored.
- She feels stupid.

- She pulls at the collar of her blouse.
- She gets up.
- She walks around the room.
- She walks for a couple of minutes.

- She stares out the window.
- She wishes the paper was finished.
- Her wishing is desperate.

- She thinks of what she could be watching on television.
- She thinks of calls she could make to friends.

- Then she sighs.
- She returns to the desk.

- She does two things.
- The things are to break the writer's block.

- First, she writes about her subject.
- She writes whatever comes into her head.
- She does this for twenty minutes.

- Then she reads what she has written.
- She tries to decide on her main point.
- She tries to decide on her support for that point.

- This work helps clear her confusion.
- Her confusion is now not so great.

- She senses the point of her paper.
- She senses how to support that point.
- She senses how to organize the support.

- She works hard for more than an hour.
- The result is the first rough draft of her paper.

- Martha sighs with relief.
- She gets up to take a break.

- She still has a second draft to write.
- She even has a third draft to write.
- But the worst part is over.

- Martha knows she has won the battle.

8 VICTIM

- The TV van hurried to the scene.
- The scene was of an auto accident.
- The lights of the TV van were flashing.

- An ambulance pulled away from the scene.
- It carried a dead boy.
- It left as the van arrived.

- The boy had backed his car out of a driveway.
- He had done so without looking.

- His car was struck by a truck.
- The truck was oncoming.
- He was killed instantly.

- The mother of the boy stood in the driveway.
- She was sobbing.
- She was talking to neighbors.

- TV lights were focused on her face.
- The focusing was cruel.
- A TV reporter approached her with a microphone.
- He asked her to speak.

- Her friends moved aside.
- Their moving was uncertain.
- Her friends did not stop the TV crew.

- Bystanders jostled in the background.
- Police moved them aside.
- The police did not stop the TV crew.

- The woman began to talk.
- The woman talked about the accident.
- The woman talked about her dead son.

- She began to cry.
- She tried to keep talking.
- The camera continued to roll.

- The reporter looked sympathetic.
- He stood to one side.
- His standing was careful.
- He wanted the camera to have a good angle.

- The woman felt obliged to the TV people.
- She felt obliged to cooperate.
- She should not have.

- The woman did not have to share her grief.
- The grief was private.

- The woman should have said something to the TV people.
- She should have said, "Get out of here."
- She should have said, "My tragedy is none of your business."

- The woman did not do this.
- The camera whirled.

PART 5
Writing Assignments

INTRODUCTION

The previous parts of *Sentence Skills* show you how to make your sentences communicate clearly. Part 5 provides a series of brief writing assignments so that you can apply the sentence skills you learned in the earlier sections of the book. Applying these skills in actual writing situations is the surest way to achieve mastery of grammar, mechanics, punctuation, and usage rules. Brief hints about composition principles are included with some of the assignments. However, these suggestions have been kept to a minimum because the primary concern in Part 5, as in the whole book, is with the mastery of sentence skills.

Sixteen Writing Assignments

Note: Make a special effort to apply the sentence skills you have already learned to each writing assignment. To help you achieve such a transfer, your instructor may ask you to rewrite a paper as many times as necessary for you to correct sentence-skills mistakes. A writing progress chart on page 336 will help track your performance.

1 FREEWRITING

In freewriting you write as fast as you can for ten minutes. You don't worry about spelling, punctuation, erasing mistakes, or finding exact words. You just write without stopping. If you get stuck for words, write "I am looking for something to say" or repeat words until something comes. Don't feel inhibited; mistakes do not count and you will not have to hand in your paper.

Freewriting will limber up your writing muscles and make you familiar with the act of writing. It is a way to break through mental blocks about writing and the fear of making errors. Since you don't have to worry about making mistakes, you can concentrate on discovering what you want to say about a subject. Your initial ideas and impressions will often become clearer after you have gotten them down on paper. Through continued practice in freewriting, you will develop the habit of thinking as you write. And you will learn a technique that is a helpful way to get started on almost any paper that you write.

Freewriting subjects Here is a series of subjects for fifteen separate freewriting activities. Remember that the only requirement is that you write for ten minutes without stopping. Once you are given a subject, you should be able to write on it for ten minutes if you get into details of the subject. If you run out of words, then write about anything—just don't stop writing.

Anything	Pets *or* weather *or* children *or* stores
Today in your life	Your kitchen *or* living room *or* bathroom *or* bedroom
The past weekend	
The place where you live *or* a person you know	Dreams *or* illness *or* money *or* exercise
Work *or* school	A valued material possession
Food *or* clothes	Anger *or* depression *or* pleasure
Housekeeping *or* sports *or* music	Married life *or* single life
Cars *or* clubs *or* television *or* movies	Men *or* women

After you have finished freewriting about a subject, rewrite the paper for your teacher. Eliminate repeated details and any thoughts that you might not want to share. As you rewrite, concentrate on making all the changes needed for your sentences to be error-free. Your aim is to produce a paper without any sentence-skills mistakes.

2 RED RIDING HOOD

Write your own updated version of "Little Red Riding Hood"—the story the way you would like to see it told. Use your imagination to invent as many specific details about the characters and their words and actions as you can think of. The more detailed you are, the more entertaining your story will be to read.

Since you will probably have the characters in your story speaking to one another, you may want to review the section on quotation marks (page 124) before you begin.

3 DIRECTIONS TO A PLACE

Write a set of specific instructions on how to get from the English classroom to your house. Imagine you are giving these directions to a stranger who has just come into the room and who wants to deliver a hundred million dollars to your home. You want, naturally, to give *exact* directions, including various landmarks that may guide the way, for the stranger does not know the area.

To help you write the paper, first make up a list of all the directions involved. Also, use words like *next, then,* and *after* to help the reader follow clearly as you move from one direction to the next.

After you have finished, give your paper to another student, who should then be able to use your written instructions to draw a map of how to get to your house.

4 COLLABORATIVE STORY WRITING

Choose one of the story openings listed on the next page and develop it for about fifteen minutes. Your instructor then will ask you to exchange your story with someone else. You will read what the person wrote and then continue writing his or her story for another fifteen minutes or so. Finally, you will exchange with a third person and spend another fifteen minutes completing the story that has been given you. Remember to write clearly and legibly enough so that your coauthors can read what you write; also, don't kill off your main characters before the final act. Have fun while you do this activity.

Afterward, exchange papers with a fourth person and proofread the completed story for fragments, run-on sentences, and mistakes with quotation marks.

Beginnings:

1. As the sun set, the lid of Dracula's coffin creaked slowly open.
2. A car was speeding down the highway.
3. It was a routine and boring lecture class until the teacher began behaving in a very peculiar manner.
4. Tony looked nervously at his watch as he waited for Lola to arrive.
5. The big stranger was standing alone at the end of the bar.
6. My husband/wife awakened me and said, "I think I hear someone downstairs."
7. I'm going to tell you about the most frightening experience of my life.
8. He/She had gone down to the beach to spend the day in the sun.
9. The trouble started when I left my English class.
10. The cool dude in the blue sports car removed his shades and said, "Get in here with me."
11. Let me tell you about the day all the appliances in my home went berserk.
12. "What's going on here?" I yelled as I walked into the room.
13. Once upon a time . . .

5 A DAY IN YOUR LIFE

Write in detail about a day in your life—your activities, feelings, and experiences during the day. A good way to prepare for this paper is to carry a pen and notepad with you through a day in your life. Make an ongoing list of things that you do, feel, see, think, hear, and say. Your aim is to accumulate a great many specific details that you can draw upon later as you work on your paper. Making an extensive list is an excellent way to get started on almost any paper.

Remember that if you are as specific and honest as possible, any day, no matter how seemingly uneventful, will be engaging to read about.

Here is the first draft of one student's response to the assignment:

A Day in My Life

Since today was very dark and rainy, I was very unwilling to get up. I got washed and went downstairs to make my breakfast. While eating scrambled eggs, I was interrupted by an insurance agent. Having to put out money really got the day off to a bad start.

About 11:30 I rode down to the post office, only to find that I had gotten nothing but bills and magazines. When I returned home, my grandmother asked me to go to the drugstore for some medication. Afterward, I had a bottle of Yoo-hoo for lunch.

In the afternoon, I went downtown to work in the music shop. It was quiet, and I was able to spend my time practicing the guitar while getting paid for doing so. I also read an article about Bob Dylan in a magazine.

At 3:30 I drove down to the elementary school to pick up my nephew and sister. When I got home, I worked on my paper for English class. After eating dinner, I drove to class.

Comments: The paper is a promising early draft: it is unified, and there is a sense of organization, with each (too short) paragraph dealing with a different aspect of the day. An occasional sharp detail appears—for example, the bottle of Yoo-hoo for lunch. However, the paper needs to be expanded with a great many more specific details. For example, here are questions that could be asked just about the writer's morning:

> What time did the writer get up?
> What did he have for breakfast?
> When did the insurance agent arrive?
> Was the agent expected?
> What was the insurance for?
> How much did the writer have to pay?
> Did the writer's meal get cold?
> What else did he do in the morning besides deal with the insurance agent?
> What were some of his thoughts and feelings?
> What bills and magazines did he receive at the post office?

A reasonably detailed account of this writer's—or anyone's—day could easily run several pages or more in length.

6 PROVIDING EXAMPLES

The two basic steps in effective writing involve (1) making a point of some kind and (2) providing specific evidence to support that point. Listed below and on the next page are three separate points followed by specific examples supporting the points. Using the spaces provided, invent two additional examples to support each point.

Point 1: Our upstairs neighbor is a thoughtful person.

Support: a. He has to get up for work at five in the morning, and in order not to wake us up with his footsteps, he moves about very quietly and doesn't put his shoes on until he leaves the front door.

b. _____

_____

_____

c. _____

_____

_____

Point 2:   My two-year-old son was in a stubborn mood today.

Support: a.   When I asked him to stop playing in the yard and come indoors, he looked me square in the eye and shouted "No!" and then spelled it out, "N . . . O!"

b. _____

_____

_____

c. _____

_____

_____

Point 3:   My landlord is incompetent.

Support: a.   He spent all Saturday afternoon plastering a large crack in my bedroom wall. An hour after he left, all the wet plaster, plus a large section of the wall, suddenly dropped to the floor.

b. _____

_____

_____

c. _____

_____

_____

Select the point for which you feel you have the best examples and develop it into a paragraph.

Suggestions on how to proceed:

1.   Supply a title (A *Thoughtful Neighbor, My Stubborn Son, My Incompetent Landlord*).

2.   Copy the point and the first supporting example.

3.   Add your own two supporting examples, which you should rewrite and expand on separate paper until they are fully developed into complete, error-free sentences.

4.   Introduce your examples with connecting words such as, "Our upstairs neighbor is also thoughtful . . . "; "In addition, my son was stubborn when . . . "; "Another example of my landlord's incompetence . . . "; "A final example . . . ."

7   BEST OR WORST JOB

Write a paper on the best or worst job (or chore) that you ever had. Provide plenty of specific details that show clearly and vividly *why* the job was your "best" or "worst" one. Look first at the student paper that follows.

Cooking at the Venture Inn

Working as a cook at the Venture Inn is the best job I have ever had. I like this job first of all because I have a steady forty-hour work week, along with a chance for overtime if I want it. Also, I can eat whatever I like, and I get a chance to take steak and sometimes lobster home to my wife. I don't have any problems with my boss; if I have to report late or skip a day now and then, all she asks is that I call her in advance. The pay is very good, averaging close to $250 the weeks that I work overtime. The last and most important reason that I like the job is that it is seasonal. This means that I will be free to go to school during the winter and then have a job to look forward to next summer when school is out.

Suggestions on how to proceed:

1. At the beginning of your paper, express in a clear, direct sentence exactly what the job was and whether it was the best or worst job you ever had.

2. Make a list (a *scratch outline*) of the supporting details that explain why you liked or disliked the job. Here, for example, is the list prepared by the author of the paper above:

   Point: Working as a cook at the Venture Inn is the best job I have ever had.
   Support: 1.   Steady work with chance for overtime
                2.   Free food
                3.   Good relations with my boss
                4.   Good pay
                5.   Seasonal job

3. Use your list as a guide to write the first rough draft of your paper. As you write, try to think of details that will explain and illustrate your supporting reasons. For instance, the writer above develops the idea of good pay by specifying his salary on the weeks he works overtime.

4. Do not expect to finish your paper in one draft. You should, in fact, be ready to write a series of drafts as you work toward a finished paper. An effective paper is almost never done all at once, and perhaps the most important step in the writing process is rewriting.

5. Use connecting words such as *first, next, then, also,* and *finally* to introduce each supporting reason.

6. Proofread the next-to-final draft of your paper for sentence-skills mistakes, including spelling. Use the checklist of sentence skills on the inside back cover of this book.

8 HOW YOU GET COMFORTABLE

Getting comfortable is a quiet pleasure in life that we all share. Write a paper about the special way you make yourself comfortable, providing plenty of specific details so that the reader can actually "see" and understand your particular method.

Following is one student's account of how she gets comfortable.

How I Relax

Here is how I relax when I get home from school on Thursday. First of all, I see that all three of my children are put to bed. Then I run hot water and add lots of perfumed bubble bath. As the bubbles rise, I undress and get into the tub. The water is soothing to my tired muscles, and the bubbles are tingly on my skin. I lie back and put my feet on the water spigots, with everything but my hair under the water. I like to stick my big toe up the spigot and spray water over the tub. After about ten minutes of soaking, I wash myself with scented soap, get out and dry myself off, and put my nightgown on. Then I go downstairs and make myself two ham, lettuce, and tomato sandwiches on white bread and pour myself a tall glass of iced tea with plenty of sugar and ice cubes. I carry these into the living room with me and turn on the television. To get comfortable, I sit on the couch with a pillow behind me and my legs under me. I enjoy watching a late movie or *The Tonight Show*. The time is very peaceful after a long, hard day of housecleaning, cooking, washing, and attending night class.

9 ANNOYANCES OR WORRIES IN EVERYDAY LIFE

Make up a list of things that bother you in everyday life. Here is one student's list of "pet peeves":

1. Drivers who suddenly slow down to turn without having signaled
2. The cold floor in my bathroom on a winter morning
3. Not having cable television to watch football or basketball games
4. The small napkin holder in my parents' home that is always running out of napkins
5. Not being able to fall asleep at night when I know I have to get up early the next morning
6. Getting a phone call during my favorite television show
7. Laying something down one minute and not being able to find it the next
8. Getting into the shower and then discovering I have forgotten my washcloth

Take the most vivid and detailed of the items on your list and develop them into a paragraph beginning, "There are a number of things that bother me in everyday life."

Alternatively, write a paper about worries you have in everyday life.

10 A SIGNIFICANT PERSONAL EXPERIENCE

Write an account of a memorable personal experience you have had and your feelings in the course of the experience. To help make your paper effective, describe just the one experience and use a time order (first this happened, then this, then this) to arrange the details. Be sure to provide as many specific details as possible to really *show* the experience to the reader. Make the experience as vivid for the reader as it was for you when you first experienced it.

11 TEN OPENING POINTS

Write a paper that develops the opening point of *one* of the following ten sentences. You may find it helpful to first make a list of supporting details for several of the sentences. Then choose the one for which you have the best support.

1. Yesterday evening was a very busy time for me.
2. The apartment needed repairs.
3. I had car problems recently.
4. The teacher embarrassed students in many ways.
5. What I had to eat and drink yesterday was probably not very nutritious.
6. Ted behaved strangely when I spoke to him.
7. State Senator Mel Grabble is a crook.
8. _____ is my favorite magazine for several reasons.
9. You could tell by looking at the room that a sloppy person lived there.
10. When my money gets tight, there are several ways I economize.

12 TEN MORE OPENING POINTS

Follow the instructions given for the preceding assignment.

1. My friend has several dangerous driving habits.
2. I passed a weird-acting character on the street.
3. The food at the place where I eat is terrible.
4. My body gave me several warning signs that I was coming down with the flu.
5. I could tell that the dog was not friendly.
6. The backyard was in poor condition.

7. The vending machine reacted in several unpredictable ways.

8. There were several ways I passed time during the dull lecture.

9. I believe the _____ (name a specific sports team) will win the league championship for several reasons.

10. My desk/pocketbook/wallet was a mess.

13 A SPECIAL PERSON

Write in detail about a person who has been very important in your life. State in the first sentence who the person is and the person's relationship to you (friend, father, cousin, etc.). For example, "My grandmother Ellie Stanton has been a very special person at several key points in my life." Then show through specific examples (the person's words and actions) why he or she has been so special to you.

14 TWELVE TOPICS

Write a paper on one of the following topics. Begin with a clear, direct sentence that states exactly what your paper will be about. For example, if you chose the first topic, your opening sentence might be, "There were several delightful childhood games I played that occupied many of my summer days." An opening sentence for the second topic might be, "The work I had to do to secure my high school diploma is one of the special accomplishments of my life." Be sure to follow your opening sentence with plenty of specific supporting details that develop your topic.

1. A way you had fun as a child

2. An accomplishment

3. Everyday pleasures in your life

4. Ways you were punished or rewarded by your parents as a child

5. A time a prayer was answered

6. A silly or embarrassing moment in your life

7. A wish, dream, or fantasy you have had

8. An experience you or someone you know has had with drugs

9. A difficult time in your life

10. Your strengths and/or weaknesses as a student

11. A crime you or someone you know committed

12. Your solution to an attack of the blues

15 TWELVE MORE TOPICS

Follow the instructions given for the preceding assignment.

1. A time of loss or disappointment
2. Some problems your child (or sister or brother) is having
3. Your religious upbringing
4. A superstition or fear
5. A disagreement you have had with someone
6. A debt you have repaid or have yet to repay
7. A bad illness
8. A favorite holiday
9. How your parents (or you and a special person in your life) met
10. Your father's or mother's attitude toward you
11. A happy time you had recently
12. Why you do or don't intend to marry (or remarry)

16 WRITING A SUMMARY

A summary gives the main idea—and often the main supporting details—of a selection, but it excludes less important supporting information. A summary is written in complete sentences and is usually written in your own words.

Read the selection below and then the several-sentence summary of it that follows.

My Self-centered Neighbor

I have a self-centered neighbor named Alice. If you tell Alice you think the dress she is wearing is beautiful, she will take the time to tell you the name of the store where she bought it, the type of material that was used in making it, and the price. Alice is also egotistical when it comes to her children. Because they are hers, she thinks they have to be the best children on the block. You waste your time trying to tell her you have seen her kids push around smaller kids or take things from parked cars. Finally, Alice is quick to describe the furnishings of her home for someone who is meeting her for the first time. She tells how much she paid for the paneling in her dining room. She mentions that she has two color television sets and that they were bought at an expensive furniture store. She lets you know that the stereo set in her living room cost more than $600, and that she has such a large collection of records that she wouldn't be able to play them all in one week. Poor Alice doesn't realize that expensive things don't always make a house a home.

Summary   My neighbor Alice is an egotist. She will talk on endlessly about a dress of hers that you admire. She believes that her children must be perfect, simply because they are hers. She brags about all the expensive furnishings in her home.

The length of a summary depends on your purpose in summarizing. The shortest possible summary of the paragraph above would be its title ("My Self-centered Neighbor"). If your purpose requires you to have more information than that, a one-sentence summary might be enough ("My neighbor Alice is self-centered."). Longer passages and different purposes might require longer summaries. For example, in writing a report on an article or book, you might want to have a summary that is a paragraph or more in length.

How to summarize: To summarize a selection, first see if you can determine its main point. Consider the title carefully; it and the first and last paragraphs of the selection may provide clues to the main idea. After you have formulated what you think is the main idea of the selection, ask yourself the question, "Does all or most of the material in the article support the idea in this statement?" If it does, you have probably identified the main idea. Write it out in a sentence.

Then write down the main supporting details that support that point. (Sometimes there are subheads within the selection that may help you determine the main supporting details.)

Finally, use the main idea and the main supporting details to write an appropriate-length summary of the selection.

Summary assignments:

1. Write a one-paragraph summary of a magazine article. Clip or make a copy of the article and attach it to your summary. Begin the summary with the title and author of the article, followed by the name, date, and page number(s) of the magazine. For example:

    A Summary: "The Buying of America," Peter T. Kilborn, *Newsweek* (November 27, 1978), pp. 78–88.

2. Write a one-paragraph summary of a television show. Take notes extensively as you watch the show; then use the notes as a guide when you write your paper. In the first sentence of your summary, indicate the network and date on which the show appeared. For example, "The March 21 telecast of CBS's *Sixty Minutes* dealt with the continuing controversy about abortion."

3. Write a one-paragraph summary about what was discussed in one of your classes at school. Indicate the main ideas that were expressed and the main supporting details for those ideas. You may also want to note any activities that went on and the purpose of the activities.

PROGRESS CHART FOR WRITING ASSIGNMENTS

Date	Paper	Comments	To Do Next
10/15	Worst job	Promising but needs more	
		support. Also, 2 frags,	
		2 run-ons,	
		and 5 dropped endings.	Rewrite
10/16	,, ,,	Support improved—good!	
		Still 4 dropped endings.	Rewrite

Date	Paper	Comments	To Do Next

INDEX